By

SHANE DALE

ISBN: 1482672022

ISBN 13:   9781482672022

Library of Congress Control Number: 2013904613
CreateSpace Independent Publishing Platform
North Charleston, South Carolina

For Jennie. I'm glad you're my girl.

CONTENTS

FOREWORDS

Great rivalries are what make college football go. In the East, there are Alabama-Auburn, Ohio State-Michigan, and Miami-Florida State. In the West, the great rivalries are Cal-Stanford, UCLA-USC, and Washington-Washington State. One rivalry tends to be overlooked when people speak of the great hatred that two teams have for each other: Arizona State and Arizona. Since 1899, the two schools have faced each other on the gridiron. At 114 years old, the Territorial Cup is college football's oldest rivalry trophy.

In the modern football era, it can be best described as the tale of two cities: Phoenix and Tucson. As the state has evolved socially and economically, Tucson has been seen as the Old Pueblo that still has the small-town, Old West feel. And then you have the growing metropolis of Phoenix. It's safe to say that Valley residents hold a certain scorn for their fellow Arizonans south of Casa Grande, while those in the south hold contempt for those in the north. It's almost too bad that Oregon and Oregon State call their rivalry the Civil War, because that is exactly what happens here in Arizona.

It's truly amazing to witness that, when rivalry week hits, the cities become Troy and Sparta. As in Greek mythology, the two Arizona towns become the most bitter of enemies who will not be content until the other is vanquished. The rivalry turns co-workers against each other, brothers against brothers, husbands against wives, and parents against kids. It makes people crazy for football and for their respective schools. The stakes are high because, for 364 days, the winner of the game has bragging rights, while the loser can only circle the calendar for the next year and hope for redemption.

As an ASU player, you are indoctrinated into this rivalry the minute you arrive on campus. You are taught to hate everything blue and red. The contentious attitude is contagious, and by the time the season ends with the annual game, you're in full hate mode against the Wildcats. As a Sun Devil, you throw insults down to them, such as "Rats," "Kitties," "Mildcats," "Tuscum Tech" and "Northern Nogales."

As your career goes forward, the hatred deepens. I went 1-2 against UA as a starter. In 1994, we had them on the ropes, but as a late field goal went wide right as time expired, I remember feeling an overwhelming sense of failure. In 1995, we again had them in our sights, leading 28-14 at the start of the fourth quarter, only to see them rally behind Tedy Bruschi and Richard Dice to win the game, 31-28. In 1996, we were not going to be denied, and we went into Arizona Stadium and ran them over, 56-14. That win made up for the close losses, but I have to admit: I would have much preferred to have been 3-0.

As the new century is now in its second decade and the rivalry enters its 114th year, there are no signs of it slowing down. Everything a fan can ask for has happened in recent years: overtime, blocked kicks, dropped punts and huge upsets. In 2012, ASU went into Tucson as an underdog and used a combination of sound defense and a pounding ground game to upset UA, 41-34. An interesting statistic that continued in that game: In the last four Territorial Cup games, the visiting team has won. So much for "home sweet home."

Moving forward, there is no question that ASU will crank up the intensity in this rivalry. With the recent head coaching changes at both schools and the fact that the two coaches, ASU's Todd Graham and UA's Rich Rodriguez, are former colleagues, it sets the stage for some very exciting Territorial Cup matchups. With Coach Graham already 1-0 in the series against RichRod, the faithful of Sun Devil Nation want nothing more than for this to be the beginning of a decade's worth of success against the hated Wildcats.

The rivalry lives on.

Go Devils! Fear the Fork!

Juan Roque
Offensive tackle, Arizona State University
1992-96

When the Cats and Devils hit the field each year for the Territorial Cup, the only thing that means anything is that moment in time. On game day, records don't matter. The Territorial Cup is the oldest rivalry trophy in the NCAA, and the Duel in the Desert is one of the most anticipated games on the schedule for players, coaches, fans and the communities.

As a player, I had the unique experience of participating in this heated rivalry. As a spectator, this great game has given me and fans alike some memorable moments. We all remember The Streak from 1982-90. I was a sophomore linebacker on the 1982 team that started The Streak by defeating the Sun Devils, 28-18, in Arizona Stadium. That victory eliminated any chance of the Sun Devils representing the Pac-10 in the Rose Bowl, and it came under the direction of the late, great Larry Smith. What an incredible feeling!

The Streak helped UA develop a strong football identity in the college football landscape. Intrastate bragging rights were claimed by fans and students. It provided an upper hand in the recruitment of local talent such as Byron Evans, Michael Bates and Vance Johnson, just to name a few.

The result of the rivalry game can have a direct effect on who will end up playing in the Rose Bowl. It also incites the intensity and passion that come along with holding state bragging rights for a full year. When a player is on the field, he is not only representing himself and his school, but the community as a whole. He carries the pride of the city with him. Through the pageantry of the game, he is also carrying the emotions of young fans. He is honoring the school tradition that has been well established. And a realization is made that he is playing for the great players that came before him and for the Wildcats of the future.

The Duel in the Desert has been watched by many fans across the country, and the rivalry is so heated that it's often been the only college football game played in its time slot the day after Thanksgiving, putting it on its own national stage.

Who could ever forget the great players and plays that have come from this great rivalry? I can still see Chuck Cecil marching 100-plus yards from the south end zone to the north end zone in Arizona Stadium after intercepting a Sun Devil pass, the crowd of 55,000-plus in the stadium going wild. There was Max Zendejas breaking the hearts of so many Sun Devil fans when, with the stroke of his foot, he sent the pigskin straight through the uprights, costing ASU a victory – and then again two years later when a win would've put the Devils in the Rose Bowl.

I was blessed to play in this rivalry game for four years. I can say that if a player loses this game, he is in for a very long off-season – and I'm thankful I only had to feel that way once in my four years.

The Duel in the Desert will live forever and will continue to be played on a big stage for years to come. In the past, I looked forward to this game through the mindset of a player. As the years have rolled on, I am now proud to say that I look forward to this game through the mindset of a big Wildcat fan.

Bear Down!

LaMonte Hunley
Linebacker, The University of Arizona
1981-84

PREFACE

It's amazing how the memories of a football game from decades ago can instantly send chills down the spines of middle-aged men.

"It's been over 40 years since I played my first game versus UA, and the hair's standing up on the back of my neck right now," one former Sun Devil told me when he was relaying his memories of the Arizona-Arizona State football rivalry in the 1970s. "It was just incredible, the intensity."

Many athletes I spoke to, both Sun Devils and Wildcats, made very similar comments. And while they were making them, one thought kept crossing my mind: *It's absurd that no one outside the state of Arizona knows about this rivalry.*

Sure, plenty of people who don't live in the state have heard of it. Maybe they've even caught a game or two on TV. But they certainly don't *know* it.

They don't know that it began well over 100 years ago – 13 years, in fact, before Arizona became a state. They don't know that the Territorial Cup is the nation's oldest collegiate rivalry trophy. And most importantly, they don't know the raw emotion that the players and fans carry – the passion they have for their school, the desire to beat the bad guys in Tempe or Tucson, the visceral reaction they feel when they hear their rival's fight song, the exhilaration that reverberates throughout their bodies when they win and the disgust they experience when they come up short.

Sure, there are plenty of college football rivalries that share similar emotional components, many of which are much more recognized on a national level. But many players – and even some coaches – from the Duel in the Desert will tell you, as they told me: There's something different about this game. Bizarre, surreal events tend to take place, especially in the fourth quarter. Often, the team with the better record does not win.

I remember a video that was played on the scoreboard video screen before the 2010 UA-ASU game at Arizona Stadium in

Tucson. The video depicted a dusty, Old West-style setting in which a grizzled ex-cowboy was telling his son (or grandson; I'm not quite sure) about the rivalry.

The boy asked him, "Who will win?" The cowboy thought about it for a second and then responded, "Depends on who wants it most."

Sounds like a cute little sports cliché, right? But the crazy thing about this rivalry is that, according to so many of the men who played and coached in it, that statement is 100 percent true. When I asked them why their rivals were able to beat them in a certain year, many responses went along the lines of: *You know, it just seemed like they wanted it more that day.*

In how many college football rivalries is that true? How often does a team with a poorer record and not-as-talented athletes routinely march into its rival's stadium and win? That's exactly what's happened over and over in this rivalry, including the last three Territorial Cup contests.

It's easy to understand why the ASU-UA rivalry doesn't earn much national recognition. Neither team has been an NCAA football powerhouse for an extended time, and rarely are both teams ranked in the top 25 when they meet. But anyone who's been privileged to be a part of this rivalry knows the annual Sun Devil-Wildcat showdown is something special. It's emotional. It's unpredictable. And it's a heck of a lot of fun.

Finally, a disclaimer that I debated sharing but ultimately decided should be addressed upfront: I'm a loyal Arizona Wildcat, Class of 2004. And while I can go on and on about how I've done the best I can to present a fair and balanced historical perspective of the rivalry (which I have) or how I interviewed an equal number of former ASU and UA players and coaches for this book (which I did), I understand that this will be a sticking point for many proud Sun Devils.

But if you do happen to bleed maroon and gold, before you toss this book aside, let me offer two points.

First, I strongly believe you have to have a rooting interest in the Duel in the Desert to fully appreciate it. Yes, I love my Wildcats. But I also love this rivalry. I love the passion, I love the history and I love the simple fact that, regardless of the records, both teams always have something extremely meaningful to play for at the end of each football season.

Second – and perhaps more importantly – my wife, Jennie, is an ASU graduate. And while she's not much of a sports fan, I quickly learned during our courtship that she's quite sensitive to any verbal jabs against her school.

Jennie has placed her stamp of approval on to this book. Take that for what it's worth.

INTRODUCTION:

The Best Rivalry
No One's Heard Of

They've been playing each other since 1899, and the winner of their annual football game receives the oldest rivalry trophy in the United States. And still, the football rivalry between The University of Arizona and Arizona State University isn't well known on a national scale.

But any former UA or ASU player or coach, or any longtime Arizona resident, will tell you that the Duel in the Desert, as it has been labeled in recent years, is just as emotional, intense - and, frankly, vicious – as any in the country.

"A lot of times during so-called rivalry weeks in college football, you might see espn.com or some publication do an assessment of what they think are the top 10-20 rivalries in college football, and they never put UA-ASU in there," said Tim Healey, the radio voice of the Sun Devils since 1998. "I really think they're missing the boat because we're tucked away in the Southwest, there are a lot of games at night, late scores on the East Coast and so forth. I think, in general, they're not as familiar as what goes on out there. And as a result, I don't think they're as familiar with this rivalry."

Dick Tomey, UA's head coach from 1987-2000, has been a part of plenty of college football grudge matches. "Of all the rivalries

I've been part of in my coaching – with Kansas-Missouri, Kansas-Kansas-State, UCLA-USC – I almost think the ASU-UA rivalry is the nastiest because I think there is so much emotion," he said. "And at times, I think it's unhealthy."

Dan Cozzetto, ASU's offensive coordinator under head coaches Bruce Snyder (1992-2000) and Dennis Erickson (2007-11), came to view the rivalry in the same way. "I'd been in the league a long time and been around every rivalry except for the UCLA-USC game, but once I got into the Territorial Cup – believe me, it was a rivalry that was far and beyond any of the other ones I've been associated with," he said. "You could call it more of a hate game. It was kind of unique because of the intensity and resentment between both schools. The magnitude of the game – it affected the whole community. It's the most important game of the year, no question about it. You've got to live in this state, and when you win that game, it's a heck of a lot easier.

"The reality of it is that, whether fans went to school (at UA or ASU) or they didn't, it seems like they pick sides. Either you root for Arizona or Arizona State. This rivalry among the fans is probably one of the most intense that I've been involved in."

ASU wide receiver Keith Poole (1993-96) said emotions definitely run deeper in the Duel in the Desert than in most college football rivalries. "I think most good rivalries are nasty, but in this one, it seems like they truly hate each other – from the fans to the players to even the cities," he said. "I've talked to a lot of people when I was playing, and even now, that won't even go to Tucson because they're scared of what will happen to their cars or that they'll get in a fight. And it's the same here (in Tempe). I guess that's the way most rivalries are, but this one has a little more nastiness to it."

ASU quarterback Jeff van Raaphorst (1983-86) compared the rivalry to the brutality of a mixed martial arts bout. "It reminds me more of MMA because you just try to pummel them until someone's down in total submission," he said. "It's not (just) about winning; it's about exerting your force and getting submission."

UA tight end Ron Beyer (1975-78) said his battles with ASU always brought out more aggression in him than any other regular-season game. "I would try to inflict as much pain on the opponents in those situations as I could," he said. "That's what it did to you inside when you worked yourself into an emotional approach to the game. It was easy to get angry and easy to get up and play these guys."

"The emotion was virtually tangible"

Anyone who comes from outside the Grand Canyon State to play football in Tempe or Tucson quickly embraces the rivalry, in large part thanks to teammates who grew up cheering for one school or the other.

Former UA defensive back, Pro Bowl safety and current NFL assistant coach Chuck Cecil (1984-87) made what many Wildcat fans consider the greatest play in UA football history in the 1986 game against Arizona State. And he quickly learned to loathe the Sun Devils when he arrived in Tucson via California.

"I walked on and redshirted my first year, and by the time I put on a uniform and actually got to participate in the game, it was – how shall I put this – I despised them, incredibly so," he said. "I still have those reminiscent feelings. Just the mere mention of the rivalry between the schools bothers me.

"It all started my freshman year when I first got there, and I don't know what it was. The emotion was virtually tangible. You could almost touch it. And it wasn't something I created; I just became a part of it. It's bigger than one player, one coach or one season."

ASU offensive tackle Juan Roque (1992-96) had the same experience in Tempe after arriving from California. "It's amazing. Literally within the first couple of weeks on campus, you really get a feel that it's just a deep-seeded rivalry," he said. "The hatred is very real. It bleeds into you. You never want to see them win a game. You despise their colors, their ridiculous-looking mascot – it's just an absolute hatred."

Mike Stoops, UA's head coach from 2004-11, said coaches learn about the importance of the Duel in much the same way out-of-state players do. "I always watched it from afar because it was always played on the Friday after Thanksgiving. I didn't know a whole lot about the history," he said. "I think you have to coach in it to appreciate it. You definitely feel that intensity, and you feel that hatred amongst the fans."

But it often comes from the players, as well. UA defensive back Heath Bray (1988-92) said there is nothing to like about ASU. In fact, Bray and his teammates grew fond of calling ASU "The Evil Empire."

"You have them wearing the mustard and rust (colors) running around the field, and you have us, the secure athletic and academic institution from Tucson, wearing the colors of our country," he said. "Those damn colors – that just makes it easier (to dislike them). They're awful. You see that and you're just like, 'That is the ugliest bunch of idiots I've ever seen.' I can't imagine having to wear that (expletive) every day going to school."

Rich Rodriguez, who replaced Stoops as UA head coach, picked up on the importance of the rivalry right away. "I think the intensity and emotion is equal to anyone I've been involved with," he said. "It's in state, it's in conference, it's in the same division in the conference, and (the campuses are) less than two hours away from each other, so there's a lot of emotion and people talking about it year-round.

"I'd kind of heard about it from afar when I wasn't here, but when you're in the middle of it, you kind of sense the intensity. It may not be on a national scale like Ohio State and Michigan was, but from an intensity and a local scale, there's no question that it's everything that a rivalry should be."

Todd Graham, who squared off against Rodriguez in his first Duel in the Desert as ASU head coach in 2012, took a proactive approach in educating new players on the importance of bringing home the Territorial Cup. "One of the things I have done is not just wait until rivalry week and tell them all about the rivalry," he said. "We have had countless players and coaches talk to us every week, coming in force, and very few have not talked about the Territorial Cup and how important it is.

"I think our guys have really learned to appreciate what it means to be a Sun Devil, and how can you do that without knowing the significance of this game? I think our guys do respect that."

"As big today as it's ever been"

ASU quarterback Danny White (1971-73) – whose father, Whizzer, was a star Sun Devil running back in the 1940s – said the ASU-UA games don't always carry as much meaning as some nationally renowned rivalries since neither team is a perennial national championship contender. But that never seems to matter.

"The only thing I think it's missing is the fact that it seems like it's never a determining factor on whether one team or the other goes to a big bowl game," he said. "But I don't think it's changed (since I played). I think it's as big today as it's ever been."

Even the guys who played decades ago remember how passionate the rivalry was – and most agree that little has changed.

"That game was always the highlight of our whole season," said Sun Devil quarterback Dick Mackey (1951-54). "That was the most important game, and sometimes if we had a so-so season but we won that one, we considered it to be pretty successful."

UA quarterback Eddie Wilson (1959-61) has kept a close eye on the rivalry in the half-century since he participated in it. "Even though football has changed dramatically from the time that I played to now, it was just as intense then as it is now – no ifs, no buts, no nothings," he said. "People who tell you it isn't are smoking something."

UA center Kyle Quinn (2008-12) grasps the significance of the Duel in the Desert as well as Wilson or any of his predecessors – and he's optimistic that, thanks to the two new guys in charge, it will soon get the nationwide recognition it deserves.

"It's very undervalued in terms of the national college picture, and I don't know if it's because we're out on the West Coast or Arizona isn't really known as a hotbed for football," he said. "But this state has got some of the most passionate fans in the country that can compete with the SEC, the Big Ten and the Big 12.

"Everybody just talks about Ohio State and Michigan or Florida and Florida State. But we have one hell of a rivalry down here with UA and ASU. It's grown a little bit in my time here, and it's going to keep growing because Coach Rodriguez and Coach Graham are going to do great things for both programs. It's going to really bring the national attention to Arizona a lot more than what it has been in the past."

Fans fill players in

While out-of-state players get plenty of help from their teammates to get them acclimated to the rivalry and fired up about winning the Territorial Cup, most of them don't need it; the students, alumni and fans take care of that for them.

Take it from ASU quarterback and Idaho native Jake Plummer (1993-96). "Right away – I mean, that first year coming up to that game – I remember fans just saying, 'You can't lose this game. You have to win this game,'" he said. "And it always struck me as kind of funny because it was a very important game, obviously, for bragging rights and to win the state battle, but all the other games were important, too."

Plummer is amused by the friction that the rivalry causes among fans and even among families. "There are a lot of families where a UA grad married an ASU grad. They fight to put their little newborn in an ASU onesie or a UA onesie. I just get a kick out of that," he said.

"I think the fans probably took it a little more extreme than we did. They really get after it wanting to win."

UA linebacker Ricky Hunley (1980-83) said the Duel tends to increase in importance for players as their collegiate careers progress. "The appreciation for the rivalry grows as you matriculate from sophomore to junior to senior year," he said. "The guys kind of understand it as they mature. You really understand what bragging rights are all about."

This was also true for UA wide receiver Jay Dobyns (1981-84). "I played some big games at Arizona," he said. "I was there when we upset USC at the Coliseum when they were No. 1. I was there when we beat Notre Dame in South Bend. I was there when we beat UCLA on national television in '83," he said.

"But none of those games compared in my mind and in my heart to the ASU game. Everything else from the ASU game was a very distant second."

∞

What is it that makes the Arizona-Arizona State rivalry so intense – especially when neither team has frequently been a national championship contender?

For starters, in the rivalry's earlier years, Wilson said most of his teammates were from Arizona and had played with or against eventual ASU players in high school.

"They knew one another, and the rivalry that they may have had in high school carried on to college," he said. "In those days, the good players did not leave the state to go play somewhere else. Back then, if there were 13 good players in the state, 12 of them stayed in the state to play."

When ASU began to import talent from the Midwest and East in the 1950s, it was up to the alumni to fill those players in on what the Duel meant to the school, the city and the state.

"The first year that I was getting acclimated to the area, I probably didn't know where Tucson was," said Sun Devil fullback and linebacker/defensive back Ron Erhardt (1955-58). "I'd imagine that less than 30 percent of the players on our team were (born and raised) Arizona people. Those guys understood it, but the rest of us were from Pennsylvania and the Midwest, and by the time we were juniors and seniors, we fully understood it."

UA quarterback and linebacker Jim Geist (1958-59) said out-of-state recruiting built upon the resentment that the Wildcats already had toward their rivals. "We always thought of ASU as just kind of an outlaw school. They paid very, very little attention to Arizona kids at all, and their coaching staff's roots were back there in Ohio and Pennsylvania," he said. "They didn't recruit locally, and a lot of people probably resented that."

Proximity alarm

ASU archivist Rob Spindler said a lot of the emotion behind the rivalry is based in geography and the simple fact that ASU and UA are the two most prominent universities in Arizona. "There has always been sort of the geographic rivalry – the fact that it's the two largest institutions of higher learning in the state," he said. "You get into that whole thing about the Mason-Dixon line, the two major cities in the state duking it out."

Stoops, who has played and coached in his share of rivalry games, including Texas-Oklahoma and Iowa-Iowa State, came to understand that geography has a lot to do with the heat behind the Duel.

"Because of the proximity between Arizona and Arizona State and them being in Phoenix, I always thought that escalated this one a little bit more than most," he said. "With Texas and Oklahoma, that's a unique venue – that game is always played in the (neutral site) Cotton Bowl – but this one goes back and forth (from Tempe to Tucson) each year, and that adds its own separate uniqueness to it."

Inferiority complex

Adding fuel to the rivalry's fire, according to Scott Bordow, sports columnist for *The Arizona Republic* in Phoenix, is a certain amount of condescension from those in Tempe toward their neighbors to the south.

"I think ASU fans feel they're superior to UA and their fans, and they feel superior to Tucson," he said. "Even though UA was the first university (in the state), I think ASU fans feel above UA.

"When ASU fans discuss the rivalry, they'll say, 'Well, we've been to a couple Rose Bowls and they haven't,' and they point out all they did that UA hasn't done. I think they feel superior in a lot of ways."

Healey agreed that the rivalry is as much about the two communities as it is about the two schools and their athletic programs. "I've always sensed that one of the reasons why this rivalry is so intense is that it kind of transcends the ASU football team versus the UA football team. It even transcends the universities, Arizona State and The University of Arizona," he said. "It's almost like these are two communities, Phoenix versus Tucson, going at one another.

"I've always gotten the sense – and maybe I'm wrong, but I kind of don't think I am – that people from Tucson think that other people in this state, and perhaps around the country, regard Tucson almost as Phoenix's ugly stepchild. And I think they bristle at that."

Dobyns sensed that condescension during his time at UA, and he took it personally. "I felt like I was representing Tucson, and I think the people in Phoenix look at Tucson as Nogales North," he said. "That inspired it, and I felt like when I was wearing an Arizona uniform and playing in that rivalry, I was representing this town. I was a representative of this community in this unfriendly war where the two communities would own bragging rights for the next year. I wanted to be a positive impact for my team, my school and my community."

Bray became annoyed by all the potshots that ASU fans would throw down Tucson's way as well as the perception that the ASU fans and athletes were more privileged than those in Tucson.

"There was, at that time, the feeling of haves and have-nots," he said. "Their budget was a lot bigger than ours."

Old Pueblo Put-Down

Sure, there are plenty of nasty college football rivalries across America. But in how many of those does a former player refuse to step foot in his opponent's town?

Danny White hasn't taken it quite that far, but he's come close, especially when he was a TV analyst for Sun Devil football.

"There was an ASU-UA game played down there (in Tucson) that I was broadcasting, and I refused to stay there overnight," he said. "I went down and did all my interviews the day before the game and then drove back home rather than spending the night in Tucson.

"I'm sure we spent the night down there when we played there, but since then, I've never spent the night in Tucson."

White was recently faced with a dilemma when his son took a job in UA territory. "I told him, 'I understand that you have to work in Tucson, but you don't have to live in Tucson. You make sure you buy a home that's outside the Tucson city limits.' So, he bought a home in Marana (just north of Tucson)," he said. "We go down and see him every once in a while. But at least I don't have to go into Tucson to see him, so that's good."

Talk to Whizzer White (1947-50) about the Wildcats and you'll soon understand where his son gets his attitude. "Like Danny and I say: If we have to go to El Paso, we hold our breaths every time we go through Tucson because it smells so bad," he said. "You can quote me on that."

Danny White clarified that he doesn't really have a problem with the City of Tucson, per se. "I have to be careful because it's not a Tucson thing; it's a UA thing," he said. "Tucson's a great town. It's a neat place and all that.

"But for one week out of the year, it's like my dad says: If they gave the world an enema, they'd stick the tube in Tucson."

This state's not big enough for the both of us

The rivalry took a giant leap forward in terms of intensity and mutual disdain during an off-field fight in the 1950s when Arizona State College sought to become Arizona State University – something that UA students and alumni were very much against, as they preferred for their school to remain the only accredited university in the state.

"One of the first things that happened when I got there was the thing about the changing of the name," said ASU quarterback Ron Cosner (1959-61). "When I first got here, we were Arizona State College of Tempe. (UA students) said the state was too small to have two universities and that they were *the* university for the state of Arizona."

Cosner said this intrastate battle between southern and central Arizona, combined with the condescending attitude from UA students toward ASC/ASU during that time, led to additional on-field bitterness and increased the passion among the players who participated in the rivalry.

"You could tell by their conversations. There was just an attitude about UA people when they talked to ASU people about how they are much better than we were," he said.

UA quarterback Ralph Hunsaker (1955-58) remembers that fight from the other side of the spectrum. "You just have pride in your own university, and you want it to be the one, so to speak, as opposed to there being two," he said. "That's just like how it was on the football field. You want to be the best school in the state, and so you try to be the best and avoid others coming up to your standard."

That mentality made no sense to ASU players such as Erhardt, and it made him and others want to pummel UA on the field that much more. "Even to those who were not born here, the idea that you could not have two universities in the same state did not make sense," Erhardt said. "I think that added a little bit to it."

Mackey said he still detects a lingering snobbery among many UA fans who still refer to Arizona State University as "Tempe Normal" – a pejorative reference to the school's original name, The Territorial Normal School at Tempe, upon its founding in 1885, which happened to be the same year that UA became an accredited university.

"Though I have some very close friends that went to UA, the general, all-around feeling is there's still an arrogance in their behavior toward ASU people," he said.

ASU wide receiver and cornerback Ben Hawkins (1963-65) said that kind of trash talk was certainly a motivational factor.

"(They would) always say something in our face about Tempe Normal, Tempe Normal," he said. "And the only thing we could do was we just had to go out and play them and show them that we were better than they were – that's all."

"A hell of a lot of UA people live up here..."

Phoenix may have replaced Tucson as the epicenter of the state, but Healey said UA still has at least one geographical advantage in the rivalry.

"The irony is that there are a lot of UA alumni and fans up here in the Phoenix area," he said. "Tucson seems more of a closed community in that you're really conspicuous down there if you happen to dare cheer the Sun Devils in Tucson."

Indeed, the fact that so many UA alums reside in the Phoenix area, but very few ASU faithful live in the Old Pueblo, is something that doesn't sit well with some Sun Devils. "I definitely remember when I was a little kid, I hated the fact that a lot of people in Phoenix were UA fans, and I couldn't understand that," said ASU wide receiver Aaron Pflugrad (2009-11). "I understand it now because a lot of people probably go to UA and come up here for jobs and everything. But as a little kid, it made me upset. I could not understand it at all."

Even Frank Kush, ASU's all-time winningest and longest-tenured head football coach (1958-79), acknowledged this disparity – but he said it adds some intrigue when ASU and UA square off in Tempe. "I thought it was good for the community because a hell of a lot of UA people live up here in the metropolitan area, and we don't have that many Sun Devil grads down in Tucson," he said.

Petty politics

Kush also suggested that political differences between Phoenix, the current capital of Arizona, and Tucson, the former capital, have made the rivalry that much more bitter.

"It got more intense because of the social contrast between southern Arizona and central Arizona," he said. "Tempe was affiliated with Phoenix, and Phoenix is the capital of the state of Arizona. It was a political thing, also, because (Tucson is) down south and they didn't have that close geographical location with the capital."

UA defensive back Bill Miller (1967-69) agreed that the political contrasts between the central and southern parts of the state are sizable. "It's always been that way, that Tucson and the southern part of the state is much more liberal and Phoenix is much more conservative," he said. "I hear from people (in Tucson) that would like to secede from northern Arizona and become the new Arizona politically."

Wildcats "the only act in town" in Tucson

Kush said the Wildcats' football program has an edge when it comes to the attention of their fans.

"I think the community makes the difference, and I think down in Tucson – I shouldn't say this, but I'm going to be diplomatic – I think they have a better metropolitan association with UA than Arizona State has with our community," he said.

Part of the reason for that, Kush believes, is the influx of professional teams into the Phoenix area in the 1980s and '90s. "When I first came here, we were the only act in town," he said. "Now, we've got more pro teams than you can shake a stick at – baseball, football, basketball, etc. – and I think that makes a difference.

"I think down in Tucson, they have an advantage of being the only act in town, which I think is great. It's great for the athletes and it's great for the university."

UA athletic director Greg Byrne, who graduated from ASU but claims (in tongue-in-cheek fashion) that he doesn't remember his days as a Sun Devil, enjoys UA not having to compete for the attention of sports fans like ASU does.

"Obviously in Tucson, we're the only game in town 365 days a year, so there's a focus down here on that, which is a lot of fun, and up in the Phoenix area, there's obviously a lot of competition," he said. "So I think from a day-to-day standpoint, (the rivalry is) very strong with our fan base here year-round, and I think it goes in different spurts up in Phoenix."

Home-field disadvantage

ASU and UA players and coaches are somewhat split on the question of whether playing their rival on their home turf actually boosts their chances of winning. Some say it makes a difference, but most said it doesn't.

UA linebacker LaMonte Hunley (1981-84), Ricky Hunley's younger brother, took the pro-home-field point of view. "I think having home cooking, it gave us motivation. It gave us a sense of security that you know you've got your people right here that are going to cheer for you and yell for you as much as possible," he said. "It helps that you don't have to travel, and staying in your own bed the night before, it does make a difference. And if you've got crazy, motivating, excited fans, you just feed off of that."

On the ASU side, van Raaphorst said he preferred to play UA at home. "I think, in my mind, home field matters," he said. "You may talk to a defensive guy that may not care, but I don't want the crowd noise (on offense). I want the comfortable environment. I want my field. I want to know where the play clock is. All of those things are so ingrained."

But recent stats don't back up the assertion that playing at home is a benefit in this rivalry. In the last 21 Territorial Cup games - from 1992-2012 - the home team has a record of 8-13, and the road team has won each of the last four contests.

"I've never been a big fan of home-field advantage anyway," Poole said. "Some teams get more fired up when they're the underdog and they're at the other person's stadium. When we played in Tucson, I think it fired us up, all their fans yelling at us. It's one of those things where I think it's not an advantage sometimes."

ASU offensive lineman Kyle Murphy (1994-97) agreed with his former teammate. "I'll be honest: I don't think home-field advantage means anything," he said. "I know (Arizona Stadium) has a tiny, cramped visitor locker room, but you know that going in and you deal with it, you adjust and you go forward. And you get enough fans from either side at the opponent's stadium.

"As a player, I always liked going on the road. I liked beating a team on their home field. It was great."

UA quarterback Nick Foles (2009-11) was similarly motivated by the ability to silence ASU's fans. "There's not a better feeling than making the crowd go quiet," he said. "When you're on offense and they're quiet, it means you're doing good things. (Home field) doesn't mean anything. Never has."

In this particular rivalry, Tomey said ASU always seemed comfortable playing in Tucson. "They'd been there before, and they had a lot of their fans at the game," he said. "I think that's true in most rivalries because most of them are still in the same state or a place you go often. I think home field matters little in those games."

The proximity of Tempe and Tucson takes away from any real home-field advantage that either team would otherwise enjoy, according to Erickson. "It's not like you've got to travel a long ways," he said. "At home, maybe noise would be the biggest difference, but it seems to me that it doesn't make any difference. That's just kind of how rivalries are."

Plummer believes that being the visitor, especially in a rivalry game, can actually help a team to focus. "Sometimes, you play even better. You hone in, you shut out all distractions, you focus and you pool all your energy into what you're doing, whereas when you're at home, it's not quite that intense feeling of everyone rooting against you," he said.

"You could make a lot about the home-and-away advantage, but good teams, they don't care. They play the same and find a way to win whether they're on the road or at home."

Graham and Rodriguez have differing views on the subject. "I think normally, the home team certainly would have a little bit of advantage with the home crowd," Rodriguez said. "To compare year to year is completely irrelevant. I think (the road team's recent success) is an anomaly and it's not something that normally happens."

But Graham doesn't think home field will make much of a difference in future Territorial Cup contests. "In rivalry games, you can throw everything else out," he said. "What I tell my players is, you are not going to remember what some person said to you hanging over the rail, you're not going to remember who had the best tweets or who talked the most trash – you are going to remember who won the game. That is one of the things that is always a challenge when going on the road, especially in a rivalry game."

Throw out the records

Most sports fans are familiar with the cliché, *you can throw the records out when these two teams get together.* But in this rivalry, that statement really does seem to apply.

"You can go in there thinking that X, Y and Z is going to happen, and it almost never does, especially when these two teams play each other," said Ryan Finley, sports editor for the *Arizona Daily Star* in Tucson and UA football beat writer for the *Star* from 2006-12. "I know it sounds like a cliché or sportswriter B.S., but certainly it seems like whenever they line up, you're going to see something that you did not expect to see in that game."

But don't just take it from the sportswriters.

"You can throw the records out; it's always going to be a hard-fought game," Foles said moments after his 2-8 Wildcats defeated 6-4 Arizona State at Sun Devil Stadium in 2011. "They can be 11-0 and we can be 0-11, and vice versa. It'll still be a hard-fought game."

ASU fullback Stephen Trejo (1997-2000) said the emotions of the game often carry more weight in deciding the outcome than the individual talent on each side. "It didn't matter if one team's record was 10-0 and the other's was 2-8; you knew you were going to get a hard-fought game regardless," he said. "You knew it was going to be physical and highly emotional, and the fans were going to be involved and crazy. From that standpoint, you didn't necessarily look at the other team's record and pre-judge how the game was going to be."

Kush, who coached in 21 games against the Wildcats, came to the same conclusion. "I think the records are insignificant," he said. "The mentality and the preparation (the Wildcats) are going to have the whole year because they hear about Arizona State, and the Arizona State people are going to hear about UA – that rivalry is there and it keeps building up."

Erickson has also been a part of many college football rivalries, and he knows they tend to function differently from other games. "Unless a team is way, way better – and I've seen it when they're way, way better and they got their rear-ends beat, too – you're going to have a dog fight from year to year," he said.

UA safety Clay Hardt (2000-03) advised gamblers to steer clear of the Duel in the Desert. "If I was betting, I'd never bet on one of those games, because you just never know what's going to happen," he said. "Usually it seems like (the team that loses is) the team that had the best chance of going to a nice bowl game. There's always a spoiler."

Healey said the fact that the team with the better record often loses these games – as was the case in 2010, 2011 and 2012 – is one of this rivalry's most important elements.

"In some ways, in my opinion, that kind of makes a rivalry," he said. "If you compare it to men's basketball, even though the schools consider themselves rivals, in the Lute Olson era, the Wildcats dominated the Sun Devils. And to me, that's not a rivalry.

"I think you have to have a situation where each of the teams has a reasonable expectation of success in the game to have a true rivalry. I think maybe that's what's made the ASU-UA games so great. Maybe there haven't been many years when both teams have been outstanding heading into the rivalry game. But I think you have a situation here where, just about every year, either team can reasonably enter that game with the expectation that they're going to have some success and win it."

Over the line?

From a 1958 incident in which UA alumni vandalized the brand-new Sun Devil Stadium in a protest of ASU's pending university status, to an on-field player brawl in 1996 in Tucson that led to police involvement, to a 2001 incident in which UA players ignited a scuffle by celebrating a victory with a dance on ASU's logo, some wonder whether fans and players have occasionally taken the rivalry too far.

"It was even the way the UA crowd would react to the players when you're coming out of that small locker room (in Arizona Stadium) one at a time, having junk thrown at you," Cozzetto said. "Some of the words that were said to the players, just the lack of respect for each team – that kind of bothered me."

Beyer said the intensity from the fans can sometimes push the players to cross a line. "It's personal and it's nasty, and now that I'm an older adult, it's like, does it really have to be that bad?" he said. "In other rivalries, it seems like there's a certain respect toward the other school's fans. But going up to UA-ASU games (in Tempe), the ASU fans are just so nasty to us. I assume we give it back to them just the same, but I don't like to conduct myself in that manner.

"If you're wearing the colors, you just want to be a little classier – particularly the younger people in groups. It's mob mentality when they get together."

Plummer recalled an on-field encounter with a former UA player that threw him for a loop before one particular rivalry game. "He pulled me over and grabbed my hand, and he said something that stuck out in my mind and kind of changed my mind about the rivalry a little bit. He said, 'You're a hell of a player, but I hate your guts,'" he said.

"And I kind of looked at him and I thought, 'Wow, I don't hate any of those guys over there.' For one, I don't know them, and two, they're just like me. They have families. They have mothers and fathers and brothers and sisters and grandmas that are watching. Why would I hate somebody who wore a different-colored uniform? If he was on my team, I'd love him, you know? So it was just kind of weird.

"I never really ever felt that way – like, 'I hate you, I hate you.' I had no reason at all to hate them. Even though they came from behind and beat us three years in a row, I didn't hate them. Of course, I wanted to beat them down – like mad, I wanted to beat them down – but I didn't ever really hate any of my opponents. I respect them, and I know some ASU fans will probably cringe when they hear me say that, but that was just me. I never really played with any hate in my mind."

Tomey said he and then-ASU coach Bruce Snyder realized that things had gotten out of hand after the on-field brawl in 1996, and they took to the airwaves to ask for civility among fans and players going forward. "I did think – and I thought Bruce thought, too – that it got over the edge," he said. "We both tried to say to our people that we need to make it a little more civil and try to (avoid) inflammatory comments and so on."

Spindler said he'd like to see the rivalry become more civil and see the two schools celebrate their similarities, much like the players who took the field in the first Duel in the Desert did well over 100 years ago.

"The truth of the matter is this great sports rivalry started in the tradition of collegiality and sportsmanship that we've lost track of, and I think that's a shame, because we really have so much in common as two institutions battling it out in the desert before they had fancy uniforms," he said. "It's kind of sad that we've lost that, and maybe someday we'll get that spirit back."

CHAPTER 1

Friendly Foundation, Wildcat Domination

That nastiness that has often come to define the Duel in the Desert was nowhere to be found in the first football meeting between The University of Arizona and The Territorial Normal School at Tempe on a cloudy Thanksgiving Day at Tucson's Carrillo Gardens Field in 1899.

In fact, it was pretty darn cordial.

"This is the thing that no one talks about," Spindler said. "The Normals took the train down to Tucson. The University students met them at the train station and gave them a tour of their new dormitories before the game."

The UA players then "had the sportsmanship and collegiality to host a Thanksgiving dinner with the whole team after the game," Spindler said.

While the friendly off-field nature of the rivalry didn't last far beyond that year, the tradition of playing on or near Thanksgiving has endured for the majority of the rivalry's history.

"Seasoned" Normals win inaugural contest

The Normals, coached by Fred M. Irish, who remained Tempe's head coach through 1906, had the better team that day – and immediately, home-field advantage was shown to not mean very much in the Duel. According to Bob Eger in his book, *Maroon & Gold: A History of Sun Devil Athletics*:

> A crowd of 300 watched the battle for the Territorial Championship Cup. After a scoreless first half, Normal right halfback Charlie Haigler and left halfback Walter Shute scored the game's only touchdowns. In those days, touchdowns were worth five points. The Normals made one of their two conversion kicks to take an 11-0 lead. They shook off a late safety by UA and held on for an 11-2 victory.

While there was a mutual respect among the players in 1899, it wasn't exactly shared among the fans in Tucson, as Abe Chanin wrote in his book, *They Fought Like Wildcats*:

> That inaugural season of '99 saw the U. of A. play its first intercollegiate game, although many Tucsonans in those days did not consider the Tempe Normal School a true university. Nevertheless, the Normal School had a seasoned team, for it had made an earlier start in football.

UA was definitely far less experienced, as it was led by head coach Stuart Forbes, who only briefly played football in Illinois, making him the most experienced UA player on the field.

Spindler's research led him to agree that the better squad won the inaugural game. "We had an extraordinarily talented team," he said. "I think the other thing was the 1899 game was UA's first competitive game, and we had played two previous games that season. We had a game in 1897, and we had been practicing since 1896 as a team. So it was pretty clear we had more experience, and we had some talented players on that team."

UA finished its inaugural season with a record of 1-1-1 after tying Tucson Town Team, then earning its first intercollegiate victory over Tucson Indian School.

The Normals, who finished 1899 with a perfect 3-0 record, might have chosen to savor their victory more had they known they wouldn't defeat UA again for 32 years.

The Cup is Created

The Thanksgiving Day game was the third and final one for Tempe that season in what was the short-lived Arizona Territorial Football League, according to Spindler.

And while the Territorial Cup was won by the Normals that year, it was not specifically created for the winner of the Duel. Tempe was awarded the cup for defeating Phoenix College, Phoenix Indian School *and* Arizona in 1899.

"The Territorial Cup is actually the championship trophy that was awarded to ASU for winning the league championship," he said. "It so happened that the third game of the season was against UA, and that victory clinched the league championship for us. So it wasn't really awarded specifically for that game."

According to ASU's Department of Archives and Special Collections, the cup itself, which was manufactured by Reed and Barton of Taunton, Mass., is composed of silverplate over Britannia base metal. In Reed and Barton's 1910 catalog, the cup design was advertised for $20 – about $500 by today's standards. The inscription on the cup still reads, "Arizona Foot Ball League 1899 Normal," and regardless of the winner of the annual Duel, it has always been ASU's property.

While the Territorial Cup has always been an important part of the rivalry's lore, it went missing sometime after the 1899 game – and it wouldn't be seen again for 81 years.

Spindler said the circumstances of the cup's disappearance are still a mystery. "The last evidence we have of the cup is that photo of the 1899 Normal squad on the steps of Old Main, which we believe was taken shortly after the game in 1899," he said.

"But there are no records that tell us what happened after that photo was taken.

"I've often speculated: If you had won a league championship cup, what would you do with that? My assumption is that it was on display in the (Tempe Normal) president's office and kept there."

Cats even the series in '02

UA and Tempe met on the gridiron only four times from 1900-1924, partly because both schools had years in which they didn't field a team. In 1902, UA earned its first victory over the Normals, 12-0, in the second-ever meeting. And for the first time in the rivalry, the game was the last of the season for both schools.

The leadership of quarterback Leslie Alexander Gillett, who doubled as Arizona's head coach that season, was instrumental in the victory and in a 5-0 season in which UA won the league championship and didn't allow a single point on defense.

The script had definitely flipped from the 1899 contest, as Tempe's side was not in the same kind of shape it was three years earlier. In fact, the Normals needed to bring in five players from the City of Tempe town team just so they would have enough personnel to compete against Arizona.

Off and on

After the 1902 game, the schools wouldn't meet again for 12 years, as UA, which had nine coaches from 1899-1913, didn't field a football team in 1903, '06 and '07, and Tempe didn't compete from 1907-1913.

In their next three meetings – in 1914, '15 and '19 – UA enjoyed shutout victories of 34-0, 7-0 and 59-0, respectively. The 1919 game had the most lopsided outcome of the rivalry's pre-World War II era.

Tempe athletic director George Schaeffer named himself head football coach of the Normals in 1914, and he headed up a team that had only one man who had ever previously played the sport.

Evolution of the "A" Mountains

In 1916, UA began a tradition that has endured in Tucson for nearly a century. According to Chanin:

> In those early days, Pomona College was one of the football powers in the West, and triumph over that team had so excited the University of Arizona students and the city folk that plans were made to erect a block "A" atop Sentinel Peak at the western edge of Tucson. Al Condron, a member of the 1914 team and student body leader who later was to lead Tucson's Chamber of Commerce, sparked the drive to construct the "A," to build for all time a tradition for the University of Arizona.

UA students raised nearly $300 – about $6,600 in 2013 money – to construct the "A."

In Tempe, the Normals constructed an "A" Mountain of their own – though the "A" didn't come right away. An "N" (for Normal) was placed on Tempe Butte near campus at about the same time as Tucson's "A" was erected. But things changed in 1925 – three years after the school adopted a new mascot: Bulldogs. According to Eger:

> For the first time, students painted a "T" on the Tempe butte. That early artwork was the beginning of a custom that has evolved into the painting of an "A" (for Arizona State), and an annual attempt by University of Arizona students to repaint the letter with their school colors.

Pop arrives, UA gets a nickname

UA became a football force in the 20th century's second decade thanks to James Fred "Pop" McKale, Arizona's football coach from 1914-30. In fact, it was under his leadership, during a UA game against Occidental College in 1914, that a *Los Angeles Times*

5

reporter noted that UA, despite losing the game, "showed the fight of wildcats," leading UA to adopt the Wildcat mascot.

Tempe's football program hadn't improved much by 1919, as the Normals didn't field a team during the World War I years of 1917-18 and had a limited number of men attending the teaching school. This led to a series of lopsided defeats at UA's hands, including a 59-0 drubbing in 1919. Coach George Cooper didn't have much to work with, as only 60 male students attended the school that year. As a result, McKale removed his starters early in the second half of the 1919 game to spare Tempe further embarrassment.

A motto born in Tucson, a hope renewed in Tempe

The 1926 season is one that UA fans best remember as the one in which star quarterback John "Button" Salmon, according to the legend, uttered to McKale what became the school's official motto, "Bear Down," on his deathbed 13 days following a car accident. That statement was relayed by McKale to his players to inspire them to defeat New Mexico State on the road later that week, which they did.

A year earlier, for the first time since the rivalry's founding,

the Bulldogs became legitimate competitors for their neighbors to the south. In fact, in the 1925 Duel, Tempe put points on the board against UA for the first time since the programs' initial 1899 meeting.

The '25 game was an early-season matchup for both the Wildcats and Bulldogs. Wrote Eger:

> The Bulldogs showed from the start that they had made up some ground in the five years since they had last played the Wildcats. They battled the Cats on even terms through a scoreless first half, then stunned the gathering in Tucson by taking a 3-0 lead late in the third quarter on a 41-yard drop kick field goal by Johnny Riggs. The Wildcats' superior depth finally paid off in the fourth quarter, however. They scored

twice in the final eight minutes to escape with a 13-3 victory. The Bulldogs had the ball on the UA 1 yard line when time expired.

More of the same

As it turned out, however, the Bulldogs' second victory – and their next points – against the Wildcats were still several years away. In 1926, '28 and '29, McKale's UA squad defeated Tempe by a combined score of 100-0.

The stability that McKale provided in Tucson was in sharp contrast to the coaching carousel up north. Tempe had five head coaches during McKale's 17-year tenure, which remains the longest in UA football history.

Tempe finally obtained some stability at the head coaching position in 1923 when it hired Aaron McCreary, who played for Tempe in 1914 and returned to his alma mater to coach all of its athletic squads.

McCreary led Tempe to a respectable 25-17-4 record over seven seasons, but he went 0-6 in his final season in 1929 – and, just as importantly, posted an 0-4 career record against UA.

A disparity in athletic resources made it difficult for McCreary's Bulldog teams to compete against the Wildcats. In 1929, UA opened Varsity Stadium, now known as Arizona Stadium, thanks in large part to the efforts of McKale, who spearheaded a committee that raised money to build what was originally a 7,000-seat facility.

Also in '29, Tempe was renamed Arizona State Teacher's College (ASTC), and former Stanford All-American Ted Shipkey took over the coaching reigns after the season.

1930: Prelude to a Bulldog breakthrough

In 1930, the Wildcats enjoyed another shutout of the Bulldogs, but there were a pair of bright spots for ASTC. First, the game was a much more competitive 6-0 contest in Tucson. Second, the freshmen, who had a separate team because the NCAA didn't allow them to compete in varsity contests until 1972, made short work of the UA freshmen in a 39-6 romp.

The freshmen and varsity results were a foreshadowing of a breakthrough the following year, when a brand-new conference was born.

"Wildcats aren't wild any more".

In 1931, the Border Intercollegiate Athletic Association – more commonly known as the Border Conference – was formed, and UA and ASTC were two of its first five members.

The Wildcats and Bulldogs were set to play that year on Halloween at Irish Field in Tempe. Fred Enke, who went on to be a longtime basketball coach at UA, coached his first and only season of football for the Wildcats that year after taking over for McKale, who led UA to an 81-32-6 record in his 17-year run in Tucson.

The game preview in *The Arizona Republic* noted that Arizona had the advantage in size, but ASTC had a big edge in speed, and it suggested that this could be a breakthrough game in the rivalry for the Bulldogs, who were in first place in the Border Conference's initial season:

> The heavyweight advantage held by the Tucson team will be off-set by speed and trickery on the part of the Tempe eleven, according to prediction … It will be the case of a hard-hitting, fighting fast team against an experienced, heavy team of Wildcats, and either of the two will have an even chance to win, the experts say.

That night, led by Norris Stevenson, who the *Republic* called "a human dynamo" and "probably the best all-around football player in Arizona" with his triple-threat ability to pass, run and kick, Tempe scored twice in the first quarter en route to an easy 19-6 win.

The intro in the *Republic* story the next day read, "Arizona's Wildcats aren't wild any more," and the writer wasn't hesitant to convey just how lopsided the win was for the Bulldogs:

> The Bulldogs of Arizona's Teachers college at Tempe tamed (UA) last night by tenaciously tearing them to bits, scattering furs over the gridiron of Irish Field … (T)he final score of 19 to 6 does not truly reflect the effectiveness with which the Shipkey-coached players ran rampant over their much heavier and experienced opponents … It was largely Stevenson's slashing play that sent the Bulldogs out in front early in the game, enabled them to widen the gap before the first quarter had been finished, and to tuck the game safely away at the half way mark.

UA's Hank Leiber, who would later become a major league baseball star, was the lone bright spot for the Wildcats, setting up their only touchdown with a 63-yard run in the third quarter. But it was Shipkey and Stevenson who "were the toast of the Valley of the Sun for many a day," according to longtime *Republic* writer Dean Smith.

Tempe went on to win the inaugural Border Conference championship that season. But just as in 1899, the Tempe contingent might have taken more time to relish the victory if it knew that another long dry spell against UA – in this case, an 18-year drought – was forthcoming.

Don't mess with Tex

ASTC and UA met eight more times from 1932-42 before both schools temporarily suspended their football programs during World War II. Tempe lost many of its stars from the '31 season, and in '32, UA returned to its winning ways with a 20-6 victory over the Bulldogs in Tucson. Shipkey, who was released due to severe budget cuts stemming from the Great Depression, was replaced by Rudy Lavik, who previously coached at what is now Northern Arizona University in Flagstaff.

In 1933, the Wildcats hired Gerald "Tex" Oliver as their new track and field coach, and he was also persuaded to coach UA football for five seasons through 1937, bringing in many top players from California. During his tenure, UA was defeated just 11 times and lost just one game by more than a touchdown.

Oliver's first contest against ASTC in '33 set the tone for the domination that his teams would enjoy against the Bulldogs, but he may have made an early mistake, as he was so concerned that UA's starters would be overconfident that he had his reserves open the game. The result: ASTC led 7-0 at halftime.

In the second half, when Oliver finally let loose a very hungry group of starters, the Wildcats scored three times in the third quarter, and they went on to win easily, 26-7.

Tex's squads went 5-0 against ASTC, winning those contests by a combined score of 122-19. The Bulldogs failed to score more than seven points in any of those games, and they were shut out twice – in 1935 and '36, when Oliver led UA to back-to-back Border Conference championships.

Unfortunately for the Wildcats, after recruiting such talented athletes as quarterback Ted Bland and fullback Walt Nielson, who would become UA's first-ever All-Americans, Oliver would be lured from Tucson.

Tex's 20-6 win over ASTC in '37 was his final Duel, as Chanin wrote that the University of Oregon of the Pacific Coast Conference was so taken with him after UA beat its team, 20-6, that it hired him away from the desert.

Goodwin opens, Lavik sent packing

In 1936, ASTC took a bite out of UA's stadium advantage by opening the 5,000-seat Goodwin Stadium, named after Garfield Goodwin, a local businessman who was a member of the 1899 team that won the first-ever matchup with UA and eventually became a member of the college's Board of Education. The stadium included lights for night games, and its seating capacity increased to 9,500 in 1940 and 15,000 in '41.

In 1937, Lavik was fired from his head coaching position after posting records of 3-5, 4-3-1, 2-5-1, 4-5 and 0-8-1. In Lavik's place, ASTC president Grady Gammage hired former Alabama quarterback Dixie Howell.

An off-field scandal

One of the first documented accounts of off-field tension between the two schools came in the late 1930s, and it was bitter enough to put the rivalry on hold.

From 1938-40, UA and ASTC didn't play each other due to some thievery that the Wildcats alleged against their rivals. According to Eger:

> Arizona officials had canceled the series in protest after A-State recruiter Tom Lillico "stole" prime recruits Wayne "Ripper" Pitts, Walt "Cowboy" Ruth and Rex Hopper off the Tucson campus in the summer of 1937. Officials of the Tucson school said they would not play the dogs until the three former Glendale stars had concluded their college careers at A-State.

Bulldogs thrive during hiatus, UA hires Casteel

UA may have dodged a series of bullets by discontinuing the series against ASTC during those three years, as Howell led the Bulldogs to back-to-back Border Conference titles in 1939-40 while the Wildcats finished second and fifth, respectively, in the conference under the leadership of coach Miles Casteel, who the Wildcats hired in 1939.

UA right end and linebacker Ray Elzey (1942, 46-47), who left to serve in the Navy during World War II, described Casteel as a disciplinarian.

"He was a tough guy. He came from the Midwest where they were tougher than hell," he said. "He had us out there running

2-on-1s all the time, and if you didn't put out full bore, he'd (make you run) 10 laps around the track.

"He was a little over the hill by the time I got down there, and we didn't always see eye to eye, either. But I liked him. I think he was a nice guy on and off the field, very respectful. And we did pretty well in the Border Conference in those days."

When the rivalry resumed in 1941, so did the Wildcats' dominance, as Casteel had righted the ship in Tucson by then. UA earned a 20-7 victory over the Bulldogs (along with a Border Conference championship) in '41, and the Wildcats enjoyed their 11th shutout in the rivalry, 23-0, under Casteel in '42.

"Loose lips sink ships"

Elzey said the Duel was a passionate game, even in those days.

"It was a bitter rivalry then. We hated ASU. Of course, they weren't even ASU then," he said. "I went to (high) school with a lot of the guys that went to ASU. We were mortal enemies when we were there, especially after what I did."

Elzey unintentionally added fuel to the rivalry's fire the summer before the '42 game when he worked at a Tempe meat market. "A man named (Johnny) Baklarz worked in the store," he said. "We chatted for a while and he told me he was a member of the Arizona State football team. He was a tackle and a huge, bulky man from Alabama."

Elzey made the mistake of talking a little trash to Baklarz about the superiority of the UA football program. "To make a long story short, I told him we were going to run his team right out of the stadium this year," he said. "I guess he remembered what I said, and he went back and told his coach, and he put it on their bulletin board for the whole season."

Fast-forward to the '42 game in Tempe when Casteel noticed that the Bulldogs – especially Baklarz – seemed to deliberately target Elzey for punishment on the field, both on offense and defense, as college football athletes played both ways until 1965.

"It became so obvious to Casteel (that I was being singled out) that he yanked me out of the game and asked me what was going on," Elzey said. "I told him that this guy Baklarz had apparently taken my boasting back to his coach, and they were using it as a rallying point for their team."

Casteel eventually put Elzey back in the game to take his medicine, and despite ASTC's bulletin-board material, UA cruised to a shutout victory. But the young Wildcat learned a lesson that day.

"Never encourage an underdog," he said. "I learned my lesson well while in the Navy, because they had a slogan: Loose lips sink ships."

Off to war

In '42, both schools scrambled to form teams during the onset of World War II, as many Wildcats and Bulldogs were called to serve in the armed forces. While UA managed a 6-4 record that season, ASTC was in especially bad shape.

The Bulldogs scraped together a team in '42 under Hilman Walker, who had been Howell's assistant. But after going just 2-8, failing to score in five games and having fewer than 20 men on the team by the end of the season, the school had no choice but to put the program on hiatus. The Wildcats followed suit, closing down their athletic programs when WWII began.

After the Allied forces claimed victory over Nazi Germany and the Axis powers, the rivalry resumed. And though it restarted the same way it ended before the war – with UA in charge – it wouldn't remain that way for long.

CHAPTER 2

Asu Uprising

As much as UA dominated the rivalry with Tempe/Arizona State Teacher's College before World War II – and ASTC would once again be rebranded, this time as Arizona State College at Tempe, in 1945 – the most lopsided defeat in Duel history came in their first post-war matchup.

With plenty of their pre-WWII teammates rejoining the squad when their football program restarted, the Wildcats resumed their rivalry with Arizona State in 1946, defeating the Bulldogs 67-0 in Tucson. UA was led by Tucson native "Firing" Freddy Enke, Wildcat quarterback from 1946-47 and son of the former UA football and basketball coach of the same name.

UA offensive lineman and defensive end Moose "Junior" Crum (1946-47) said he and his teammates didn't take the younger Bulldogs too seriously. "We didn't consider it that much of a rivalry. The big rivalry came later on," he said. "Most of us were veterans and were older – 21-22 years old."

Crum said he remembers the '46 game well – and not just because of the score. "I scored the only touchdown I ever scored in college," he said. "I took a lateral off tackle. Our fullback drove through the hole and was heading for a touchdown, and (the Bulldogs) grabbed him, and I was following him. He lateraled to me and I scored."

The view from Tempe

From the Tempe perspective, ASC quarterback Sid Glenn (1947-48), who served as an assistant coach in '49, said the rivalry was "vicious" back then, and UA definitely had one major advantage.

"I'll tell you this: The scholarship situation was so lopsided at the time. A number of years later they started to equalize them out, but most of the legislature were people who graduated from UA," he said. "I think we hadn't beaten them in 20 years or so. Every game was important, but that game (was especially important)."

Casteel's Wildcats finished 4-4-2 and in fourth place in the Border Conference in '46. ASC head coach Steve Coutchie, who had coached at Mesa High School the previous 18 years, resigned at the end of his first and only season in Tempe after posting a 2-7-2 record and an eighth-place conference finish.

Devils and Angels

The 67-0 game led to a needed change in the ASC football program, and President Gammage promised that better things were ahead. ASC received assistance from a civic group called the Phoenix Thunderbirds that joined forces with ASC boosters to improve the Bulldogs' athletic programs. The combined entity was named the Sun Angels by member and well-known vegetable grower M. O. Best.

The Sun Angels then pitched an idea for yet another new nickname for the school – the Sun Devils, which the student body approved by a vote of 816-196 in November 1946. Berk Anthony, an artist with Walt Disney Productions, designed a new mascot named Sparky to reflect the name change.

Meteor lands in Tempe

The newly branded Devils didn't turn the rivalry around right away, but they sent warning shots down south in 1947 and '48.

First, ASC hired Notre Dame assistant coach Ed Doherty as its new head coach before the '47 season.

"He was a great coach and a great man – a real character builder," Glenn said. "He was tough but fair, and probably one of the best offensive minds in the country at that time. He gave us some plays that were very tricky-type stuff. We were making a pitch fake, then a dive fake, then back to a pitch – which was always to Wilford, of course."

Mesa High star Wilford "Whizzer" White, who was nick-named "The Mesa Meteor," starred at running back for the Sun Devils from 1947-50. Whizzer learned to dislike UA before his first collegiate game, and even before he decided to play football in Tempe, after witnessing the Wildcats attempt to, in his opinion, run up the score against their rivals.

"I went down to the Arizona State-UA football game in Tucson when they beat us 67-0, and (the Wildcats) had their first-string players in the game at the end. I eliminated UA (from college consideration) that night," he said. "I couldn't see having their first string – Freddy Enke and all those guys – in at the very last minute of the game. I realize there's no love lost between the schools, but that was a little bit far out for them, to have their first team out there when it was that bad."

Doherty, White, Glenn and the rest of the Devils began to turn the dial on the rivalry with much more competitive contests – a 26-13 loss in Tempe in 1947 when most of ASC's players were freshmen, and a 33-21 defeat in Tucson in '48, a game featuring the most points the Sun Devils had ever scored against UA to that point.

Glenn remembers the optimism that the team had heading into the '48 contest. "We practiced in the area of the hotel (in Tucson), and we left ahead of time earlier than we did to go to other games," he said. "Coach put a lot of new stuff in, and we were really hyped up for UA. But they were very strong, very good and a physical team, and they beat us."

But Glenn said the Devils could sense that the rivalry's tide was slowly starting to turn. "It started to equalize after (the '47 game), and our team progressively got better," Glenn said. "'48 was better, and '49 was much better."

Doherty rallies the troops

Under Doherty, the Sun Devils turned the Duel on its head, and in 1949, they enjoyed their first win over the Wildcats in 18 years.

White said Doherty placed an emphasis on beating UA even before the 1949 season began.

"I suppose that, because of the fact of what the record (in the rivalry) had been up to that point, that was a game we pointed toward all year long," he said. "That week of practice is almost indescribable because it was so hyped up, in fact almost to a fault – you're so keyed up and hyped up that you make mistakes, so we had to cool it a little bit.

"The practice leading up to the game, there was no way to describe it. We knew that if we beat them, that would complete our season."

Angels give Devils their due

Perhaps the biggest catalyst for the flip in the rivalry's script was Casteel, who resigned as Arizona head coach and headed north to become executive director of ASC's newly formed Sun Angel Foundation.

Greg Hansen, longtime sports columnist for the *Arizona Daily Star* in Tucson, said Casteel's transition played a key role in enhancing the influx of talent and bringing in needed revenue for athletics to Tempe by developing the embryonic organization. "They hired him to do it, and he did it," he said. "I know he wasn't a big-time coach (in Tucson) and that they weren't great or anything like that, so he didn't have a big legacy here. But it's funny how his legacy became not coaching (UA) but starting the Sun Angel Foundation."

Crum agreed that Casteel's move was an important rivalry milestone. "He helped Arizona State recruit money and players," he said. "That's when Arizona State started on their upswing."

UA, which had won 11 in a row against ASC, was still favored by oddsmakers to win the 1949 game in Tempe, according to Jeff Metcalfe of *The Arizona Republic*, partly because there was speculation that the Devils' star player might not make it onto the field. "White suffered a slight concussion during practice but had no intention of sitting out," he wrote.

White didn't just suit up; he bowled over UA's defense in '49, rushing 45 times for 145 yards and two touchdowns that evening as part of a 34-7 rout in front of 18,000 fans at Goodwin Stadium. A *Phoenix Gazette* sportswriter noted that White "bounded into the air with all the fervor of an exuberant kid on Christmas morning" upon scoring both of his TDs.

UA safety and halfback Karl Eller (1949-51), a Tucson native who would become a successful ad executive and ultimately saw Arizona name its business school after him, was also impressed with Whizzer. "He was a tough cookie. He was very fast and a solid player," he said. "We beat him in high school but couldn't beat him in college."

White recalled an early touchdown he scored in that game that one UA player, Tucson native Fred Batiste, didn't appreciate. "It was a sizeable gain, and I went into the end zone and crossed the goal line, and I was almost out of the end zone when Freddy hit me from behind," he said. "I came up a little bit disturbed and had a few words with Freddy, and I think that kind of fired us up a little bit, too."

UA placekicker John Carroll (1949-50) said the final score had him shaking his head. "I remember I was really surprised that the score wasn't more in our favor because we moved the ball fairly well; we just couldn't score," he said. "But I think they were a better team. Whizzer White was a great athlete. He passed effectively, and he also ran."

Carroll said the Wildcats were a despondent group following the loss. "I remember at the end of the game, a lot of these veterans and really tough hombres were in tears having lost to them," he said. "And I said, 'Come on you guys, we play Michigan State (next week). Let's look ahead.'

"And one of the guys, Roy Rivenburg, a senior and kind of the all-star of the team – he was a center and linebacker – took me aside and said, 'John, I wouldn't say anything.' It was good advice."

UA didn't recover in time for its next game; it lost to Michigan State, 75-0, the following week.

For the Devils, the game was a culmination of a journey that Doherty was hired specifically to lead. "That was the game that we pointed to, and it took us two years under Coach Doherty that we finally came about, and it was a big night," White said. "After that many years of being beat by them, it was quite a thing.

"And then we beat them down there."

Encore performance

Carroll recalled that UA coach Robert Winslow, who was hired to replace Casteel but led the Wildcats to a record of just 2-7-1 in '49, wanted to beat ASC so badly that season that he tried to teach his players a move that wasn't exactly legal in college football.

"We had a bad season that year, but before the (ASC) game, the guys really wanted to win, and so Coach Winslow was out teaching them how to do a block that had been outlawed – the chop block. And he spent a whole week before the game teaching them that," Carroll said. "We had a line coach – a great guy and also a war veteran named Carl Mulleneaux. He said, 'That block won't work. Anyone who's a good football player can get out of it, no problem.'

"So Winslow tried several times to put that block on Mulleneaux, and Mulleneaux knocked him to the ground each time."

Carroll said Mulleneaux's upstaging of Winslow ultimately got the assistant fired. "So you can see that the team at its core was not great that year," he said.

The Devils topped their '49 performance with an even more lopsided win in 1950 in what was their first victory over the Wildcats in Tucson since their inaugural contest 51 years earlier.

In front of a then-record crowd of 27,000, White scored a pair of touchdowns on 1- and 57-yard runs, and backs Manuel Aja, Mark Markichevich and Marvin Wahlin also had big games in a 47-13 thumping.

ASC fullback and linebacker Bob Tarwater (1951-53) said the role that White played in the rivalry's momentum shift can't be overstated. "I think they couldn't catch up with him," he said. "He ran in the open field and broke plays. If the hole wasn't open on the left side, he'd reverse field and outrun them back on the other side. He was just a good open-field runner."

White said beating UA on its home turf was especially satisfying. "It's hard to describe what the feeling was during and after the game," he said. "It was quite a chore after so many years of not being competitive against those guys, and it was something to beat them on their home field."

Glenn didn't get the chance to beat UA during his playing career, but he savored it as president of the ASC student body in '49 and '50. "It was a personal feeling of victory because we hadn't beaten them in so long," he said. "It was a great feeling, and we knew there was a turnaround in the college right then and there. And things kept getting better."

A 60-pointer of their own

In 1951, the Devils once again piled points on the Wildcats in a 61-14 demolition in Tempe, which remains the most lopsided victory they've ever enjoyed in the series.

ASC didn't miss a beat in the rivalry in '51 even though Doherty had been replaced as head coach by offensive guru Larry Siemering, who led the Devils to a 6-3-1 overall and 4-1 Border Conference record in his only season in Tempe.

"He was so creative. He had a great offensive creative mind, and it was really a pleasure learning from him and learning offense the way that he was teaching it," said Sun Devil quarterback Dick Mackey (1951-54). "We were very successful with it, too. We really took to it."

Tarwater also appreciated Siemering's approach to offense. "He had lots of ball-faking and so forth; you wouldn't know whether the ball was going through the middle or off tackle and around," he said. "To me, he was the best (coach) I had, and we beat (UA) pretty good that year."

It was Siemering's tricky offensive schemes that had the Wildcat defense guessing – mostly incorrectly – in the '51 game, as Tarwater and three other backs set an NCAA record by each rushing for over 100 yards. "He used the fake up the middle, and the plays that were working were around the end," Tarwater said. "The halfbacks would fake it up the middle, and then it would be a lateral around the ends, and UA just didn't get it schemed."

Whenever UA began to catch on to the misdirection, Tarwater said, Siemering would change things up again and give the ball to a halfback who'd dart up the middle untouched. "He'd be through the hole and behind the linebackers before they knew what was happening," he said.

One and done

Unfortunately for ASC, ball fakes weren't the only trickery that took place in Tempe that year, as Siemering resigned after the '51 season when it was revealed that an ASC player, who was competing under an assumed name, violated NCAA rules by playing for the Devils after he had played for Indiana the previous season.

"I really believed in him, and he really did teach us a lot," Mackey said of Siemering. "I always wondered why that occurred, having an ineligible player play for us. We really did not need him at the time. If the coaches would've sat him for a year, that would've been fine, but it didn't happen that way."

It was Siemering's departure that would help swing the rivalry back in the Wildcats' direction in the mid-1950s.

Winslow goes three and out

After the '51 beating at the hands of UA's newly adept rivals, the administration had seen enough. Winslow was fired after three seasons, a 12-18-1 record in Tucson, three Border Conference finishes of fifth place or worse and an 0-3 record against the Devils, including a combined score of 142-34 in those losses.

"He was probably the worst coach we ever had," Eller said. "He and his staff, most of them came from Southern Cal, and he was a very tough guy and pretty good recruiter, but he didn't have a very successful three years. That's when they hired Warren Woodson."

Woodson comes to Tucson, "Cloud of Dust" Clyde lands in the Valley

The Devils and Wildcats both introduced new head coaches before their '52 campaigns.

Warren Woodson, who had coached Hardin-Simmons University in Texas since 1941, was brought on board at UA. Don Bowerman, who played four different positions for the Wildcats from 1953-56, said Woodson was great with X's and O's but not so much in the character department.

"Woodson was an offensive genius. He could make changes at halftime that just did wonders. But his personality was severely lacking," he said. "I thought he was sarcastic, and he coached by intimidation."

Another Wildcat who didn't care for Woodson's personality was "The Cactus Comet" Art Luppino (1953-56), arguably the greatest running back in UA history. "I couldn't relate to the man. I didn't understand him and he didn't understand me," he said. "We didn't have much to do with one another.

"I thought he was strange. He didn't have any relationship with the players that I know of. He was a cynic, he was very sarcastic and he was so different from a high school coach that it was a disappointment."

Meanwhile, ASC hired Clyde Smith, who – perhaps ironically in light of the Siemering scandal – coached at Indiana from 1948-51.

The difference between Smith's and Siemering's offensive philosophies could not have been more stark, Tarwater said, noting that Smith's conservative, grind-it-out philosophy contrasted dramatically with Siemering's wide-open, misdirection style. "Being from the Midwest, Coach Smith's philosophy was three yards and a cloud of dust," he said.

And Mackey said that approach didn't attract a lot of talent to Tempe. "He was very conservative, and we really started to lose good recruits," he said. "I can't just point the finger at him, but it was difficult."

Johnson saves the Devils

In 1952, ASC notched its fourth straight win over UA on a rainy November day in Tucson – though with a final score of 20-18, it was a much closer contest than the Devils' previous three victories.

The game was also Mackey's first as starting quarterback. But the hero of the day was running back John Henry Johnson from St. Mary's College, Calif.

The '52 season was Johnson's last as a Sun Devil, and he went on to have a 13-year NFL career at running back – but the most important play of the '52 Duel came with Johnson on defense and the Wildcats moving the ball deep in Sun Devil territory in the final minute.

"We were ahead by two towards the end of the game. It was the last play of the game, and he intercepted the ball (in the end zone) and saved us," Mackey said. "That was really a good game. He was an amazing athlete."

ASC finished that season with a 6-3 record and a Border Conference championship, while UA ended Woodson's first season at 6-4 and in third place in the conference.

Woodson wouldn't have a great deal of overall success at Arizona, but he would have plenty against the Sun Devils.

Cats regain the upper hand

Johnson's late pick kept UA from scoring at the end of the 1952 game, but the Devils didn't do much to keep the Wildcats out of the end zone in their next two matchups.

"I don't think we had as much talent. I think at that time they had some better athletes, and we just collapsed," Mackey said. "We were really sliding down during that time, which was pretty hard to take."

From the Wildcats' perspective, their 35-0 win in 1953 and 54-14 win in '54 against the Sun Devils righted the ship. On the ASC side, Mackey said it wasn't a lack of talent but rather a lack of direction that was the problem. "We felt that a lot of it had to do with the fact that our preparation was not to the point that it should have been in both games, because we did have the talent," he said.

Luppino remembered the Devils' 1953 and '54 squads the same way. "I remember that Tempe was not a very good, well-coached football team," he said. "They had good athletes, but they weren't in good condition and they didn't seem to jell. They always had a lot of talent up there, but sometimes maybe too much."

In 1954, Luppino was No. 1 in all of college football in rushing yards, return yards, all-purpose yards, and points scored – and ASC was just another one of his victims.

"We were the superior team. In fact, it was a mismatch," he said. "I don't know if it was because they had a lot of injuries or we played exceptionally well, but it wasn't a very good football game - for the fans, anyway. It was one of those games that was one-sided, and the motivation (for the losing team) disappears."

The road to Arizona State University

In 1953, the Arizona Board of Regents approved ASC's first two individual colleges: the College of Liberal Arts and the College of Education. The following year, the board gave ASC permission to create two additional colleges.

As the state's only university since 1885, UA resented this development, and its members who served on the Board of Regents were afraid that university status for ASC was right around the corner.

"They were concerned about funding, ultimately," Spindler said of the UA contingency. "They felt it was not a wise use of public money to fund two universities in the state. They felt (UA) could serve the needs of the entire state as far as education.

"I think that was probably their strongest argument. They also had some concerns about whether we could achieve the level of quality that they had achieved as the land-grant college in Arizona and a long history of research that we did not have until the mid-to-late '50s."

The 1954 measure to allow for the creation of the additional colleges in Tempe was approved by the Board of Regents in a highly contested 5-4 vote – though the board decided not to rename Arizona State College at that time.

"The modern-day Board of Regents was formed in 1946 right after the war, and historically there had been very, very few (ASC) graduates as members of the Board of Regents," Spindler said. "So between the concerns of the University of Arizona, a UA-packed Board of Regents and members of the legislature who were opposed, it was really an uphill battle for this institution to become a university. And I think that one way of expressing that frustration was on the football field."

Sun Devil running back Bobby Mulgado (1954-57) remembers the off-field fuss but said he didn't let it get to him. "I know there was a controversy about us becoming a university. I think it's because they were against everything we wanted to do," he said. "But we were there to win, win, win – it didn't make any difference what we were. It was for Arizona State, and showing them what we had."

But a name change in Tempe, and the fears of many in Tucson, would be realized soon.

Devine and Kush head west

Under Clyde Smith's direction, Luppino said the disarray among the ASC players was palpable. "They never seemed to have the same 11 guys on the field from one game after another, and there was a lot of shuffling around," he said. "That was until Dan Devine came along. He added a new dimension to their program. They were very lucky to find a man like that."

Devine, a young Michigan State assistant, was hired in 1955 to head ASC's talented but dysfunctional football squad – and he got immediate results, leading the Devils to a 7-1-1 record in '55 heading into their meeting with the Wildcats at Goodwin Stadium.

But it was an assistant coaching hire that would be Devine's most important contribution to Arizona State football. Frank Kush, who was a defensive lineman for Devine at Michigan State, was serving in the Army and coaching the Fort Benning football team in Georgia when he got a phone call from Devine before the 1955 season.

"I got the fortunate call from him that he was taking the head job at Arizona State, and he wanted to know if I'd be interested in coaching," he said. "I kind of got elated and jumped at it. My wife, my son Dan, who was only a couple months old, and I went back to Michigan – and I drove and I drove and I drove, all the way across the southwestern United States."

Suffice it to say that Kush, who would serve as offensive and defensive line coach under Devine, was less than impressed with the comparatively small Goodwin Stadium when he finally pulled into Tempe on a Sunday. "As a student, I had the opportunity to play at Michigan, Notre Dame and all those places. So I was looking for the same (kind of stadium), and I couldn't find it," he said. "I stopped and asked a guy, and he said to turn right on College (Avenue), and I came right through the campus.

Then I asked another guy about the stadium, and he said, 'Go back, it's on your left-hand side.' That was my first experience with Goodwin Stadium."

Comet crashes Devine's debut

Luppino put on a show for Devine and Kush in their first game against the Wildcats, as he scored the only UA touchdown of the game off a 20-yard rush in the first quarter.

Kush still remembers his first Duel, in '55, specifically for the dominance of Luppino, who led the NCAA in rushing yards for the second straight season. "I thought he was one of the great running backs I'd ever seen," he said. "We had some good ones when we were at Michigan State and we were national champs, but I thought he was elusive, good at acceleration and read blocks really well."

Mulgado answered Luppino's score with a 1-yard TD run in the second quarter, but he missed the PAT – and it proved to be crucial, as neither team scored in the second half. The final score: UA 7, ASC 6.

Another defensive play from an offensive star

UA quarterback Ralph Hunsaker (1955-58) remembers playing well as a freshman in the '55 game, but like Johnson three years earlier, his most important contribution came on the other side of the ball.

"I recall knocking a pass down in the end zone that was intended for Bobby Mulgado that would have meant a win for them," he said. "We didn't throw the ball as much in those days, but I went 13 for 19 in passing, which I thought was pretty decent for a freshman."

Luppino, who was also playing defense during that sequence, said he can still visualize the crucial play that Hunsaker, a Mesa product, made to seal the win. "It was the last play or the next to the last play of the game, and Tempe threw a bomb, and (Mulgado) was obviously going to catch it," he said.

"And Ralph came out of no place, and he came up and just slapped the ball out of this guy's hands.

"I can still see that. And the last time I spoke to Ralph about 10 years ago, oddly enough, *he* can still see that. It's just imprinted on our minds. Of course, I was the happiest guy in the stadium. But that was the end of that. We took possession and there was just a few seconds left."

The play gave UA, which was just 4-4-1 heading into the matchup, its third straight victory over ASC – and the 1955 game became one of the earliest examples of the Wildcats defeating a more talented Sun Devil squad.

Replay reveals deflection

When asked about the '55 game, Mulgado didn't mention the TD he scored – only his PAT that sailed wide right. "It wasn't a good memory, but it's something I'll always remember," he said.

Bowerman, however, is convinced that UA lineman Eddie Sine deflected Mulgado's kick. "He got a finger on their extra point and made it go wide," he said.

A 2009 *Arizona Republic* story by Bob Young confirmed Bowerman's assertion. "It wasn't until later that film revealed that (Sine) actually had grazed the ball with a fingertip, sending it just wide in a 7-6 UA victory," he wrote.

The '55 game is still tied for the lowest-scoring contest in Territorial Cup history – and for the next 55 years, it would be the only game in the rivalry decided by a blocked extra point.

Bowerman booted

Thanks to Bowerman, the scoreless second half of the '55 game literally became a slugfest, as late in the game, he tackled Mulgado on a special-teams play and then promptly got ejected by the officiating crew.

"I had broken my finger in practice a couple weeks before and had my hand in a cast. And for some reason, maybe it was the excitement of the game, but after I started to get off the pile, I just popped him one right in the face with the cast. And he didn't have a facemask," he said. "And of course their bench and their coaches saw it, and the officials saw it, and my butt was gone."

The incident was one of the earliest examples of unsportsmanlike play in an increasingly heated rivalry.

Devine Gets It

Despite the loss to the Wildcats in his Duel debut, Sun Devil running back Leon Burton (1955-58), who followed Devine to Tempe after he originally committed to play for him at Michigan State, said the entire team loved playing for him.

"He was just open. If we wanted to talk to him, he was just like a dad, and you could talk to him," he said. "And he took care of his ballplayers. If there was anything he could do for me, he was there. You couldn't ask for a better coach as a mentor for you."

Kush said he and Devine's different coaching styles meshed well. "Dan Devine was a very intelligent, knowledgeable guy," he said. "He wasn't the same kind of jackass I am – a disciplinarian. But he knew the game extremely well. He was one of those intellectual coaches that did a commendable job."

With his connections in the East and Midwest, Devine was the first coach in the rivalry to specifically target those parts of the country for recruiting purposes. "UA took care of in-state kids and a few out-of-staters, and ASU with Dan Devine and Frank Kush all had connections in Ohio and Pennsylvania, and they recruited heavily out of that area," recalled UA linebacker Jim Geist (1956-59).

But ASC fullback, linebacker and defensive back Ron Erhardt (1955-58) said Devine grasped the importance of the UA game soon after that '55 contest, and he made sure his out-of-state recruits did, as well.

"I distinctly remember that the week of the (1956) game, we practiced at old Goodwin Stadium, and they would play the UA (fight) song throughout the whole practice at full blast so that we would be used to it," he said. "I guess that added a certain element of excitement for most of us because we were anxious to not be making mistakes out in practice, and because of going down to Tucson and playing them, we knew we were going to face that, and we didn't face that with any other team that we played. So that was pretty exciting.

"And, of course, everybody on campus was pretty open about making sure that we knew that this was a very important game and that this made the season for us."

Kush said Devine understood the Duel in the Desert thanks to another big rivalry he'd been a part of. "I think Dan Devine learned that, being at Michigan State and the rivalry he had between Notre Dame and Michigan State, it was very similar to the rivalry that (the Sun Devils and Wildcats) developed here in the state of Arizona," he said.

Off-field fight escalates

As Arizona State grew along with the city of Tempe and the Phoenix metropolitan area, there was a growing feeling of inevitability that ASC would soon become ASU, meaning that UA would have to share the state with another university for the first time in seven-plus decades.

But that didn't mean that Arizona's first university wouldn't fight against that development until the bitter end – and the administration made sure that its football players were a part of that fight.

"Hell, they made us take petitions around the neighborhood that said, 'One university's plenty for the state of Arizona,'" Bowerman said. "They had us, the athletes, going around the neighborhood getting people to sign petitions to try to keep them from making a university out of them. I (only) did it because I was told to."

Hunsaker still remembers the emotions involved from the Wildcat side of the university fight but said the passion for the issue lay less with the athletes and more with the administration and alumni. "It was a big fight. There were petitions going on at the UA against them becoming a university," he said. "But to be honest with you, I didn't really talk much with my teammates about that issue. I really didn't carry on much of a conversation about it."

But the Sun Devil players sure did, and Erhardt said he and his teammates didn't understand why UA was so vehemently opposed to ASC's growth. "Although all of us came from different areas, it made no sense to us that this was taking place," he said. "We were as good as they were and we were so excited to be getting an education, and (we were) at the beginning of some pretty substantial growth in Tempe and Arizona that we were very excited about."

Burton said the university issue revved up him and his teammates. "That was one of the things about UA – at that time they didn't want us to become a university. (Beating them) was one way that we could prove in a sense that we can handle them and show them that we were a university, especially in the sporting portion of it – that we were competing for (Arizona State), and it was a rivalry for us," he said.

"We took it as a rivalry, and we didn't lose."

Sun Devil shutout

The Wildcats kept the Normals/Bulldogs/Devils from scoring in 13 of their first 30 meetings.

In 1956, the Tempe contingent finally returned the favor.

As part of a 9-1 season, Devine and the Devils ended the Wildcats' three-game winning streak in the Duel and beat UA, 20-0, in Tucson on Nov. 17. ASC players carried Devine off the field after his first rivalry win.

Hunsaker said there was no mystery behind the shutout. "They just had better players, there's no doubt about it," he said. "They recruited very well.

"Mulgado was an excellent player. They had Leon Burton, who was probably one of the top players in the nation my last two years. They had a really good team."

Hindering the Wildcats in the game was that Luppino, who had been hampered with injuries most of the season, wasn't his typical explosive self. But Erhardt said he and the rest of the defense were instructed to focus on him anyway.

"Luppino did some great things, and being a linebacker, he was one of the guys I was instructed to key in on. And because of the great job the guys on our front line did, we were pretty much able to shut that game down," he said. "One of the things we focused on all week was the fact that we did have enough of a defense that we could stop them from scoring.

"Our defensive coach, Al Onofrio, did such an outstanding job of preparing us for the game that we knew their tendencies thanks to his scouting and looking at film for tens of hours. We knew what they were going to do, and therefore the job became to stop (Luppino). The coaching staff was tremendously prepared for all of the games, but this one in particular."

Luppino, who still managed to gain 66 yards on 10 carries in what was his final Duel in the Desert, said the outcome wouldn't have been much different even if he had been at 100 percent.

"I think they'd have won. We had a lot of guys that weren't healthy, but we weren't a good football team to start with," he said.

Woodson let go

In 1957, UA decided to replace Woodson, who was let go following five mediocre years in the Old Pueblo and three victories against ASC sandwiched in between a pair of losses.

Aside from his team's performances, Bowerman said there were two additional reasons for Woodson's departure. "The boosters' club at the time was called the TownCats, and they were heavy hitters downtown. (Woodson) was trying to tell them to leave him alone and let him coach football, and they didn't take to that very well," he said. "Plus, there was the fact that, at the time, we had a university president named Richard Harvill who I thought was anti-athletic all the way."

In Woodson's place, UA hired ex-ASC coach Ed Doherty, who had led the Devils to back-to-back bowl appearances in his final two seasons in Tempe.

Hunsaker didn't think as highly of Doherty as he did of Woodson. "How do I say this? I kind of felt like Doherty was sort of at the end of his career, so to speak, and I didn't think his heart was in it as fully as Woodson's," he said. "I didn't enjoy playing for him quite as much as I did Woodson, and part of that was our record. Our records under him were terrible. And he wasn't good on the recruiting end."

Geist said Doherty, who was the backfield coach for the Philadelphia Eagles a year earlier, tried to install his "atomic bomb" pro-style offense at UA, but it didn't take. "We didn't have the talent and skills to execute it, and it was really a mess," he said. "We were just terrible."

For his part, Doherty complained of being unable to recruit in-state talent as effectively as Devine was due to what he thought were academic standards that were much higher in Tucson than in Tempe.

Regardless of the reason, the Wildcats went 1-8-1 in 1957 and 3-7 in '58 under Doherty. And the only thing uglier than their overall record during those two seasons was their performance against the Sun Devils.

Ranked Devils destroy Cats

As the momentum toward an ASC name change continued to grow, so did the Devils' stranglehold on the rivalry in what would be Devine's third and final season in the Valley.

ASC beat UA, 47-7, in what was the final game of the season for both teams and what turned out to be the final Duel at

Goodwin Stadium. The win capped ASC's first-ever perfect season (10-0), as the Devils finished with a national ranking of No. 11 in the final Associated Press poll, the best mark in school history at the time.

Quarterback John Hangartner played a major role in the win, as did Burton and Mulgado, who led the NCAA in total points that season with 96 and 93, respectively. In fact, the Devils led the nation in points per game (39.7) and rushing yards per game (444.9) in '57.

"Basically, we felt at the time that UA had nothing as a university, and they never did want us to be a university," Burton said. "And we wanted to prove that we were a stronger football team than they were at the time."

In contrast to the ASC squads of the early '50s, Erhardt said the '57 team acted as a high-functioning, unified unit thanks to Devine and Kush. "It was really one of the most cohesive things I've ever done in my life," he said. "Everybody was together, everybody supported everybody, and if somebody did make a mistake, you tried to help them cover it by performing to a higher level. We really functioned as a team.

"I think Frank and Dan made a great combination. They split up the responsibility, and Frank was teaching us things that all of us big players in high school had never been exposed to. The relationship we all had and the great relationship between Dan and Frank and all the other coaches – there was never any disagreement about anything. They probably disagreed in their meetings about what was going to happen, but once they got to the field, they knew what they wanted, and we performed to the best of our abilities. I really knew what a team was like my junior and senior years."

In particular, Erhardt said the coaching staff did a great job of helping ASC maintain its focus going into the emotion-packed rivalry game that season. "We were undefeated and we knew it, and we wanted to make sure that they wouldn't have an opportunity to come back and beat us," he said. "So we poured it on pretty heavy, and I think we were able to play the game accordingly."

Beginning of the Kush era

The University of Missouri took notice of Devine's success out West and offered him a job that he couldn't pass up, and he left Tempe to coach Mizzou after the 1957 season.

In his place, the Devils made perhaps the single most important move in the history of their football program, as well as the rivalry, by promoting Kush to the head coaching position.

Erhardt said Kush was more hands-on than Devine and was much more of a perfectionist than his predecessor. "Frank was really a teacher to the extent that he stood out there and showed you which way your feet were supposed to go when you made contact and where your hands were supposed to be, and of course, once we got that principle down, it was a matter of pretty outstanding compliance with what he wanted," he said. "He repeated it until you got it right – and obviously, that meant putting in a little extra time after everybody left.

"He surrounded himself with great assistant coaches that could handle the other things – the offenses, the defenses and the scouting – and he taught the guys what to do, not only on the field but as a matter of intensity and not giving up. Most of the teams that we played, we were in a lot better physical shape than they were. The games were not as hard as the practices were, so that made it easy for us. Of course, Frank had a standard that exceeded the 100-percent level, because that obviously wasn't enough for him. And I think all of us performed to that level. We all did things that we didn't think we could."

Geist said the '58 squad that Devine built and Kush led was one of the most efficient he'd ever seen. "That team was probably the best team of anybody I played against," he said. "If they had played a major schedule, I think they would have been nationally ranked at that time.

"They were so much better than we were most of the time I was there that it wasn't much of a rivalry. They just absolutely ran all over us."

Welcome to Arizona State University

On Nov. 4, 1958, 18 days before that season's game between the Wildcats and Sun Devils, Arizona voters overwhelmingly passed Proposition 200, which officially changed Arizona State College's name to Arizona State University. Students celebrated the victory with an on-campus dance and a rally just before midnight.

"If you look at that referendum, it didn't authorize research, it didn't authorize reorganization, it didn't authorize degree programs – all it did was change the name," Spindler said. "The battle over establishing colleges and research programs and broadening curriculum in some ways was already won earlier in the '50s when regents authorized the formation of several colleges to the point that *The Arizona Republic* came out and said, 'This is already a university; all we need to do is change the name.' The election only changed the name, but symbolically, that was a huge deal for the institution and the citizens of Arizona.

"The pressure (to expand ASC) and the growth of the metropolitan area of Phoenix ultimately resulted in the name change. For years through the late '40s and '50s, they kept pushing forward proposals to expand curriculum and to become more than a teachers' college. And it was clear that there was a demand to broaden the education offerings in the Valley that, ultimately, UA couldn't provide."

Prop 200 "burned into Sun Devil lore"

A month before the measure went up for a vote, however, a handful of individuals decided to tell Tempe what they thought of Proposition 200 by defacing ASU's brand-new stadium.

On the day of the first-ever game at Sun Devil Stadium, school officials noticed that vandals had apparently made their way into the stadium and burned the words "No 200" into the middle of the field. While the perpetrators were never found, the natural suspicion was that it was the handiwork of UA students or alumni.

Prop 200 "was literally burned into Sun Devil lore that year," wrote Richard Ruelas of *The Arizona Republic*.

Erhardt was taken aback by the vandalism. "Most of us at this stage had been playing 7-8 years of football and played in some pretty intense championship games – but that kind of thing, we'd never experienced that," he said. "It was, in my judgment, kind of a juvenile thing to do."

Erhardt said the act was an early example of some people taking the rivalry too far. "They had the tradition of painting the (Tempe Butte) 'A' red, and I guess we went down there and painted our colors, too, but I don't think we did anything on their field," he said.

Devils shut out Wildcats again

Tempe Normal won its first-ever meeting with UA. So did Arizona State University.

The Sun Devils enjoyed the passing of Prop 200 and earned a measure of revenge for the defacing of Sun Devil Stadium by going down to Tucson and shutting UA out for the second time in three seasons. The 47-0 win in Kush's first Duel as head coach, with Burton leading the way with three touchdowns, gave the Devils their second straight shutout of the Wildcats on their home turf.

"All of us had played in (high school) championship games where we came from, and we played in big stadiums with a lot of excitement. But I think that was probably the most emotional game that I've ever played in," Erhardt said.

And while payback was on the mind of ASU fans for the bitter university fight that UA had waged – an *Arizona Republic* story the day after the game quoted one ASU fan as saying, "We won this one like Proposition 200" – Erhardt said Kush made sure that his players were in the right frame of mind heading down to Tucson.

"I can recall the name-change committee taking us down to a parade in front of the legislature with our letter sweaters on, showing that we were as big a school as they were," he said. "But I think the day before the game, Frank's concentration was of course more on the game and being sure we were ready for the game. The university issue kind of stopped the night before the game, and you had to stop and study your plays."

Can't stop them

Erhardt said Kush wasn't a fan of trickery in his offensive scheme; his style was more of the grind-it-out, stop-us-if-you-can variety.

"Everybody in the stadium, whether it was the ASU fans or whether we played someplace else, knew what we were going to do," he said. "And when we got within the (opponents') 10-yard line, we were going to get in a certain formation and we were going to run the same play."

In practice, Erhardt said, Kush would have his defense focus specifically on stopping the run – the idea being that the offensive line and running backs needed to be able to move the pile forward, even if the opposing defense knew exactly what was coming.

This was the strategy that Kush employed during his thumping of the Wildcats in '58. "I remember (ASU offensive linemen) Tom Ford and Ken Kerr, in particular, would look at the other side of the line and say, 'You guys know we're coming here, don't you?'" Erhardt said. "And we did it so intensely, and our mechanics were excellent. That's what I remember happening in that game."

A new era

With both schools finally on equal academic footing, ASU knew it had the capacity to keep up with its neighbor to the South, both in education and on the gridiron.

But as far as the Duel in the Desert was concerned, the first half of the Frank Kush era was a mixed result for both universities.

CHAPTER 3

Kush and the Ultimatum

With the university issue in the rearview mirror and Frank Kush at the helm, ASU's football program was at the beginning of an unprecedented era of stability.

UA, meanwhile, was in a state of flux.

In 1959, new Wildcat athletic director Dick Clausen replaced Doherty with former Kansas and SMU assistant coach Jim LaRue – who was Clausen's second choice after his first preference, Dallas Ward, was forbidden by his wife to move to Tucson to take the position.

It all worked out pretty well for the Wildcats, though – at least in LaRue's first few seasons.

"Jim was a fine man, and still is," said UA offensive tackle and defensive lineman Dave Areghini (1961-63), a Phoenix Central High School graduate who was recruited by both LaRue and Kush. "He was a very good tactical football coach."

As is common in this rivalry, the head coaches had much more respect for each other than most of the fans and players did.

"I knew Jim LaRue, and I thought he was a good teaching coach and a disciplinarian," Kush said. "He did a good job recruiting. We competed against each other in recruiting, not only (in Arizona) but a lot of times in Pennsylvania."

LaRue said the feeling was mutual. "I had a lot of respect for (Kush) because he had a situation that I'm sure was similar to mine, and he was always respectful to me," he said. "I had no complaint about him or the way his program is run. I didn't have any right to.

"I haven't talked to Frank in a long time. We weren't old buddies, but I think we both had respect for each other."

Areghini said LaRue focused more on in-state talent than Kush did. "Jim got a hell of a recruiting class my senior year in high school, but outside of myself and one other player, I don't think anybody stayed for four years," he said. "Frank focused on out-of-state (athletes) and got some great talent.

"(LaRue) started off with some great recruiting years but lost a lot of players, primarily through academics, and he just didn't seem to be able to continue recruiting. He recruited Bobby Thompson, Joe Hernandez and some other people, but he just didn't seem to be able to recruit enough of those."

But Areghini said LaRue did highlight the importance of beating the Sun Devils. "Jim really focused, as did his assistants, on ASU," he said. "It certainly appeared that they did a lot more intelligence on the ASU players and their schemes, and they just talked the week before the game about how important this was – not to get everybody so psyched up that we were nervous, but particularly because it was the last game (of the season)."

UA quarterback Eddie Wilson (1959-61), a Chandler High School grad, said LaRue set the tone for the rivalry as soon as he set foot in Tucson. "That year, almost from the get-go, there was a commitment made that there was one team to beat, and that team was going to be ASU," he said. "And of course, all of the in-state products who were in that squad for those next three years, they bought into it. We all did, because in many cases, we were recruited by ASU.

"There was nothing against ASU – we respected them, and hopefully they respected us – but by golly, when we teed it up, one of us was going to win, and we wanted it to be us."

LaRue doesn't recall much about his head coaching days, but he still remembers the bitterness of the rivalry. "I know we were anxious to beat Arizona State, and we thought they were a dirty word," he said with a laugh.

Kush welcomes Devils to hell

To say that Frank Kush was a tough, demanding head coach is to note that it gets a little warm in Tempe in July. And more than one ex-Sun Devil said Kush was a fair man in that he treated everyone the same: equally badly.

Of course, most of his players didn't enjoy it at the time. "I think every single one of us felt that way. When you look back and think about how he treated us, which was all the same, I'll give him credit for that – but it wasn't very good," said ASU offensive guard and linebacker John Folmer (1963-65), who now serves as chairman of the Sun Bowl committee.

"But you don't really realize what kind of a man he is until you're away from him. He used to have a policy where he would take the seniors the last week (of the season) on the town for a couple of nights. And I remember he talked to us as a group and said, 'This is football, guys. This is fun. Wait until you get a kid who gets sick on you, or you've got to make mortgage payments you can't do. That's hard.' At the time you go, 'Yeah, right.' But later on in life, you start thinking about some of the things he told you that final evening you were with him. And it stuck with me forever."

Like Folmer, ASU quarterback Ron Cosner (1959-61) said he came to understand and appreciate Kush's hard-hearted approach. "I've coached 44 years of high school sports," he said, "and in the back of your mind, every time you coach, whether you yell at somebody or pat them on the back, you are trying to get those people to be a better athlete or get them to the point where you think they could be. I think that's what Frank was doing."

Kush's kids escape in '59

Most ASU fans won't argue that Kush built more high-caliber football teams in Tempe than any two other Sun Devil head coaches combined. But his team hit a rough patch in the rivalry almost immediately after he took over.

In 1959, ASU had just enough to win its fourth straight game, and its eighth in the last 11, against UA with a 15-9 victory in Tempe.

Wilson said that, although the Cats were just 4-5, they gained some momentum heading into Tempe by defeating Texas Western (now UTEP) the week before the '59 Duel. "We were playing some pretty good football, and so now we're coming up against ASU, and the drums are beating," he said. "We came up against those guys and they were favored, because I'll tell you, Frank Kush had them rolling.

"But Jim LaRue turned that program around in that 1959 season, not so much in the win-loss record but in the caliber of football that was being played. And he emphasized the fundamentals of rock 'em, sock 'em – if you did not block, you did not play, and if you did not tackle, you did not play."

With ASU leading by a soccer-like 3-2 score at halftime in front of a then-state-record 32,300 fans, Sun Devil quarterback and future Canadian Football League pro Joe Zuger scored on a 1-yard run in the third quarter, then threw a 9-yard touchdown pass to fullback Joe Camut later in the third. UA responded with a 3-yard TD run by running back and Mesa High grad Warren Livingston in the fourth quarter, but a late interception secured the Devils' victory.

ASU had a much better record than UA going into the game, but as is often the case in this rivalry, the records – along with the game's location – didn't seem to matter.

"We played them even-steven," Wilson said, "and then late in the game, in the last few minutes, I threw an interception, and that killed us. The game was over.

"The next day, the *Tucson Citizen* headline was, 'Late Interception Kills Cats.' I was very upset with that – not that it wasn't true, but I became determined that it wasn't going to happen again."

And it didn't – at least not while Wilson was in town.

Tucson bottles up its emotions

While ASU won its fight to become a university, there were still plenty of off-field issues for the schools to bicker over.

"A big issue when I was an undergraduate was where they were going to locate the medical school, and that kind of added to the rivalry," Areghini said. "It did end up in Tucson – it never really had a chance to end up anywhere else – but that kind of added fuel to the fire.

"You would start the first day of practice off, and not so much the players but the alums – particularly the old-timers – all they were talking about is, 'You've got to beat ASU.' That's how big the rivalry was. Until we got close to that game, we really didn't focus on it – but boy, the outside crowd really did."

ASU center Fred Rhoades (1958-61) said Tucson fans were quite hostile to Sun Devil players back then – which was unfortunate for him and his teammates, who played in an era in which glass bottles were still allowed in college stadiums.

"You didn't like to go down there too much because people were throwing bottles and things like that," he said. "I think that's changed now for the better, but you used to go down there, and oh, man, you were booed and really hit hard and stuff like that. But I guess you had to think that was the way it was going to be, anyway. That's the way it was, and you just had to live with it."

Rhoades said Sun Devil fans conducted themselves in a classier manner. "I think it was the nastiest down in Tucson," he said. "I don't know why, but that was just the way it was from the area they were in. I'm sure a lot of them got treated a little rough here, but I don't remember (our fans) going through the stands and doing that."

Folmer can attest to that, as he recalled an unpleasant incident following a game in Tucson. "We were playing UA down there and I was coming off the field, and my wife was a cheerleader," he said. "And I was walking with her, and a fan threw a paper cup of water that hit me directly in the face.

"One of the first things I did was look up, and (the fan) was yelling and screaming at me and so forth because I'd been kind of ornery in that game, like I had a tendency to do being a linebacker."

'We're going to walk back'

While any loss was unacceptable, Folmer said Kush viewed losing to UA as the absolute worst.

"He just said, 'If we go down there and lose, we're going to walk back. You go to Tucson and let those jackasses beat you, we're going to walk you back," he said.

"He didn't mean that. I don't think."

ASU quarterback and retired U.S. Marine Corps lieutenant general John F. Goodman (1964-66) said Kush definitely treated the UA game differently from all others. "There was always the next game, and (then there was) the Arizona game," he said. "The week of the Arizona game, we didn't practice on the practice field; we practiced at the big stadium. There was an entirely different atmosphere. He ran the speakers in the big stadium at full blast. You couldn't talk (to each other).

"We prepared completely differently. There was an intensity from the first day of practice that week until the game was over. It was distinctly and measurably different."

Take three, times two

The Sun Devils took four in a row from UA from 1949-52 before the Wildcats won three straight from '53-55. When ASU won another four straight in the series from '56-59, UA once again responded with three consecutive wins of its own.

"I think they had some great athletes, and I think their coaches did a commendable job," Kush said of the Wildcats' winning streak against the Devils from 1960-62. "I don't know whether we got complacent or we mentally lapsed."

In 1960, UA went into its meeting with ASU in Tucson with four straight wins. But Wilson said the 7-2 Sun Devils were still the heavy favorites.

Livingston, who would later play defensive back for the Dallas Cowboys, lit up the field in the 1960 Duel, Wilson recalled. "Warren was also our premier student-athlete. The guy was phenomenal; all he did was carry his books around all the time," he said. "He had a career day that year."

Livingston scored on a 60-yard run on Arizona's second play from scrimmage to set the tone, and the Wildcats added a 29-yard TD pass from Wilson to Hernandez along with a 5-yard rushing score from Thompson as part of a 35-7 rout that *The Arizona Republic* called one of the most unexpected results in the rivalry to date. ASU's only score was a 58-yard pass from Cosner to Bob Rembert.

Rhoades doesn't recall ASU playing poorly that day; he said UA was just that much better. "They just came on stronger, and we weren't ready for them or whatever," he said. "But you try to get up for every game, and we just didn't get it done, really."

Wilson said the win sounded the alarm throughout the Grand Canyon State that the Wildcats weren't about to take a permanent back seat in the rivalry to Kush and Co. "It was a huge upset," he said. "It sent a message throughout the state: 'Hey, UA is for real.'"

If football fans in Arizona didn't get that message in 1960, they certainly did the following year.

Unnecessary roughness

The Wildcats and Sun Devils have both fielded some outstanding teams, but they've rarely both been great in the same season.

The 1961 game was an exception – and that year's Duel lived up to the hype.

It also got nasty that November night in Tempe.

"That was a hard-fought football game," Cosner said. "The biggest thing that came back to me was I ran the ball one time, and (after the play) I was laying on the ground and the officials took the ball off of me, and a linebacker for them came up and stomped on my chest and didn't get a (penalty) flag for it. I had cleat marks on my chest."

Both teams were loaded with special players at the skill positions. ASU boasted a pair of underclassmen – running back Tony Lorick and wingback Charley Taylor, who would both play in the NFL – along with Zuger, a senior. On the UA side, LaRue's squad had the tremendous senior trio of Wilson and halfbacks Joe Hernandez and Bobby Lee Thompson.

Both teams had seven wins heading into the game: The Wildcats were 7-1-1, the Sun Devils 7-2. And for perhaps the first time in the Duel's history, both programs were receiving national attention.

"In my senior year, both teams again were rolling, and this time, the nation was aware of it," Wilson said. "We came into the final game, and there was a lot riding on it nationally. Most of the people at that time east of the Mississippi weren't aware that Arizona had even become a state back in 1912.

"Sun Devil Stadium was packed. It was a night game, as was the previous year in Tucson, and it was for all the marbles. There was no shying away, babe."

Kush had already become ASU's all-time winningest head football coach earlier that season, surpassing Devine, who had compiled a 27-3 record in three seasons.

The buildup to the game was tremendous, and 40,100 fans – once again, the most ever to watch a sporting event in Arizona at the time – packed Sun Devil Stadium in what was the final Border Conference game for both teams.

UA running back and defensive back John Goetz (1961-62) can still feel the intensity that the Tempe fans brought to that game. "The crowd was pretty tough out there," he said. "They had a guy in the first row of the stadium right behind our bench.

If I wasn't on the field, I was always down at one end (of the sideline), and this guy was 10 yards behind me. And he had this air horn, which he played pretty continuous from about an hour and a half before the game and all through the game. This air horn was so loud, he had to have a compressor there, or have it plugged in someplace."

About halfway through the game, Goetz said he'd had enough of the noise. "I turned around and yelled at the guy and told him where to put it," he said.

Satisfied with the verbal lashing, Goetz then turned back to the field. "And all of a sudden, a big tackle named Tony Matz, the captain of the '60 team and a graduate assistant, said, 'The guy's coming over the wall.'"

Matz told Goetz to behave himself and not turn around while Matz, well, defused the situation. "The guy came over the wall, and I think Tony took care of him pretty well," he said. "That's my recollection of the game."

Bobby Lee lifts Cats

Boosted by the partisan home crowd, ASU took an early lead in the '61 game. But the Wildcats, who had plenty of speed on offense and had become accustomed to come-from-behind victories in that season and the previous one, remained confident.

"In that time, we won nine games coming from behind, which compares favorably with John Elway up at Stanford," Wilson said. "Our team was electric, explosive and had really great speed. I think it was faster than the way they're playing today. Our overall team speed was that fast.

"It was a good football game. ASU got up to a 13-3 lead at halftime, and we were bringing up the rear a little bit. Then we got started in the second half."

Wilson opened the second-half scoring by throwing a touchdown pass to running back Walter Mince to cut the margin to 13-10. That set the stage for what Wilson called one of the most impressive plays in UA football history.

"We had the ball in our own territory on the 33-yard line," he said. "We ran a play that was a triple cross, where all three backs crossed (each other). I faked to Hernandez coming to the right and then gave the ball to Thompson.

"I no sooner handed the ball off than I heard this crash. I looked, and Bobby had slipped a tackle, but he got hit again, then again, then a couple more times. Finally, he's at the line of scrimmage after six clean hits, and he broke free.

"Bobby Lee, to make a long story short, got hit by nine players – six of them behind the line of scrimmage."

With Thompson finally out in the open, ASU's Nolan Jones was the only remaining player who had a chance to bring him down before he reached the end zone. "But Hernandez, who had faked going to the left side of the line – he got Nolan Jones out of the way with the last block, and Bobby scored from 67 yards out," Wilson said.

Wilson called it "the greatest run I ever saw – and I'm talking about Walter Payton, everybody. It's the greatest I've ever seen in my life."

Goetz said the block that Hernandez unleashed on Jones, a second-team All-American, was a tad unnecessary. "It was about 15-20 yards behind the play. Bobby was going into the end zone, and Joe Hernandez cheap-shotted him into the Arizona State bench," he said. "The guy just sort of sauntered around and got blindsided. Of course, (Hernandez) should've been penalized, but he fortunately did not, because that won the game for us."

Areghini, however, thought the hit was legitimate. "We were looking to make sure Bobby was heading across the goal line," he said with a laugh. "It was all very clean; he hadn't scored yet. It was just an amazing part of that play."

A 5-yard Wilson touchdown run put the game out of reach, and the Wildcats earned another improbable victory over the Devils by a score of 22-13.

It was Thompson's game-winning score that Wilson remembers the most from that game. "I'm not blowin' smoke here. I'm telling you, in this rivalry, you have John Jefferson making 'The Catch' for ASU (in 1975), and you have Bobby Thompson making

'The Run' for UA," he said. "Very little has been made of it over time, and that's a mistake."

UA finished the season with an 8-1-1 record – its best mark during LaRue's tenure – as well as an Associated Press top-20 ranking. "That was a big ballgame – and I've coached in many big ballgame rivalries," said Wilson, who came back to UA as an assistant coach from 1967-71.

Cosner, who was head football coach at Marcos de Niza High School in Tempe from 1973-89, said that game – along with his other experiences in the Duel during his ASU career – still leaves a bad taste in his mouth.

"I will not go to Tucson unless I really and truly have to," he said. "I'm kind of like (ASU quarterback) Danny White. I don't like staying down there."

Enter the WAC

After 31 years, the Border Conference disbanded following the 1961 season. Both ASU and UA had plenty to boast about during those years: The Devils won seven Border Conference championships compared to UA's three, but the Wildcats got the better of the rivalry, going 16-9 against the Bulldogs/Devils during that span, including an 11-game winning streak from 1932-48.

In place of the Border Conference, the Western Athletic Conference (WAC) was formed in 1962, and UA and ASU were two of its six charter members, along with BYU, Utah, New Mexico and Wyoming.

"Amazing upset" opens rivalry's WAC era

After losing Wilson, Hernandez and Thompson to graduation, UA was relegated to mediocrity for most of the 1962 season. But as has been established many times, a win in the Duel can make up for a lousy year.

"'62 was an amazing game. They were a 7-1-1 team, and we were about a .500 team (4-5) and had a lot of injuries," Areghini said. "And we kind of patched the team together and beat them down in Tucson."

Trailing 17-13, UA made decisive plays on defense and special teams in the fourth quarter. Wildcat captain Ken Cook came up big by blocking an ASU punt, then making a catch inside the Sun Devil 5-yard line to set up a 1-yard touchdown run by fullback Ted Christy.

In the game's final moments, UA's Jim Singleton caused a crucial turnover. "ASU ran a play with (halfback) Larry Todd, who took a pitch like a reverse and was going to throw a pass, and the (receiver) was going to be wide open," Areghini said. "And Singleton – a big, tall, lanky defensive end – got a hold of his jersey, spun him around and knocked him down before he could get the pass off."

Singleton's play caused Todd to fumble, leading to a UA recovery that sealed the Wildcats' improbable 20-17 win – their third straight in the rivalry – and prompting the Tucson fans to chant, "You choked, Tempe, you choked."

Areghini said the game was yet another instance of UA playing above its talent level to upend a favored ASU squad.

"I think in the '61 game, we were clearly better than they were," he said. "I mean, the talent we had, particularly at the skill positions, were clearly better with Eddie Wilson, Joe Hernandez and Bobby Thompson.

"And then in the '62 game, it was almost a fluke that we beat them. It was just one of those games where we got breaks. We had a tough season and we were just determined to go out with a big game. And we played over our head, and they had a letdown. That was an amazing upset."

Three years of glory

Areghini still savors those wins over talented Sun Devil squads, and he still can't quite put a finger on why the Wildcats were able to win three straight against them.

"(Kush) had talent; it's just for some reason or another, we had their number," he said. "Being a Phoenix kid, it sure meant a lot to us to have won the years I was there then, and it's just something that, until the day I die, that (game) will always be a mark on my calendar. It just means so much."

Kush said UA's head coaching switch in '59 shook up the rivalry in the Wildcats' favor. "They changed coaches, and I think that makes a difference," he said. "The changing of coaches not only changes the philosophy but changes the recruiting and everything else."

But the Wildcats wouldn't earn back-to-back wins over the Sun Devils – let alone three in a row – for another two decades. In fact, after its winning streak from 1960-62, it would take UA 17 years to earn its next three victories over Arizona State.

Bucking the '60s trend

An influx of talent in Tempe led to another highly successful campaign for the Sun Devils in 1963 – and this time, it propelled them to their first 1960s victory over the Wildcats.

ASU's backfield was once again loaded, featuring future NFL running backs Lorick and Gene Foster, and the Devils also boasted the wingback combination of Taylor and newcomer and New Jersey native Ben Hawkins, ASU's first-ever first-team All-American and a player who would lead the NFL in receiving yards in 1967.

Hawkins (1963-65) said Kush was so determined to break through in the Duel after three straight losses to the Wildcats that he changed up his offensive scheme just for that game, electing to switch to a more passing-oriented, pro-set offense. "Charley was the halfback, and (Kush) stuck me out as a wide receiver. We hadn't run that all year," he said.

The beginning of the '63 game, however, must have had Sun Devils fans thinking: *Here we go again*.

"We get up to ASU, and (UA halfback) Rickie Harris runs the opening kickoff back for a touchdown. We miss the extra point, so it's 6-0. Then, we kick off, they fumble and we take over at their 20-yard line," said UA halfback and kick returner Floyd Hudlow (1963-64).

UA attempted to run a specially designed play following the fumble recovery. "We actually had planned during the week several plays that we thought would work against ASU," Hudlow said. "Bill Brechler was our quarterback at the time, and we had a special play where I'd just kind of sneak across the middle into the end zone.

"I was wide open in the back of the end zone; there wasn't anyone around me whatsoever. I don't know how that happened, but it did. And Bill started to throw the ball, but just after he let it go, one of the defensive linemen for ASU tipped it away."

The Cats ended that possession with a missed field-goal attempt, and it was all uphill from there, as the Devils regained their composure and took it to the UA defense with their new offensive look the rest of the game. "They were up for it and they wanted it very bad, and it showed, and they just stopped us," Hudlow said.

Lorick's 12-yard touchdown run put ASU up for good in the first quarter, 7-6. A 61-yard run by Hawkins gave the Devils a 21-6 lead at halftime, and more Lorick magic in the second half – an 18-yard rushing touchdown in the third quarter and a 42-yard interception return in the fourth – was more than enough for the Devils, who outgained the Wildcats in total offense, 325-81.

The final score: ASU 35, UA 6. The win was the Devils' eighth straight victory after opening the season with a loss to Wichita State, while the defeat, followed by a loss to New Mexico the following week, capped a second straight .500 season for the Wildcats.

If anything, the game demonstrated to the ASU faithful just how important beating UA was to Kush, who was willing to set aside the ground-and-pound offensive philosophy to which he was devoted.

"We had never shown them a pro set, and it just threw them off," Hawkins said. "We threw the ball a lot, plus we were able to keep our sweeps and our traps (in the running game), so that was an extra added tool for us."

One last '60s surge

In 1964, just like in '62, a seemingly more talented Sun Devil team fell to a very average Wildcat squad.

"From everything we had seen on film, the UA guys played so far above themselves in that game, and we came in flat, which shocked me. We hadn't been flat all year," said Goodman, who played primarily on defense in the '64 game. "I was surprised at how our defense was just absolutely flat. We were so much faster than them, but it didn't show.

"But they came to play, and we showed up and we weren't ready to play. And then the offense just sputtered. We had three All-Americans on the team, so it was surprising. But if you're not ready, you're not ready."

Hudlow said Arizona's 30-6 win at Arizona Stadium in '64 was a measure of sheer willpower. "We went nuts," he said with a laugh. "It was almost a reverse-type situation (from the '63 game). We just took over the game, and we wanted it bad because of the previous year.

"They were pretty well favored – by two touchdowns or more, if I remember right. But we just wanted it, and we went out and got it. ASU was the better team, but we just wanted it worse."

With the Wildcats leading 15-6 in the third quarter in front of a statewide TV audience, Hudlow scored on rushes of 58 and 7 yards to give UA a 27-6 advantage and seal the deal.

Hudlow said the Devils moved the ball effectively – ASU quarterback John Torok passed the ball well throughout the game – but they simply couldn't find the end zone. "They just went up and down the field until they got to the 20, and then we were able to shut them down," he said.

The Wildcats scouted ASU's prized running backs well in the week leading up to the game. "Coach LaRue was really smart as far as that he showed us a lot of films in our meetings of ASU playing other good teams and showed us the great plays that (their running backs) were making," Hudlow said. "It was awesome, and we took over."

Hawkins said ASU underperformed because it was a young team that had never experienced the level of intensity that the rivalry game always brought. "When you go down to Tucson, it's like going into the lion's den," he said. "You've got to listen to the people in the stands, listening to whatever they want to call you. A lot of times you'd hear the 'Tempe Normal' stuff.

"A lot of guys that came in were junior-college transfers and first-year players. A lot of times, when you're first involved in something like that, unless you have enough guys around you who have been through it before to be able to clue you in on what it's going to be like, you really don't understand the intensity of it, and you get sort of caught off guard. UA had players that had been there before.

"It was like going down into the lion's den and trying to beat the lion in his den. They had a lot of momentum. We got a rude awakening, put it that way."

Goodman, who got his first taste of the rivalry at the varsity level that year, said he thought his team was prepared for the Arizona Stadium crowd due to the noise that Kush piped in during team practices. "But the stadium was noisier, particularly at the bench, than even when we practiced for it," he said. "And both teams were unusually emotional. The intensity was high. Emotions were high."

When he and his team arrived in Tucson, Goodman said he was surprised to see the ASU sideline positioned right in front of the UA student section – "At no other place that we ever played was that the case," he said – and he was even more perplexed at the nastiness of the fans. "The student-body section was absolutely hostile. They threw stuff at us. They yelled at us," he said. "It was just constant, and it was just distinctly different."

Like some ASU players who came before him, Goodman thought some of the behavior was over the top. "The yelling and that sort of thing (is OK), but throwing stuff crossed the line," he said. "All three times we played in Tucson, they threw stuff at us.

"What surprised me was the degree to which it wasn't just the student body. It was people who lived in the neighborhood. It was parents. It was intense."

But Goodman gave credit to the Wildcats for just being better that evening. "Frankly, on some of those nights, it happens," he said. "Every ball would always hop their direction, but that usually comes from hustle and preparedness. It doesn't come from, 'We got a bad break.' It was just their night, and they came to play and really took it to us. And I have to tell you, Kush was not happy."

While Kush often made his players hit the practice field right after a disappointing performance, Folmer said there was one bright spot after the loss.

"We didn't have a very good time coming home that game. Frank was not very happy with us. But we got home so late, we couldn't practice," he said. "I remember, on paper, we had a heck of a lot better football team, but you know, they just snuck up on us. It was not a pretty picture."

The script of the underdog Wildcat squad defeating the favored Devils is one that Goodman has seen acted out many times since his playing days. "More often than not, when ASU is highly ranked and they're playing in Tucson, I just don't think all the coaches and players really appreciate what it's like to go into a highly emotional game on foreign turf," he said. "I don't know why. I've watched it and been frustrated over the years watching Arizona State go down there and do that.

"But in an emotional game, it really has nothing to do with the record or the skill; it has to do with that day, period."

Kush cools off Cats

The Wildcats won four of the first five Duels in the 1960s. The rest of the decade belonged to Frank Kush.

The 1965 showdown featured a pair of very speedy defenses in what would be the lowest-scoring game between the schools in a decade.

"The hitting was absolutely amazing. Both defenses flew like you wouldn't believe," Goodman said about ASU's 14-6 late-November win, which featured the lowest point total for the Devils in a win over the Wildcats since the inaugural 1899 game. "It was a very intense defensive game."

With ASU trailing 6-0 in the first half following a 91-yard punt return by UA running back and defensive back Wally Scott, fullback Max Anderson ran 80 yards for a touchdown with 11 seconds to go before halftime to put the Devils ahead.

Kush, who broke character with his offensive plan two years earlier at home to help ASU end its losing streak in the series, was reluctant to do so again, according to Goodman. "Kush went in with a very conservative game plan," he said. "He insisted that we try to run the ball against UA up and down the field. But we just didn't have the horses."

Kush's run-first approach frustrated Goodman a number of times throughout the '65 season. "He hated passing," Goodman said. "He bought into that (idea): If you put the ball in the air, three things happen, and two of them aren't good."

But with ASU leading just 7-6 in the fourth quarter, Kush finally gave in to Goodman's pleas. "All year he'd been trying to insist on establishing the running game, and it was only in the fourth quarter of games that he would turn me loose," he said. "And so when he finally turned me loose, we went down and scored."

Following an interception by defensive lineman Curley Culp, who went on to be a five-time NFL Pro Bowl selection and was inducted into the Pro Football Hall of Fame in 2013, Anderson scored on a 17-yard pass from Goodman with less than 10 minutes left in the game.

After losing four of their first five games in '65, the Devils won five straight to close the season.

Hawkins said ASU's underclassmen made a big impact in the '65 Duel. "We got a lot of help from the younger guys who had come in and hadn't played before, and they were able to keep the University at bay," he said.

Before he was Mr. October, he was Mr. November

Folmer said two of the underclassmen standouts on defense in '65 were Culp, who would be named the WAC Lineman of the Year two years later, and future Major League Baseball Hall of Famer Reggie Jackson, the man who became known as Mr. October with his postseason heroics for the New York Yankees.

"I remember (the Wildcats) were double-teaming Curley, and it freed me up, and I had a field day. I made a lot of tackles," Folmer said. "They were also giving respect to Reggie. People don't realize or remember: He was a heck of a football player. He would knock your ass off.

"But he did the same thing with a little baseball, too. So we didn't see him anymore."

Jackson left football behind to play baseball for the Sun Devils in 1966 before embarking upon his 21-year pro baseball career.

One loss outweighs two wins

When Folmer was asked what he remembers more about the rivalry – the two games he won against UA or the one he lost – he didn't need time to think about it.

"The loss. Don't like to lose to the Kitty Cats. Wasn't any fun," he said. "And I'm sure our people are just as bad, but their fans were just terrible. Some things never change, do they?"

Folmer's wife and daughter both attended UA, which he said makes the week leading up to the Duel very interesting. And the fact that he became the Sun Bowl committee chairman is a fascinating footnote considering the controversial events that occurred with that committee three years after he graduated from ASU.

And despite UA's dominance of ASU in the early '60s, Scott (1965-67) said the consensus around the state was that the Sun Devils, not the Wildcats, were the team to beat in the desert.

"During my time – and this is just my personal opinion – I just felt like we were more of a stepchild to them," he said. "Even the attitude in Tucson was that they had better athletes and better coaching. So we had a chip on our shoulder."

Goodman leads ASU rally in Tucson

They faced more rowdy Arizona Stadium fans (33,500 of them) and were outgained by over 50 yards in 1966, but the Devils won their first game in Tucson in eight years, 20-17, thanks to some late-game heroics from Goodman, whom Kush once again waited to unleash until the final quarter.

"The first and fourth quarter absolutely belonged to us, and in the middle we got mired down again with having to try to run the ball," Goodman said. "In the first quarter, I was allowed to throw, and in the fourth quarter, Kush turned the offense (back) over to me. In between, we wanted to run the ball."

Going up against future WAC Lineman of the Year Tom Nelson along with Bill Lueck – the brother of Bob Lueck, who was Goodman's center in 1965 – Goodman preferred to put the ball in the air, despite the punishment he knew his body would take, because he had guys like Hawkins and future All-WAC wingback Wes Plummer to throw to.

With ASU trailing 17-13 in the fourth quarter after UA quarterback Mark Reed connected with Fritz Greenlee on a 70-yard touchdown pass, Goodman once again begged Kush to let him throw. "I was surprised when UA got the ball in the fourth quarter and moved it as well as they did. Their quarterback really engineered a very good drive," Goodman said, "and when we got the ball back, I turned to Kush and said, 'Give me the offense. I'll score.' He said, 'Go ahead.' And we did."

Goodman found Plummer for a late, game-winning 19-yard touchdown pass – but it came at a painful price. "Bill Lueck absolutely hammered me when I released the ball. It hurt like crazy, and I broke a rib," he said. "So I didn't see the touchdown pass; I was flat on my back in pain."

Despite the teams' records going into the game – ASU was 4-5 and UA was 3-6 – Goodman said both teams played at a level far above those marks. "It was just one of those really good games; hard-hitting and intense," he said. "There was nothing off-color or derogatory, but there was a lot of talking on the field. There were a lot of guys who really cared (about the rivalry)."

LaRue's last stand

After the Wildcats opened the 1966 season in the same way that they closed their '65 campaign – losing six out of seven games – a coaching change seemed inevitable. And unlike earlier in the 1960s, LaRue didn't have a win over ASU to ease Tucson's pain, as '66 was his final season at UA.

Though the Wildcats' struggled at times under LaRue, Scott said he enjoyed playing for him. "I'm partial to Jim LaRue. To me, LaRue was more of a laid-back kind of guy. He knew the game, and to me, he was more of a defensive-oriented coach," he said. "Jim, to me, was more of a coach-player guy where you can relate to him."

LaRue, who still lives in Tucson, said he's proud of what he and his staff accomplished in his eight seasons, leading UA to a 41-37-2 record, including a 1964 WAC championship and a 4-4 record against the Sun Devils – the best mark of any Arizona coach against Frank Kush.

"I think I did a good job while I was there," he said. "You just go out there and do the best you can. You do the best recruiting you can and get some good coaches to help you, and you always have fans that help you."

"A year of turmoil"

After the Wildcats' second straight loss to the Sun Devils, President Harvill replaced LaRue with Darrell Mudra, who had spent the 1966 season coaching the Montreal Alouettes of the Canadian Football League.

Scott was less than thrilled with Mudra's approach and his lack of emphasis on defense. "Mudra came in and he had his Ph.D. in psychology and all that. He was a little more standoff-ish, if you know what I mean," he said. "He came from Canada, and I think his expertise was more offensively minded."

Scott, who was a co-captain during his senior season, said the team didn't take too well to the Mudra regime. "A lot of us had some issues with the new coaching staff, and I think that didn't help us during the year because it takes a while to mesh," he said. "We were seniors and had been with a different coaching staff for a couple years. We got used to them. And then we were in a different defensive scheme, a different offensive scheme, and I just think we didn't mesh. It was a year of turmoil, as far as I'm concerned."

Mudra did inherit some talented defensive players, such as standout linebacker Rusty Tillman, who would play and coach in the NFL. But the Wildcats' instability was in sharp contrast to the consistency that Sun Devil players and fans had come to enjoy under Kush, who entered his 10th season as head coach in 1967. And it showed on the football field in the two years Mudra was in charge in Tucson.

Kush invests in fine Art

Kush's long line of future NFL running backs in Tempe continued with the addition of Art Malone from Eloy, Ariz. Malone was named to the '68 and '69 All-WAC teams and, after being drafted by the Atlanta Falcons in the second round of the 1970 NFL draft, played seven professional seasons with the Falcons and Philadelphia Eagles.

"The one thing I remember probably the most about Art was his explosion off the snap and his ability to hit holes so quickly and with such power," said ASU quarterback Ed Roseborough (1967-68). "I think his ability to get to full speed so quickly and have the ability to cut the way he did – he delivered quite a blow, and he put the leather to some people on numerous occasions. He was just a very hard hitter, intense, and just so determined to gain that yardage. There was nothing lackadaisical about him when it came to carrying the football."

And while Kush was a run-first man, he convinced another future NFL pro, wide receiver J.D. Hill, to come to Tempe via California.

Roseborough said Hill was one of the fastest men on the planet. "He could lull you to sleep and blow by you without the person knowing it happened," he said. "He ran a 4.4(-second) 40 at a time when that was pretty much unheard of. That was the one thing he could take advantage of anytime he wanted to.

"But the thing that impressed me most was his hands, because not only did he have explosive speed but he had probably the best hands of any receiver I've ever thrown to – and I threw to a lot of different pros at different tryouts, but I'll tell ya, I've never seen anybody that had hands as good as J.D. He was a lot of fun to throw to."

Hill and Malone would both score as part of a rout of the Wildcats in Mudra's first season.

'67 Duel a "joke" of a game

The Devils survived a couple of tough contests with UA in 1965 and '66, but their fans didn't have to sweat out the '67 result, as ASU blew out the Wildcats, 47-7, at Sun Devil Stadium. The win provided a climactic end to an 8-2 season in which ASU handed Wisconsin its first home-opening loss in 19 years – a game that earned the Devils some national attention in their first-ever meeting with a Big Ten opponent.

Against UA, Roseborough threw three touchdown passes, including a 48-yarder to Hill that gave the Devils a 21-0 first-quarter lead. Anderson had two scores – a 15-yard reception from Roseborough in the first quarter and a 61-yard run in the second – and Malone scored the Devils' final points on a 3-yard run in the third.

The Wildcats pulled off a huge Big Ten win of their own in '67 – a 14-7 win at Ohio State in the second week of the season – but couldn't capitalize on it, finishing 3-6-1 in Mudra's debut season.

Unlike in the very competitive losses to ASU in the previous two seasons, Scott said the team was demoralized heading into the '67 Duel. "Our record was bad, and I think when we went into the game, it was just more of the fact that we wanted to get the season over with," he said, noting that the game got so out of hand that Mudra pulled the seniors in the fourth quarter. "I don't think we were as motivated. I think that was probably one of the issues."

ASU linebacker Ron Pritchard (1966-68), who was named to the All-WAC team in all three of his varsity seasons and had a nine-year NFL career with the Houston Oilers and Cincinnati Bengals, said '67 was all about an abundance of talent on the Tempe side. "That was a joke. We just had better athletes, period," he said. "There was just no way they could match up with us."

Roseborough said everything just clicked that day for the Devils. "Everything we did worked, it seemed like, and it was just one of those games that it was just very easy," he said.

The Ultimatum Bowl

Mudra's second season in the Old Pueblo was much more fruitful than his first, as he led the Wildcats to an 8-1 record going into their post-Thanksgiving clash with the Devils at Arizona Stadium.

But with a bowl berth on the line for the winner of the 1968 Duel, Mudra decided to let his words, rather than his players' performance, do the talking.

Following UA's win over perennial WAC powerhouse Wyoming the previous weekend, the Wildcats were on the brink of a conference championship, which would mean a bid to the Sun Bowl in El Paso, Texas. This was a big deal considering that there weren't nearly as many bowl games up for grabs in 1968 as there are today; in fact, there were only 10 bowls that year. And neither team had been invited to a bowl in well over a decade – UA hadn't been since 1949, ASU since 1951.

Rather than risking the Wildcats missing the postseason for the 20th straight year, Mudra, who knew that only one WAC team would be invited to a bowl, took matters into his own hands. He went to the Sun Bowl committee and laid down an ultimatum: Agree to invite the Wildcats to the Sun Bowl before their game against the 7-2 Sun Devils or his team would refuse to grace El Paso with its presence.

"Mudra had told the Sun Bowl committee that there was no way that (ASU) could win the WAC, and (UA) *could* win it," said UA defensive back Bill Miller (1967-69).

Wildcat tight end Ted Sherwood (1966-69) said Mudra's argument went like this: UA had beaten Wyoming, which had beaten ASU earlier in the season. Therefore, the best the Devils could do was tie the Wildcats in the WAC standings.

"He took it to the press and said, 'Hey, worst-case scenario, we're going to be tied for the WAC conference lead, and best-case scenario, you're going to have to end up taking Wyoming or Arizona State, and we'd have beaten both of them," Sherwood said.

"(The Sun Bowl committee was) backed into a corner. I guess they had a choice: They could take either Wyoming or Arizona State because they were committed to taking the winner of the WAC conference, and if we beat Arizona State, we'd be the outright winner, and if Arizona State beat us, there would be a three-way tie. But Mudra said he was going to turn them down (if they made their decision after the ASU game)."

Miller said he and his teammates weren't happy with this development. "We did not support Darrell Mudra's move. We wanted to win on the field," he said. "I think we pretty much as players thought that was a terrible power move that Mudra did that."

But the Sun Bowl committee gave in to Mudra's demands and agreed to invite UA to El Paso before the ASU contest, which led a local sportswriter to deem the 1968 ASU-UA game "The Ultimatum Bowl."

Sherwood knew the unhappy Sun Devils would be determined to take out their frustrations on the field in front of the Wildcat faithful. "Of course, that just infuriated Frank Kush, and I'm sure he had his own way of stirring up his players," he said. "And he had a lot of talent to begin with.

"Ron Pritchard and their gang of J.D. Hill and Malone, they were really upset about it. Kush made a huge issue out of that."

Sherwood said the players tried to look at the ASU game as one that they still needed to win in order to earn their bowl bid, despite Mudra's manipulation tactics. "The players came into practice one evening before the game and we said, 'Hey, let's leave it on the line, we want to play for it. This game is for the (WAC) championship,'" he said. "I think (Mudra) was afraid to do that for fear that we wouldn't get asked if we lost."

Kush said he played up the disrespect card during practice that week. "That's always a motivating factor, not only with the athletes but with the community and the other segments of the institution," he said. "I think the mental aspects were there, so we were motivated. We wanted to go prove that we could do it, and that's what we did."

Roseborough is still very unhappy about the Sun Bowl's pre-game announcement. "What a bunch of garbage that was," he said. "That was definitely in the forefront (of our minds). We knew what had happened and we knew we were a better team than them, and we thought it was B.S. that they would force the Sun Bowl committee to make that decision before the game, especially because we had better stats and everything than them. I'm surprised the Sun Bowl committee caved, but they did."

Like many former athletes who played decades ago, ASU defensive guard Ted Olivo (1968-71) doesn't remember much about his playing days – but he remembers the week leading up to the Ultimatum Bowl as clear as day.

"All I know is they gave them the ultimatum – either you pick us now or we're not going to go. Well, they picked them, and it was kind of like, 'Whoa,'" he said. "And then we went down to Tucson and Coach Kush, he played (UA's) music when we were practicing, and he drilled it in us: 'Hey, they're mocking us. They don't even want to give us a chance to play for the Sun Bowl.'

"There was a lot of extra motivation there. A lot. Instead of saying, 'OK, the winner of this game is going to go to the Sun Bowl,' we were insulted.

"And we went down (to Tucson) and it wasn't even a contest."

Determined Devils clean Cats' clocks

Playing in his first Duel in the Desert, ASU quarterback Joe Spagnola (1968-70) said there was an immense satisfaction in laying a 30-7 beating on the team that was prematurely picked to represent the WAC in the postseason.

"It started off with a bang, with Art Malone just tearing up the ground with them," he said. "That was probably one of the more joyous games I played for ASU, beating them down there."

Malone scored twice in the first quarter – on his first and sixth rushing attempts of the game – and those tallies were followed by a 42-yard touchdown reception by Hill from Spagnola that gave ASU a 21-0 lead at the end of the first. UA's only touchdown came via a return of a blocked punt in the second quarter.

Malone rushed for nearly 200 yards in the game, and the Devils outgained the Wildcats 274-0 on the ground.

Wrote *Arizona Republic* writer Steve Weston the next day: "Arizona and Arizona State buried the hatchet last night. The hatchet, however, ended up being buried in the Wildcats' skull."

Roseborough said the hostile crowd wasn't a factor for the focused Devils that night. After all, following Mudra's demands and the Sun Bowl committee's willingness to acquiesce, the 1968 Duel had essentially become their bowl game.

"What I really remember is any celebration that was done was strictly on our bench, and that was all that mattered to us," he said. "You sort of block out all the negativity – and beating them the way we did, we kind of shut up the crowd anyway."

Pritchard remembers the silence in the Arizona Stadium stands that evening and the fun the Devils had in making it so quiet. "We went in there and humbled them is what we did," he said. "In fact, this is kind of funny: I played the guard position for a couple plays just for the heck of it, just kind of goofing off.

"They were 8-1 going into that game, and we were 7-2. But that was a no-gamer, believe me."

The memory of that win is still one of Olivo's favorites. "It's funny: Your memory fades, but that's the one I really remember the most, because we had a lot of fans down there. (It was) the Ultimatum Bowl and this and that, and there was a lot of excitement," he said.

Miller said Mudra's manipulation didn't do the Cats any favors, as it not only riled up ASU's players but its students and alumni, as well. "There was an angry confrontation from ASU fans who pretty much blamed us as players (for the ultimatum) instead of the coaches, where it belonged," he said.

Mudra quits on the Cats

The Devils' win allowed Wyoming to become the '68 WAC champion. But it was the Wildcats that went on to the Sun Bowl, where they were blown out by Auburn, 34-10.

And Mudra, who had just coached in his second game against ASU, decided not to stick around until the end of the bowl, according to his players.

"Mudra quit at halftime of the Sun Bowl," Miller said. "He got his doctorate (degree) while he was at UA, and he believed that if band members would get academic credit, the same should be true of athletes. Harvill told him no just before the game."

In an apparent act of protest of the administration's decision, Miller said Mudra gave the team his farewell address at halftime. "He said, 'Dr. Harvill has turned me down, and I believe very strongly that you guys spend way too much time and we don't pay you, so you deserve some sort of academic credit (for playing football) – and it's unfair, especially to those of you who are P.E. majors, that varsity football does not gain you any academic credit,'" he said. "And he said, 'I'm a man of my word, and so I've quit as head coach. Go have a good second half for me, guys.'"

Miller said Mudra thought the announcement of his resignation would fire the Wildcats up after halftime.

It didn't.

"We just went off as flat as hell in the second half and got our butts kicked by Auburn," he said. "But it does go back to the heart of the ASU-UA rivalry, where Mudra played that card to leverage us into the Sun Bowl. When he quit at halftime, it was like he quit on us."

In Mudra's defense, Hansen said Harvill was notorious for not investing in UA's football program. Therefore, it was good news for the program when Harvill retired in 1971. "Harvill was just not going to spend any money on football, or on sports altogether, and LaRue just ran up against that after he had that one great year in 1961," he said. "That was why Darrell Mudra quit after going to the Sun Bowl that year. He didn't want anything to do with Harvill."

UA defensive end and Mudra recruit Bob Crum (1970-72), the son of Moose Crum, verified that account. "(Mudra) wanted to turn it into a football-oriented school, and Harvill's comment was, 'We're not going to have a football factory here,'" he said.

In spite of the success that UA tasted in '68, Sherwood said he wasn't sad to see Mudra go. "I never really thought Darrell Mudra was a great football coach," he said. "I think he was very much of a personality, a guy who was good in front of the camera and the press, but I think he surrounded himself with a number of people who were really good X's and O's people.

"And I would consider Bob Weber one of those guys."

A new coach in Tucson, a similar result in Tempe

Bob Weber, who served as Mudra's assistant in 1967-68, was named UA head coach in 1969, becoming the Wildcats' fourth coach of the Kush era at ASU.

Miller said Weber had a great strategic football mind but didn't necessarily have the personality to be an effective leader in Tucson. "I think that Bob Weber was an excellent assistant coach. I didn't think he was a (great) head coach," he said. "No offense to him, but he wasn't charismatic. At times – at least to me, as a fifth-year senior – he appeared indecisive."

Weber's first season at the helm was similar to Mudra's: The Wildcats went 3-7 overall and 3-3 in the WAC in '69.

Meanwhile, led by Spagnola, Malone and future seven-year NFL cornerback Windlan Hall, the Devils were enjoying another seven-win season. They headed into the UA game in Tempe with five straight victories, the WAC lead and a 79-7 victory over Colorado State a week earlier.

Nonetheless, the underdog Wildcats went into Sun Devil Stadium with confidence and determination. "I know, when we went up there my senior year, it was a big issue to us because the class that I was in, which was a small class at the time, had not won a game against ASU," Sherwood said. "Of course it was in Tempe, and they were favored significantly in Sun Devil Stadium. But I remember each of us standing in the locker room and imploring the rest of the team that this was our last chance. We were asking them to stand with us and give everything that they had."

The Wildcats did that, and they were able to compete with the much deeper and more talented Devils for three quarters. In fact, Sherwood's 21-yard touchdown catch from quarterback Brian Linstrom gave UA a 24-19 lead in the third quarter.

But ASU eventually took charge, and just like in the '55 game that UA won, 7-6, via a blocked extra point, special teams were among the '69 Duel's deciding factors.

Lenny Randle – who, just like Reggie Jackson, also played baseball at ASU and later enjoyed a lengthy MLB career – returned an Arizona punt 57 yards for a score to give the Devils the lead for good. In the fourth quarter, Malone cemented his place in rivalry history by scoring his second TD of the game on a 3-yard plunge. ASU added a pair of late field goals for a 38-24 win and its first WAC championship.

Spagnola remembers the impact that Malone made in that game and throughout his collegiate career, which ended that night. "He probably hit the line of scrimmage faster than anybody I'd ever seen," he said. "There were countless times when I couldn't turn around fast enough and he'd pretty much run me over. So that gave him the advantage over everybody, because he hit the line of scrimmage so fast that nobody could react to it.

"And he was one tough son of a gun. He was a punishing runner. Defensive tackles would come to hit him, but he'd strike a force on you first."

ASU also got two touchdowns in that game from halfback Dave Buchanan, who was the 1969 WAC Offensive Player of the Year. "We had so many talented running backs that if one went down, we had two or three to back him up," Spagnola said.

Regardless of the talent level in Tucson, Spagnola said he never expected anything less than an aggressive challenge from the Wildcats, and the '69 game was no different. "From what I remember from that game, it was just a typical ASU-UA game where we both hate each other, there was a lot of calling names, under-the-huddle antics, stuff like that," He said.

"But the end result was the same: We beat ya."

While the Wildcats came up short against their rivals for the fifth straight season, meaning Sherwood was never able to get that coveted win against the Devils, he said the effort level from him and his fellow seniors was befitting the end of their careers.

"We ended up losing, of course, but it was a game that I think we gave everything we had as far as leaving it on the field," he said. "We just didn't have the talent that Arizona State had."

ASU's "obnoxious fans"

Plenty of ASU players from that era complained about the nastiness of Wildcat fans in Tucson. Sherwood left UA in '69 with a similar opinion of the Sun Devil contingency.

"God, they were friggin' obnoxious," he said. "I had never played (anywhere else) where they had more obnoxious fans. They had these horns that would sound like a big foghorn, and they were yelling and screaming and throwing crap at you. They were just crazy.

"Of course, they always caught us coming out of the dressing room and would just throw all kinds of crap. I can specifically remember that my senior year. You're always used to the noise and people yelling and booing when you play, but I just felt like their fans were really obnoxious fans."

Snubbed again

ASU won the '69 WAC title, but Malone and his fellow seniors would never appear in a bowl game during their collegiate careers, as the Devils were once again overlooked for postseason play by the Sun Bowl, which decided instead to invite a 5-4-1 Georgia team.

But the back-to-back Sun Bowl snubs may have been a blessing in disguise, as they were a catalyst for the creation of the Fiesta Bowl, which would be played on ASU's home field.

Devils' dominance a preview of things to come

Roseborough said the formula for ASU's dominance of its in-state neighbor in the late '60s included two ingredients: superior athletes and coaching stability.

"I just feel we had dominant personnel," he said. "We had a lot of outstanding athletes: Curley Culp, Ron Prichard, J.D. Hill, Max Anderson, Art Malone, (halfback) Larry Walton. I think the better athletes decided to play at Arizona State in Tempe, and Arizona kind of took a back seat for a while.

"And I know they had some difficulties with their coaching. They weren't some of the greatest coaches in the world, and of course Kush was, so there was a distinct advantage right there."

Those advantages would continue deep into the next decade, when Arizona State would take the next step from regional contender to national powerhouse.

CHAPTER 4

Devils' Domain

With yet another rebuilding job taking place in Tucson under Bob Weber, ASU's program kept humming along with Frank Kush entering his third decade at the helm.

And he was as hardnosed as ever – which some players enjoyed and others didn't.

"I loved playing for him. He was like my father away from home," Spagnola said. "I could've gone to other schools, but when I met Frank and saw his desire to win, it was the place to be for me.

"And if you do the right things and you don't make mistakes, he stays off your back," Spagnola added with a laugh. "To me, he was always a good guy."

In 1970, quarterback Danny White, the son of Sun Devil legend "Whizzer" White, signed with ASU on a baseball scholarship but later joined Kush on the football team.

"He loved ASU, ASU football and winning a lot more than he did the players, and he wasn't afraid to admit that," White (1971-73) said of Kush. "We knew that his concern for us ran through

ASU football. If we were successful on the field, he would be our best friend for life, but if we weren't, he'd act like he didn't even know you.

"He was old school to the old-school guys. He was the Woody Hayes of ASU football, and he didn't care about rules, he didn't care about what the rest of the world thought about what was cruel and how you treated people when it came to players. He wanted us to be mentally tough. That was his mantra. He said, 'I don't care who your mommy and daddy are. You're going to be the best you can be, or you're going to be out of here. It's as simple as that.'"

White said Kush placed a heavy emphasis on beating the Wildcats – but he didn't need any additional motivation in that area.

"The intensity for me came more from my family than ASU or the team, having been raised in an environment of, 'Beat the Wildcats,'" he said. "There was more pressure from my family, I think, than there was from Coach Kush or my teammates. It was the double whammy for me, just because of the history and my dad having played against them during the years when ASU really kind of turned it around, because UA had really dominated the rivalry series up until then.

"But (Kush) put a lot of emphasis on it for a number of reasons. It was the in-state rivalry, it was the last game of the year, it had bowl implications – there were a lot of reasons for that game to be a big game other than just the fact that it was UA. But there's no question about it: He made sure that we all understood that what we had done to that point was anticlimactic – that it would all be lost if we lost to UA."

Kaji

ASU offensive guard Steve Matlock (1970-72) said Kush had assistant coach Bill Kajikawa set the tone for the out-of-state players whom Kush recruited – both in terms of what to expect as a Sun Devil football player and what it meant to beat the Wildcats.

Kajikawa played football for the then-Bulldogs, then served as ASU's freshman coach from 1937-78. The Phoenix Union High School grad who his players called "Kaji" also coached ASU's basketball team from 1948-57.

"On your very first day when you'd show up as a freshman at ASU, you line up out there, and Kaji was about 5-foot-6 maybe, but he would sit there in a very gentlemanly, sincere (way), never raise his voice, never say a foul word," Matlock said. "He was just an incredible role model and mentor for a bunch of knucklehead freshmen coming to ASU."

Matlock recalled Kajikawa's annual speech to the incoming players. "He would say, 'Boys, this is just like home. Look to the left and look to the right, because not everybody's going to make the journey. And the only thing you guys have got to understand is there's one game you have to win every year, and if you're focused enough to win that one, you'll probably win enough other ones to make it worth your while – and that's to beat the guys down south,'" he said.

Kush would then follow up on the comments of Kajikawa, who passed away in 2010 at the age of 97. "Frank talked about it on the opening day: 'Boys, we want bragging rights at home, and you don't lose to UA,'" Matlock said.

"And then, it was just a matter of one game at a time. You have the other 9-10 games you've got to go through before you ever get to them. But there was never a situation when that wasn't a balls-to-the-wall game."

Such was the case in 1970, when a permanent place in NCAA football lore – not to mention a major milestone in the history of the football program – would be lost if the Devils came up short against the underdog Wildcats. And they very nearly did.

Weber's Wildcats

UA offensive lineman Jim Arneson (1970-72), whose brother, Mark, also played at Arizona, was signed to play football under Darrell Mudra but ended up playing for Weber.

"I think Bob Weber was one of those examples of a great coordinator or position coach who didn't quite make it as a head coach," he said. "I don't have anything bad to say about Bob Weber other than he wasn't able to get out of his players what he'd hoped."

Bob Crum said Weber was a better person than a head coach. "Bob Weber was the nicest guy ever, but he was not a strong personality," he said. "Our team had a whole lot of issues."

In 1970, which was Weber's fourth season in Tucson but just his second as UA head coach, the Wildcats neared the end of another mediocre year. They beat Wyoming, 38-12, in their second-to-last game of the season to end a four-game losing streak, and they headed into a December matchup with ASU in Arizona Stadium with a 4-5 record.

"Overconfident" Devils not "mentally ready"

Entering the 1970 Duel, the Sun Devils were a perfect 9-0 for the first time since 1957, having beaten their opponents by an average of more than 25 points per contest.

"There was a lot of excitement because of the fact that we could go undefeated," said ASU defensive end Junior Ah You (1969-71), who later starred in the Canadian Football League. "When we got to 6-0, we thought there was a potential to be undefeated. It got more exciting as the next game came along."

But the kind of domination that ASU had grown accustomed to that season might have caused some of the players to do the unthinkable: take Arizona lightly.

"It was an ugly game. We obviously went in there overconfident," Matlock said. "We went out there and we weren't mentally ready to play, and they were."

Considering that ASU had averaged over 38 points per game to that point in the season, the halftime score was remarkable: Sun Devils 0, Wildcats 0.

Spagnola had the same complaint about ASU's offense in the '70 game that Goodman had raised with Kush more than once.

"We were pretty much a 50-50 club as far as running and passing," he said, "and from what I recall, we got to be a little too conservative against UA in that game."

Crum remembers it the same way: ASU's cautious approach, combined with UA's underrated defense, made for a competitive, low-scoring contest.

"I think Frank played really conservative in that game, and we really played tough. But Frank could've cranked it up if he wanted to," he said. "We had some pretty good players on that team. We had (future NFL defensive back) Jackie Wallace. Bill McKinley was a real talented defensive end who played in the pros. We had a defensive tackle named Jim Johnson, who was just a stud.

"UA was not short on athletes when I was there. We just weren't very well orchestrated."

Missing the point

Arneson recalled the Wildcats' kicker, Steve Hurley, being booted off the team days before the Duel. Apparently, Hurley wasn't satisfied with the footballs he was supplied with during team practices.

"All I remember is (Hurley) was complaining because the balls that he was using in practice were the older footballs," Arneson said. "That bothered him; he said something about it and he got kicked off the team."

If they had to do it over again, the UA coaching staff might have been more willing to appease Hurley. In his place, defensive lineman Al Mendoza was called in for kicking duty against ASU.

"So we missed an extra point and three field-goal attempts of 30 yards or (closer)," Arneson said. "If it wasn't for that, we probably would've won the game."

Considering that the game's final score was 10-6 in ASU's favor – it was the Devils' narrowest victory in their undefeated 1970 season – Arneson is probably right.

ASU finally opened the game's scoring in the third quarter when Spagnola found Hill for a 7-yard TD pass to make it 7-0.

The Devils added a field goal in the fourth quarter, and the Wildcats got a late touchdown pass from quarterback Bill Demory – followed by that missed extra point – to complete the scoring.

Ah You said there was a feeling of relief after ASU survived with its undefeated season intact. "It was so intense, it was a low-scoring game, and you didn't know if the game was going to go one way or the other," he said. "We were hanging on for dear life hoping we can get the ball back and run out the clock."

ASU wingback Steve Holden (1970-72) said it wasn't a lack of effort that caused that game – in which the Devils turned the ball over seven times – to be such a nail-biter. "Sometimes, when you go in with too much emotion, you're too hyped up and excited, and you make a lot of mistakes," he said.

But Spagnola said a win is a win – especially against Arizona. "I recall going into that game that we were favored by a couple touchdowns, so from that matter, it was a little bit of a disappointment," he said. "But the end result was we won the game, and close or not, we ended up undefeated for that season. Then we were on our way to our first big bowl game, and I was pretty excited about that."

Maybe the best ever

The Devils finally got their long-awaited bowl invitation from the Peach Bowl in Atlanta, where they completed their perfect season by beating North Carolina, 48-26. The win allowed ASU to earn some national respect with a ranking of No. 6 in the final 1970 Associated Press poll.

His opinion being admittedly subjective, Spagnola said the 1970 team was the best Sun Devil squad of all time, especially when one factors in the lopsided margins of victory – the UA game notwithstanding – and the toughness of the players.

"I think we had more talent and more want, you know. We wanted to win it more," he said. "We played with broken fingers and things like that. Today, they take (players) out for 2-3 weeks."

But Matlock said the ASU team that deserves that best-ever label came a year later. "I don't think there's any question the best team I played on would be the '71 team. We just had more weapons," he said.

White gets starting nod with Fiesta Bowl on line

Matlock said the 1971 Duel remains his all-time favorite. "The 1971 ASU-UA game was by far the most memorable game I played in – and I played in three bowl games, and we won all of them," he said.

The Devils came into the game with a 9-1 record – they had a 21-game winning streak broken earlier that season by Oregon State – and the players knew they were competing for a bid to the first-ever Fiesta Bowl.

Matlock said the loss to the Beavers turned out to be a positive. "We had a quarterback by the name of Grady Hurst who was a really good athlete out of Los Angeles but not a really good leader," he said. "So after he threw five picks against Oregon State and we lost, the next week, Frank started the baseball player."

Kush said he was enamored with Danny White's athletic ability. "In high school he was a baseball player, a basketball player, a football player, and he came from what I call a mental athletic background. His dad was a great football player," he said. "We had some pretty good quarterbacks – Joe Zuger, Danny White, Dennis Sproul – so we were fortunate.

"But Danny White, to me, he could do it all. Hell, he could punt. He could kick off. He, to me, was the epitome of high school athletes."

The next Malone

Joining the Devils' roster in '71 was Art Malone's brother, Ben, who was every bit as skilled as his older brother, according to Kush, and was his kind of player.

"Ben and Art, to me, were both extremely talented, and above all, they were mentally determined and had that great desire, both very intelligent, didn't make any mental mistakes, and they both ended up playing pro ball," he said. "The Malone family, they lived across the tracks down in Eloy. But they had the personal discipline at home, and I think that's what made them successful."

ASU had plenty of talent in the backfield in '71, including Woody Green and Brent McClanahan, both of whom later played in the NFL. But Matlock said Ben Malone was in a class all by himself.

"No. 1, Benny was the hardest-working guy out there," he said. "He was so quick off the ball, and (as an offensive lineman), you didn't have to blow anybody over; you just had to get there quick, make contact and go.

"But the real difference between Benny and Brent McClanahan and Woody was Benny made sure that he helped up every lineman after every play and brought you back (to the huddle) and say, 'Great job, come on guys, let's do it.' If he got stuffed, he'd say, 'OK, my fault, let's go.' He would stay after practice and do agility drills by himself. And he had a smile like a 1958 Buick grill – just a big old smile."

And Matlock suspected payback for the Ultimatum Bowl might have been on Ben Malone's mind in his first Duel in '71, just as it was for his brother three years earlier. "Art was the one who beat UA really bad in the Ultimatum Bowl," he said. "It was a little bit of revenge maybe, and he played just incredibly well."

Benny bowls over Cats in Tempe

The Wildcats, who still hadn't found their legs under Weber, got more than they could handle from Ben Malone and his backfield mates in '71.

Malone rushed for over 100 yards and a touchdown, Green scored two TDs of his own and the ASU defense held UA to 168 yards of total offense in a 31-0 rout – the Devils' third shutout of the Wildcats and their first since Kush's first season as head coach. White added 171 yards and a TD pass in his first Duel start.

"I couldn't wait for the game to start, and it was just a track meet, basically," Malone (1971-73) said. "We had a lot of speed all around, and UA, they played the game the way that we expected to play. We were just fortunate enough to take advantage of opportunities, and I think we had a little better team than they had at that particular time."

Arneson said the '71 game was "ugly" for the Wildcats, both on the field and on the sidelines. "That was the only time I played at Sun Devil Stadium, and we just got our butts kicked," he said. "During the game, I remember two guys on our team got in a fight (with each other). Now that's ridiculous.

"I remember coming out after the game thinking we just got our butts kicked offensively and defensively. I give them credit; they beat us soundly in that game."

Matlock said he and his fellow offensive linemen were instructed to contain Arneson's brother, Mark, a consensus All-American in '71. "We just literally kept running it at him," he said. "We had the best offense in the country, and we just said, 'We're going to run it right here, and you know we're going to run it right here, and see if you can stop it.' And from my standpoint of being an offensive guard, it was a pretty cool challenge."

The Devils were up to the challenge, racking up 235 rushing yards on 58 carries. "It wasn't even a contest. We were possessed," Matlock said.

Devils continue to earn national attention

ASU secured its third straight WAC championship with the Duel win and advanced to the inaugural Fiesta Bowl, where White passed for two touchdowns and Green ran for three TDs, including the game-winner late in the fourth quarter, for a 45-38 victory over Florida State.

Ah You said the 1970 and '71 seasons were the two that let the rest of the country know that ASU was a top-tier contender - and certainly the best football team in the Grand Canyon State. "I think those years, people started taking ASU seriously," he said. "Going back East and beating North Carolina (in the Peach Bowl) – people got to see ASU play, because we hadn't played in that part of the world before. That could have been the years that turned around the status of ASU football."

Devils run, Cats fight

Not much had changed in terms of the two programs' football fortunes in 1972. The Devils lost a couple of close games to Wyoming and Air Force but were otherwise having another stellar season, while the Wildcats were nearing the end of another losing campaign under Weber's direction.

Not much had changed in Kush's approach to beating UA, either: ASU ran the ball no fewer than 72 times at Arizona Stadium in '72, allowing White to throw just 12 passes.

"Kush was like that. He loved running the ball straight ahead and taking the fight to your front line," said UA left guard and long snapper Jay Bledsoe (1972-74). "He was pretty adamant that he wanted to go after your center of gravity – your front folks on defense – take the wind out of them and throw the ball as a changeup. Most of the time, his receivers were pretty wide open because of the effectiveness of the running game."

The Devils took an early 14-0 lead thanks to a 56-yard TD pass from White to Holden and a 2-yard run by McClanahan. But this time, UA didn't go away easily, as Demory threw two first-half touchdown passes, cutting ASU's lead to 21-14 at half-time. Demory threw for three scores in the game, including two to Theopolis "T" Bell, who played nine NFL seasons and led the Wildcats in career TD receptions until 2011.

Demory had a solid outing against ASU that day, but UA offensive guard Don Proietti (1972-74) said he never reached his full potential as a Wildcat. "There were a lot of expectations coming in that he was going to be a team leader, and I think he had a disappointing year," he said. "He was a good-looking, tall kid, and he was a good passer, but he always fell below what the expectations were."

The Devils put some distance between themselves and the Wildcats with another McClanahan TD run, this one a 1-yarder, in the third, and then took a 17-point lead on a field goal. UA would get back to within 10 points in the third quarter on a 1-yard reception from Bell, but White closed out the Cats with his second TD throw of the game, an 8-yard pass to senior wide receiver Ed Beverly. Final score: ASU 38, UA 21.

Matlock, who was a co-captain on the '72 ASU team, had to sit out the game due to a knee injury. He said the game's competitive nature was another example of the Devils taking the Wildcats a bit too lightly.

"That was another case of maybe a little premature (celebration) on our part, that we're the big boys coming in here," he said. "They were good. Bob Crum and Jackie Wallace, they were really good athletes. But they weren't good enough to overcome the offense that we had."

ASU boasted two running backs with over 150 rushing yards in the '72 Duel – Green (172) and McClanahan (153) – and gained 363 yards on the ground overall.

"We actually played them pretty tough; our offense did a great job. But they were just so good," Crum said. "Their offense was unbelievable. They had a bunch of tough guys on their offensive line. Against us, it was just boom-boom – they were just hitting us. It was like some of those fights when Muhammad Ali would just hit 'em at will.

"Their running backs hit the line so much faster and harder than anybody we played. They were such a great team."

Sticks and stones

Ben Malone still remembers the emotion from the UA fans that fueled another tough Wildcat effort in Tucson. "It was a very hostile environment down there – a lot of noise, a lot of fans, and of course back in those days, it was a full house when those two teams met," he said.

Malone said he was careful not to get in a shouting match with the pro-Wildcat crowd. "They would say things to us, the fans, but that ignited us. That made us want to play more because they couldn't do anything but just (keep) talking," he said. "The guys who could (play) were out on the field. We respected them and just went out on the field and let our play do our talking."

Kush said he did his best to get his players to focus on the field and not the fans in every game he coached against UA, regardless of whether it was in Tucson or Tempe. "I prepared our guys (the same) whether we were going to play down in Tucson, Timbuktu or wherever," he said. "I think the only contrast you may have is the mental factor and the physical factor of traveling here and there."

That's it for Bob

While the Devils had clinched their fourth consecutive WAC championship and were enjoying their third straight bowl win – a 49-35 Fiesta Bowl victory over Missouri – the Wildcats were looking for a replacement for Weber, who was released following four straight sub-.500 seasons and an 0-4 record against the Tempe contingent.

Proietti said that he felt as though Weber, similar to Mudra, had quit on the team in '72, as the coach seemed to know he was on his way out.

"I can remember from that ('72 ASU) game, his halftime speech was unbelievable," he said. "He said, 'Men, I just want to say one thing to you: When you go out onto the field, the (home) fans are going to boo you.' And I remember him saying that, and it was like, 'Really?' It was shocking. It was like he already knew he was fired and wanted to kind of give us a word of advice: 'Just expect you're going to get booed and be ready for it.'"

UA defensive end Rex Naumetz (1971-74) said he doesn't recall Weber ever placing much of an emphasis on beating ASU.

"I don't believe that his coaching staff brought out the intensity of this rivalry like Coach Young did," he said.

New coach, new tone

After being freed of the anti-football Richard Harvill when he retired as school president in 1971, UA hired Jim Young to replace Weber as head coach. Young had served as defensive coordinator at Michigan the previous four seasons.

Proietti said the personality differences between Weber and Young were quite stark. "Weber was very cerebral, very reserved, very quiet, and pretty much had all his assistant coaches do the work," he said, "whereas Young was a real people person, a real positive personality, really believed in a positive mental goal setting and all that kind of stuff.

"He was a very important person in my life. He had a real good approach to life in general – very structured and goal-oriented. None of that was I ever exposed to with Weber. Young was also the master of putting in time for any opponent – particularly ASU."

Naumetz said Young, unlike Weber, made beating the Sun Devils one of the Wildcats' top priorities. "The intensity between the Bob Weber and the Jim Young era was like night and day," he said. "The Bob Weber era, it was brought up as a rivalry, and everyone knew it was a rivalry, but ASU absolutely handed our tail ends to us just about every time we played them, and (the coaches) really didn't do much to kind of motivate you.

"On the other hand, when Jim Young came in, the intensity was shown from the very, very first meeting that he ever had with us."

Naumetz recalled that, shortly after he was hired, Young called a special all-players meeting on a February afternoon in a conference room inside Arizona Stadium. "All the players were notified that the first meeting with our new head coach was at a specific time and place, and you'd better not be late," he said.

"So we're sitting down (at the meeting) and Jim Young is up in front, and he's pacing like a caged cougar, back and forth. And when it came 4 o'clock, he told (an assistant coach) to close the door, and everyone who was late wasn't allowed in."

Bledsoe also remembers that meeting well. "He sits up there, and as more and more guys come in, 4 o'clock hits, and he looks to the back of the room and says, 'Lock the door.' Pretty soon, you hear more scratching and knocking at the door. He told them to go away and come back when they were ready to play football," he said.

Naumetz said Young talked at length during that first meeting about how important it was to beat Arizona State. "So from the very, very first day that we met Coach Young, we knew that we were going to change, and we knew that we had to beat our rival," he said. "That's how it was. He came from Michigan and the Michigan-Ohio State rivalry, where you knew you had to beat your rival."

Young's recollection of that initial meeting matches that of his players. "We had a 4 o'clock meeting, and some of the players came a little bit late. So yeah, I locked the door because I wanted to establish a disciplined program and responsibility between the players," he said. "I guess the sense that they still talk about it put the point across to them."

Young said he was well aware of UA's rivalry with ASU – and the fact that it really hadn't been much of a contest for nearly a decade. "I knew ASU was our No. 1 rivalry, but any time they'd beaten you eight straight years, you better focus on that," he said.

To further illustrate his point, one of Young's first purchases as UA coach was a large picture frame that he showed to his team. "I said, 'This frame will go up in the hallway (with a picture of) the first team to beat Arizona State, and you men will be a part of that,'" Young said. "We had that frame put up in the hall by the locker room."

Young's disciplined approach instantly translated to on-field results, as the Wildcats won eight of their first nine games in '73.

"We had a lot of talent, so coming out West, he wanted to come out with more speed and passing and thought we had talent for that at the skill positions," Bledsoe said.

The Wildcats were slated to take on the Devils in Tempe following their second loss of the season, a tough 27-26 defeat to Air Force. They would face another talented ASU squad that entered the Duel with a 9-1 record but was a game behind UA for first place in the WAC standings.

"We just really turned that whole season around, and it was just like living a dream," Proietti said. "We were just playing so well, and it was a big success.

"So going into that ASU game, everybody had really high hopes because we were playing for the right to go to the Fiesta Bowl. They had to beat us to go to the Fiesta Bowl, and all we had to do was tie them or win."

Young has Cats watch "horror film"

The night before the '73 ASU game, Young gathered the UA players in a room in their Tempe hotel to watch a movie – something that Proietti said had become a tradition that year.

"We'd have a movie before we went to bed that Friday night, just to get our mind off the game – like a Western or some fairly recent movie," he said. "And he said, 'Tonight, we're going to do something different: We're going to watch a horror film.' And we all thought (it would be) some great slasher, blood-and-gore film.

"So he doesn't say anything, he turns the lights off, runs the projector, and on the screen comes a total black screen, and it's just black for a few seconds. Then you see these white letters dissolve onto the black screen."

On the screen, one by one, came the years and scores of the previous eight UA-ASU games – all of which, of course, were in the Sun Devils' favor.

"Nobody said a word," Proietti said. "And when it was over, he turned off the projector and he said, 'That's it. Go to bed.'"

"Honed in" Cats vs. "steamroller" Devils

Naumetz said Young had the Cats whipped into a frenzy heading into the 1973 Duel in Tempe.

"I remember the intensity," he said. "We were just honed in on the game, more so than any other game during the season.

"It got to the point where guys were tense and nervous. I know there were a couple receivers on the team that, the night before the game, got in a little fisticuffs, you might say, and a lot of that was just tension that was building up inside while getting ready for this game."

Meanwhile, Frank Kush's son, Dan (1973-76), who joined ASU as a placekicker that season, said the Devils were plenty confident that they would make it nine straight wins over the Wildcats.

"I'm playing with Danny White, Benny Malone, Woody Green – just tremendous athletes. We were just a steamroller going through teams, and it was like, 'Hey, this is a game we expect to win, and let's go do it,'" he said.

In the '73 Duel, UA hung tough with White, Malone, Green, wingback Morris Owens and the rest of the Devils for the first 30 minutes. The Cats fell behind by 10 points twice in the first half but responded each time with a touchdown. A 4-yard TD pass from quarterback Bruce Hill to halfback Willie Hamilton with less than two minutes remaining in the second quarter cut the Sun Devil lead to 22-19. ASU countered with a TD pass from White to Owens right before halftime to take a 28-19 advantage.

Naumetz said the Wildcats believed at halftime that they could continue to challenge the Devils the rest of the game – but that belief subsided after the first play of the second half.

"We were all hyped up and ready to go, and we were playing them closely in the first half," he said. "And in the second half, we fumbled the (opening) kickoff, and they took it right in (for a touchdown) and ended up pounding our butts. That was a huge letdown for us.

"I hate to say this, but it appeared that once the opening kick-off for the second half was fumbled and ASU promptly just stuck it into the end zone quickly – I was on defense on that play, and you could see the body language on some of the players; it was slumped shoulders."

The Devils outscored the Wildcats 27-0 in the second half. For the game, ASU amassed over 700 yards of total offense and forced seven UA turnovers. Owens caught three TD passes from White, and Green (192 rushing yards) and Malone (147 rushing yards) each had a touchdown run in the second half.

Final score: ASU 55, UA 19. And that meant another Fiesta Bowl appearance for the Devils.

"We just got beaten by a very good football team," said UA offensive guard Bill Parks (1973-75). "We were hanging in there, and at one point we thought our magic was working. And then, with their talent they had, they just steamrolled us."

Even Young, who did everything he could to get his team fired up for the game, acknowledged that his Wildcats were just outmatched.

"They had some great personnel, and we weren't up to the challenge that year," he said. "They just kept coming at us."

Two-point eruption

With the game out of reach in the second half, Kush and the Devils went for a two-point conversion following a touchdown rather than attempting the usual extra-point kick. Bledsoe said that didn't sit well with UA defensive coordinator Larry Smith.

"It didn't take much for Smith to get too fired up about something like that," he said. "He was starting to think they were starting to run the score up."

While Bledsoe suspected that the Devils went for two just because mathematics suggested that they should in that situation, Smith obviously didn't see it that way. "Smith was beside himself," he said. "That instilled – I wouldn't call it hatred, but pretty damn close, into Larry Smith. He never forgot that."

It's safe to say that Smith – who would eventually because UA's head coach – wouldn't soon forget that play.

"We're still playing"

UA defensive back Joe O'Sullivan (1973-75) remembers some taunting on behalf of a few ASU players toward the end of the '73 game.

"They beat the (expletive) out of us, quite frankly, so I think there was a little mocking going on at that point – like, 'You guys may be up and coming, but you're not even in our category,'" he said.

But despite the lopsided nature of the second half, Naumetz said he and the Cats never let up against their rivals.

"I remember one of the touchdowns that they had punched in on us, and they're going in for the extra point, and once again I'm on defense as a defensive end," he said. "Woody Green steps in to block me, and I hit him as hard as I could. I can't put it verbatim, but what he essentially said is, 'Why are you guys doing this?' And basically, I said, 'F you. We're still playing.'

"That's how I felt about it. If we're down 55-19, it didn't matter, and I'm still coming at you like it was the first play of the game. I wanted to hit somebody just as hard on the last play of the game as if it was the first play."

1973: The end of an amazing ASU era

The Sun Devils' third straight Fiesta Bowl win – a 28-7 victory over Pittsburgh – marked the end of the collegiate careers for the outstanding offensive trio of Danny White, Ben Malone and Woody Green.

All three went on to enjoy success in the NFL. White won a Super Bowl with the Dallas Cowboys, with whom he spent 13 seasons. Malone played seven years with the Miami Dolphins and Washington Redskins. And Green played for the Kansas City Chiefs from 1974-76.

Malone still loves reflecting on his days in Tempe. "The wins were great because we love the fans, and it was exciting back in those days to play football and carry the torch and pass it on to the younger kids now," he said.

Is it still a point of pride to have an unblemished record against the Wildcats? "Oh, yeah. The Cats never beat us," Malone said. "They played great football and they were coached well. They just didn't have the horses that we had back in those days. They had great athletes, but in college football, you can have a couple of marquee players that can be the difference in the season."

Despite the concussions that he sustained during his NFL days, White can still recall boasting about his unblemished record against UA following the '73 season – much to Frank Kush's dismay.

"I remember getting up at the football banquet after my senior year and kind of bragging a little bit about us beating UA three times," he said. "I don't remember exactly what I said, but I said something to the effect that I'm 3-0, I'd always be 3-0 the rest of my life, and there was nothing they could do about that.

"And Coach Kush comes up to me after the banquet and says, 'Nice going. That's easy for you to say. You don't have to play them again.' And he was serious. He was intense. That just kind of showed you how he felt about the rivalry."

Indeed, if White had known what was ahead for his alma mater the following season, he might have chosen his words more carefully.

Visualizing victory

In 1974, Young proved that the Wildcats' eight-win season the year before was no fluke, as they were 8-2 and looking forward to getting another crack at the Sun Devils, this time in Tucson.

Naumetz said Young was a big believer in visualizing one's goals in order to achieve them. Case in point: According to Naumetz, before the start of the '74 season, Young had placed a plywood board over the entry to the UA locker room.

"To get to the locker room, you almost had to duck down on your knees to get under this," he said. "He would put sayings on there, and they were all painted on there."

The week leading up to the Duel that year, Naumetz said, Young painted a large ASU logo on the board. "So when we left (the locker room), we had to see it and we had to bend down to get underneath it," he said. "I think Coach was playing mind games with us: They beat us, so now we've got to bend under them all the time.

"That was the only time I've ever seen anything like that. Jim Young was not going to let us lose this one."

During the week of practice before the '74 Duel, Young emphasized to his players that they would have to play better against ASU than they did the previous week in a narrow 21-14 win over Wyoming, and he ensured that by having full-contact scrimmages.

"I said, 'We're going to have very short practices this week, but we're going to hit in every practice.' We did full-blown scrimmaging, because I felt that toughness would beat Arizona State," he said.

With Malone, White, Green and others gone, the Devils had a down year by Kush's standards, and they went into Tucson with a 6-4 record and losers of three of their last four.

"In '74, we had just a lot of, I'll say, junior people – not experienced, maybe not the best guys around – and we were just struggling," Dan Kush said.

But that didn't mean that his dad didn't expect the Devils to march into Arizona Stadium and win, just as they had done in the previous nine seasons and in four straight trips to Tucson.

"I'll admit that, once we got to that week of practice, you could just see that everyone was at another level. Things were dialed up a little higher," Dan Kush said. "You (could see that) in everyone, from the seniors to the captains to the coaches."

Another defensive Duel

The '74 game closely mirrored the defensively oriented Duel in Tucson four years earlier, as the Cats and Devils battled to a scoreless tie through three quarters.

"Sooner or later, something was going to happen, and the breaks were going to go to our side. We never lost faith that we were going to win that game," Naumetz said.

"On offense, we had (quarterback) Bruce Hill, we had 'T' Bell, we had (wide receiver) Scotty Piper – we had a very, very good offense with a lot of speed, so we could have scored from anywhere on the field at any time. And when we finally did score, it was our job to make sure there was no retaliatory score coming back."

Bledsoe said Young's intense practices allowed the Wildcats to do something that year that very few teams ever did against the Devils under Frank Kush. "We outhit them, which was abnormal for ASU," he said. "I think both defenses were good enough to win that game, but our offense was a little sounder than them. They could not throw the ball to save themselves, and we shut down their running game cold.

"If Kush couldn't run the ball on you, his offense started to fall apart because he couldn't fall back on his passing game. (All-WAC defensive tackle) Mike Dawson dominated the line of scrimmage that game."

Halfway through the fourth quarter, UA linebacker and Tucson native Mark Jacobs intercepted a pass by first-year ASU quarterback Dennis Sproul on the Sun Devil half of the field. Three plays later, Wildcat kicker Lee Pistor scored the first points of the game, giving UA a 3-0 lead.

ASU failed to respond offensively, and Arizona halfback Willie Hamilton scored the only touchdown of the game late in the fourth to ice the Wildcats' 10-0 win.

After nearly a decade of frustration and futility against their northern neighbors, the Wildcats not only broke through with a win in the Duel; they shut the Devils out for the first time in 21 years.

"I was very confident that our defense was going to keep them from scoring because we knew our players and we were very confident. We felt great about it," Naumetz said. "On the other hand, I felt we had a very good offense, and I was very confident that our team would be able to punch something in."

The victory wasn't enough to get UA a bowl berth or even the WAC title – BYU took that honor in '74. But knowing that it would be BYU that would be invited to the Fiesta Bowl, O'Sullivan said he and his teammates treated the ASU matchup as their bowl game.

"The coaching staff made beating that team that year one of the primary goals," he said. "That almost became our bowl game, because I think that year, BYU actually beat us in Provo, and they made it to the Fiesta Bowl, and we were hoping to go to the Sun Bowl, but we didn't have an expectation of that. So beating (ASU) became our bowl game, and I think we felt very confident throughout that game that we would win."

Parks said the Wildcats would have won the game by a wider margin had they not built it up as such a monumental hill to climb. "We were over-concerned that the team we played before (in the early '70s) would show up, but they didn't have those players; a lot of them were gone," he said.

"We weren't boasting until the (final) gun went off, and it took us 'til the locker room for us to really let loose from what we tasted. You've got to realize: The guys before me, they hadn't won for nine years straight. I think the fans themselves didn't know what to think because they hadn't been there awhile."

In O'Sullivan's mind, the win allowed Tucson, which was being dwarfed in population and economic growth by Phoenix and its growing suburbs, to regain a lost sense of pride.

"I think the ASU-UA rivalry in the '70s really fell along the lines of the way that Tucson people think of Phoenix," he said. "Tucson people think of themselves as the smaller town, much like San Diego does with Los Angeles: It's a smaller, Podunk town - it's ugly - and Phoenix is big, has pro sports (teams) and all that kind of stuff.

"And so I think UA people had a chip on their shoulder toward ASU, not only because of ASU's record but because they represented Phoenix, too."

Framed

Young, who had all of his players sign a pledge before the season that they would give everything they had physically, mentally and emotionally to beat the Devils in 1974, said he was on a mission to show that the Wildcats could be every inch as tough as Kush's squad.

"Arizona State was a very tough program at the time. Frank Kush was a great coach," he said. "They didn't think Arizona could stay with them physically, I think, and we wanted to prove that we could."

All of Young's tactics that year – the pledge, the plywood board, the intense workouts that final week – allowed him to fill that picture frame that he purchased and reserved for his first team that beat the Sun Devils.

"The first year, it stayed empty, and the second year, we beat them," he said. "And so we put the 1974 team up in that frame."

Kush takes a walk

For the first time in a decade, a class of ASU players got to see what Frank Kush was like after a loss to Arizona.

Or they would have if they'd been awake.

"We were really flat, didn't do very well, and everybody had to ride the bus (that night) back up to ASU," Dan Kush said. "And so it's late, and by the time we get up to Tempe, everybody on the bus is sleeping. And so we come up the (Interstate) 10 and took the 60 up to Rural Road and went north on Rural until we got to campus.

"There's a traffic light between Southern and Broadway on a street called Alameda, and we lived off Alameda. I was on the back of the bus sleeping, but my dad was so pissed that he lost that he got off the bus there and walked a quarter-mile to his house."

Most of the players slept through their coach's early exit. "We all kind of wake up and stumble out of the bus, and it's kind of like, 'Where's my dad at?'" Dan Kush said. "One of the assistant coaches said, 'He got so pissed off, he walked home,' And I said, 'Great,' because he was my ride home."

High-tech advantage

It took just one season for Frank Kush to turn ASU back into a national contender. In 1975, the Devils were firing on all cylinders, especially on the defensive side.

Joining ASU that season was defensive lineman Al Harris, an eventual NCAA All-American and 12-year NFL star. Harris was recruited out of Hawaii by both ASU and UA, and one of the reasons he picked the Devils was their technological advantage.

"That year, (UA) had beaten ASU, and they showed me a film of them beating ASU," he said. "But back then, money resources must have been different, because it was the old reel-to-reel kind of film, but it didn't have sound, and they had a tape recorder from a guy narrating the highlights of the season.

"I really liked it, but then ASU had their highlight film, and theirs was more how you see today's highlight films – no tape recorder. And that told me that ASU was at a different level in their athletic department. And I just remembered how ASU was insulted that they even lost to UA."

With more seasoned players such as Sproul, All-WAC half-back Freddie Williams, second-year wide receiver John Jefferson and future nine-time NFL Pro Bowl cornerback Mike Haynes, along with defensive newcomers Al and John Harris, the Devils were enjoying an undefeated season when their Tempe showdown with the Wildcats came around.

"We only had 5-6 seniors on that team and a bunch of really talented underclassmen, but the senior leadership on that team was very, very strong," Al Harris said. "I think after that '74 debacle, they had come out refocused."

Down in Tucson, UA was enjoying its best season yet under Jim Young, going 9-1 – its only loss coming at home to New Mexico in October – prior to the ASU game.

And never before had both teams been so highly ranked before the Duel in the Desert; ASU was No. 8 in the AP poll, UA was No. 12.

"That was our best team (in 1975), because the key figures on that team were sophomores in '73 and seniors in '75," Young said.

Fans trade chants in "shaking," "rocking" Sun Devil Stadium

Harris said the packed Sun Devil Stadium crowd, which included quite a few Wildcat fans that night in 1975, reminded the players just how important this particular Duel was.

"The big thing I remember is how huge that game was because there was so much riding on it," Al Harris said. "The mountains (behind the stadium) were full of people from both sides. UA came out and painted their colors up on the Butte.

"It was rocking. The whole stadium was shaking the whole time, and you're hearing fans chanting on each side against each other: 'A-S-U, 'U-of-A.' It had an Ohio State-Michigan kind of feel, with everything on the line.

"That was the first time I was in a rivalry like that (kind of) fervor. There was so much at stake and so much pressure in that game. You had a bunch of guys that were future NFL players on ASU's side, and UA's side, too. Bruce Hill and Mike Dawson – they had a really good team. Both teams had a lot of speed at the skill positions."

Dan Kush didn't play in that game due to a torn hamstring, but he remembers the enhanced media coverage that surrounded it. "It was just a very important game. We win that one, we're undefeated on the season and WAC champs," he said.

The Catch

The Sun Devils ended the first quarter of the '75 Duel with a 3-0 lead, but the Wildcats struck twice in the second. Their second touchdown of the game came via a Williams fumble that set up a 10-yard run by Hill to give Arizona a 14-3 advantage with two minutes left in the half.

Then, Sproul engineered a late drive that culminated with the most talked-about play in Duel history on the ASU side.

With just seconds left before halftime and ASU at the UA 8-yard line, Sproul appeared to overthrow Jefferson on a pass in the end zone. But the overthrow allowed Jefferson to display his athleticism, as he dove for the ball at full stretch, reached it and then brought it into his body as he hit the ground in the back of the end zone.

The extra point following Jefferson's touchdown grab cut the Wildcats' lead to 14-10 at halftime – and, just as importantly, it gave the Devils significant momentum heading into the locker room.

Frank Kush has a framed photo of The Catch, as it's still known in Tempe, in his sixth-floor office in ASU's Intercollegiate Athletic Complex.

"John Jefferson, to me, is the epitome of what college football is all about," Kush said. "He wasn't the biggest guy, he wasn't the fastest guy, but he had the ability, almost like it was a vacuum, that he would suck that ball into him. And that's why he played pro ball and did a commendable job."

Cats question catch

Many of the Wildcats who played in the '75 game are quick to insist that what's known as perhaps the greatest catch in ASU history wasn't a catch at all.

"I just know that the play kind of broke down a little bit, and (Jefferson) was trailing along the back side of the goal line. The ball was thrown, and he was literally horizontal to the ground," O'Sullivan said. "As he caught the ball, he landed on the ground with his elbows, and the ball bounced out. But the referee called it a touchdown.

"When you look back at the game film, the ASU band was right there at the goal line and they were getting ready to take the field. You can see Arizona players pointing at the ball, and you can see an ASU band member's feet pointing at the ball (on the ground)."

Would the officiating crew have reversed the call on the field if it had the benefit of instant replay in 1975? "No question about it," O'Sullivan said. "That wouldn't have taken any time. But of course, I'm not exactly objective here."

Parks was on the sideline during the play, but he said the film he viewed after the game suggested it wasn't a catch. "If they had instant replay as they do now, it would've made it easier for a lot of us," he said. "I remember seeing (the UA players') faces in disbelief."

Young said Jefferson's grab was an amazing display of athleticism, but he also questions whether the touchdown call on the field would have held up under further review.

"We had the lead and (Jefferson) made a diving catch, which I know they would look at in instant replay today, because three things took place at the same time," he said. "Did he hit the ground before he went out of bounds? Did he hold on to the football when he hit the ground? It was a great catch, and I don't necessarily like instant replay, but I might have liked to see that."

Dan Kush said the questioning of The Catch by UA personnel is likely a case of people seeing what they want to see rather than seeing anything conclusive on video.

"I think it's sour grapes," he said. "I've watched that replay more than a half-dozen times because the media always replays it. I'm not sure, even if he did drop it, if the replay would've showed it, because his back would've been against where the cameras typically are at ASU. There were two officials, each on one side of the end zone, and they called it good.

"John wasn't the fastest guy or the biggest guy, but he had a great set of hands and great focus and attention. He had to have the best set of hands and the most concentration and focus of any receiver I've ever seen. That was a guy I just never questioned. I don't see the ball hitting the ground."

Al Harris said it was definitely a completed catch in his mind, but he also understands the other perspective.

"From the footage that I saw, it was a catch. It was a fantastic catch," he said. "If I'm on UA, I'd probably say it wasn't a catch. But the bottom line is: It was ruled a catch, and it'll go down as a catch.

"That'll always be disputed, but the bottom line is what it is, and officials can't change it."

Frank Kush agreed that the officials made the right call – and they certainly weren't influenced by the partisan Tempe crowd, as one Wildcat suggested. "One thing I learned is the officials call it the way they see it, and I don't think they're biased one way or the other," he said. "Even today, I watch a call, whether it's a pro game or a college game, and they call it the way they see it. And I think that's what happened in that particular ballgame."

The only thing that ASU and UA players from the '75 game seem to agree upon is that The Catch was a game-changer. "We thought we could overcome that, but we never did," Parks said. "ASU seemed to grow after that and did better, and we didn't. I think Jefferson's catch won the game for them."

The momentum that may have resulted from The Catch helped the Devils to go ahead, 17-14, in the third quarter with another touchdown pass from Sproul to Jefferson.

The Penalty

Hill, the 1975 WAC Offensive Player of the Year, made sure the Wildcats didn't go quietly, as he connected with halfback Dave Randolph on a 53-yard touchdown toss to give UA a 21-17 lead late in the third quarter. But on ASU's next possession, Sproul engineered an 80-yard touchdown drive, capped by his 1-yard touchdown run, to give the Devils a 24-21 advantage.

Then came a play that Wildcat players remember as vividly, and angrily, as The Catch.

Early in the fourth quarter, Hill threw a 77-yard touchdown pass to Piper that appeared to put Arizona back on top. "I was the left tackle and Piper was the split end," said UA offensive tackle Bill Segal (1975-79). "He ran a pass (pattern) and Bruce Hill hit him, and it was just beautiful.

"And all of a sudden, this yellow flag came at me, and I thought, 'Oh my God, I've done something wrong.' So, I went up to the ref and I said, 'What was that for? Holding?' He said, 'Offsides,' and he called the touchdown back."

Piper turned out to be the one who was flagged for being off-sides on the play, but Segal is certain that the play was legal. And at that point, he and the rest of the offense thought the fix was in. "I looked around and we all just thought, 'Oh my gosh, that (referee is) Frank Kush's brother,'" he said. "Obviously it wasn't, but it was just a real tough call.

"I've never seen replays of it, but I know he didn't throw the flag before Scott caught the ball, because I remember the play being completed, and then the flag came out. I'm not saying anything; it was just a weird call in my book."

O'Sullivan remembers his coach's reaction to the call. "I thought Jim Young was just going to melt down on the sidelines, and that was not characteristic of him," he said.

Young asserted that, if the touchdown had been allowed to stand, UA would've won that game. "It would've been *that* catch and not Jefferson's catch (that would've been remembered) if they hadn't called it back," he said.

From Segal's perspective, the offsides call changed the scope of the game more than Jefferson's TD grab did. "And that flag came awful late. Not that we hold grudges now," he said with a laugh.

Given a second chance, Kush's defense held tough the rest of the way as ASU won, 24-21, maintained its perfect season and locked up another WAC title and Fiesta Bowl bid.

The best Duel ever

Al Harris still thinks highly of the '75 Wildcat squad that, despite ending the season in the AP top 20, was not invited to a bowl game.

"I'm telling you, and I'm convinced of this: That UA team would've knocked off one of those top-10 teams," he said. "They were that good. We were very, very fortunate to beat them.

"I've always said that to people: The 1975 UA team got ripped off (by not being invited to a bowl game). They had a heck of a team. We barely beat them at ASU, and because only one team could win the WAC championship, they had no place to go."

Young, whose Wildcats finished the season at 9-2, said the '75 game should be considered one of the best in UA-ASU history. "When I was there, and I think for a good number of years (afterwards), it was considered the best game," he said. "I don't know whether it still is because that was years ago now, but at that time and for the next 20 years, I'll say that it was still the No. 1 game."

As for the '75 Sun Devils, Harris said they are in a class by themselves.

"I would say, from a focus standpoint and a vision standpoint, I can't think of an ASU team that was better," he said. "I think in each era, you get bigger and bigger teams. We were probably bigger than the guys in the '60s, so it's almost impossible (to compare). But I don't know if any team's focus was better than ours.

"That's why I'd put ourselves ahead of the '86 team (that won the Rose Bowl): We wouldn't have lost to that (1986) UA team. We just had a different type of vision than that team."

Dan Kush, who kicked the game-winning field goal in the Fiesta Bowl against Nebraska to cap the Devils' undefeated season in which they finished with a national No. 2 ranking, agreed that the '75 ASU squad was probably the all-time best – not because of individual talent but because of its team play. "I think the records and rankings would probably dictate that," he said. "We didn't have the Danny Whites, Woody Greens, Benny Malones. We didn't have a lot of the big names – just a lot of talented, hard-working, good football players."

"Playing for pride"

Both teams took a giant step back in 1976. In Tucson, the Wildcats experienced their first and only losing season under Young, partly because they were literally limping through an injury-plagued year.

"Our quarterback, (Marc) Lunsford, had been out for the season," Young said. "Earlier in the year, when we played UCLA, we lost eight starters in one week – four in the UCLA game and four in practice.

"We had a good team at the start of the season – we beat Auburn in that first game. I thought we were going to have a good year, but I really felt that the injuries had a lot to do with the season."

ASU's rare down season under Kush in '76 was primarily due to the loss of senior leadership, according to Al Harris, who sat out much of that season with an Achilles injury.

"Frank would tell you to this day that he blames the '76 season on himself because he didn't realize how immature we were," he said. "We lost those key leaders that we didn't have on the '76 team."

So, with no conference title or potential bowl game on the line, the '76 Duel in the Desert was solely for satisfaction and rivalry bragging rights. "It was one of those games where we were playing for pride that year – and you know what, if your season's in the toilet, that's the game you want to win, because at least you have bragging rights in the state," Harris said. "It was just one of those typical ASU-Arizona games: It's November, it's cold and windy out there, and at the end of the day, other than to yourself personally, it doesn't matter if you win or lose – you're playing for yourself and the team."

Harris had planned to sit the UA game out, as he was still nursing an injury. But his head coach had other ideas.

"Our defensive coordinator, Larry Kentera, advised me not to dress for the UA game because I hadn't dressed for the previous two games. I could run but I couldn't push off or anything at that point," he said.

Harris said Kentera knew that if he suited up for the game, Kush would make him play. "He said, 'Don't dress because Frank will play you. This is the UA game,'" he said. "But I said I'd dress just kind of to support the guys and show them I'm out there."

But Kentera was right. When UA took a 7-0 lead into the second quarter, Kush started looking in Harris' direction.

"I'm on the bench, and whoever took my place was really struggling at that position," Harris said. "And Frank would glance back at me during the game, and I'm thinking, 'Oh, gosh, it looks like he's going to put me in.' He'd go back and ask, 'How you feelin'?' And he kept walking back and forth, back and forth, and every time they'd run a play at (my position) and get yards, he'd look back at me.

"That's how desperate (beating UA) was for him. He looks back at me again and says, 'Well, what do you think? Do you think you can go?' And I said, 'Coach, I can't even run. I can't push off.'"

But Kush didn't care. "Next thing you know, I hear this: 'Harris! Get in!'" Harris said. "I can't push off; I can only jog. I don't have any lateral movement. It looks like there's a cast on my leg. And my defensive coordinator was probably going absolutely nuts: Here's this up-and-coming guy, and his career could be over."

Predictably, the Wildcats ran at the hobbled Harris as soon as he went in – but then he caught one of the biggest breaks of his collegiate career. "Fortunately for us, they came at a play right at me, which was OK; I could anchor, but I couldn't go anywhere," he said. "So I tackled the guy for a loss. And they never ran at me again."

And led by quarterback Fred Mortensen, who threw for 213 yards and two touchdowns, and linebacker Gary Padjen, who had five tackles and an important fumble recovery, the Devils finished a crummy 4-7 season on a high note by beating the Wildcats, 27-10, in Tucson.

Young packs for Purdue

Arizona wound up with a 5-6 record in '76, which was Young's last year in Tucson, as he decided to go back to the Big Ten by accepting a job offer to become head coach at Purdue.

None of his teams were invited to a bowl game during his four seasons in Tucson, but Young still appreciated what he was able to accomplish at UA – and he developed an appreciation for ASU and its longtime coach, as well.

"To me, I respected Arizona State. You have to, particularly with Frank Kush as the coach," he said. "I wanted to beat them in the worst way, but I didn't hate them.

"Frank Kush was a truly great coach, a very tough coach, and very successful. I think it's tough to be successful over a long period of time at the same place, and he certainly built that. I used to get charged up to recruit against him and challenge him on the football field, but he did more for football in the state of Arizona as a college coach than anybody I know of, certainly in the last 60-70 years. He is the dominant football individual in the state of Arizona."

Bearcat becomes Wildcat

In Young's place, UA hired University of Cincinnati head coach Tony Mason, who had led the Bearcats to three consecutive winning seasons from 1974-76.

"(Young and Mason) were complete polar opposites in style and personality, but I got along with both of them," said Wildcat tight end Ron Beyer (1975-78). "Tony Mason, God bless him, I remember he was just such a dynamic personality coming in, and Jim Young was more of a quiet, confident guy. He was a serious presence – not a big personality like Tony Mason. Tony brought more flair and contact, and if he liked you, he'd let you know it."

UA defensive back Van Brandon (1978-81) said he loved playing for Mason. "Tony was a great coach," he said. "The one thing I remember about Tony Mason is he told us on our recruiting trip that at the University of Arizona, we don't drive Volkswagens; we drive Cadillacs. It meant that we weren't a small guy; we were a big guy."

Segal said Mason's grasp of the Duel's importance, however, wasn't as sharp as Young's. "I don't think he understood the intensity of the rivalry," he said.

But his players certainly did. UA linebacker Corky Ingraham (1977-78) said Sun Devil Stadium was the second-loudest stadium he played in during his collegiate career, behind only Michigan Stadium in Ann Arbor. "But that wasn't a rivalry; that was just an inter-regional game," he said. "At Arizona State, I don't want to say it got personal, but they were nasty. They were aggressive fans, and it was an extremely loud place."

Devils get back on track

While the Wildcats were experiencing an up-and-down year – they were just 4-6 but had won two straight games going into the Duel in 1977 – the Sun Devils were 8-2 and eyeing another WAC championship and Fiesta Bowl bid.

But ASU fullback and linebacker Jeff McIntyre (1977-78) said the Wildcats were ready. "I just remember (UA) came out hard, and we had expected it. And it was a fight," he said.

But as was the norm in the Kush era, it was a fight in which the Devils remained standing. After Sproul threw a 46-yard touchdown pass to wide receiver Chris DeFrance on the seventh play of the game, John Harris returned a punt 55 yards for a score to give the Devils a quick 14-0 lead. Fullback Mike Harris then scored on a 31-yard run to give ASU a 21-0 advantage in the first half.

"I remember John Harris' (punt return). That was a huge momentum play," Al Harris said. "We had a lot of pride in returns. I think that had been ASU's moniker over the years: to have really good return people. We had a lot of speed."

The Devils' defense did the rest, as the Wildcats' only points came on a 1-yard TD run by wide receiver Harry Holt late in the first half, and the only second-half scoring came via a tackle of Lunsford in the end zone for a safety. Final score: ASU 23, UA 7.

Out with the WAC, in with the Pac

The win earned the Devils a co-conference championship with BYU – their seventh and final WAC title – and another invite to the Fiesta Bowl, where they lost for the first time, 42-30 to Penn State. UA managed to close its season on a winning note, defeating Hawaii, 17-10.

The 1977 Duel was the last for both teams as members of the Western Athletic Conference, as the Cats and Devils joined the Pacific 8 Conference before the 1978 season, turning it into the Pacific 10 Conference (Pac-10).

Beyer said the move to a new conference didn't change the rivalry's dynamic. "I wasn't up on the history of the Pac-8," he said, "and since we were new (to the conference), we didn't know who Washington was or who Oregon was.

"But we certainly knew who ASU was, and boy, was it energetic."

No wins, no offense, no problem

Though the Wildcats carried a two-game winning streak into their first Pac-10 Duel in the Desert in 1978, it was another mediocre 5-5 season in Tucson when the time came to face the Sun Devils at Arizona Stadium.

And just by perusing the box score, one would assume the '78 matchup was a blowout in the Devils' favor. Total offense: ASU 440, UA 162. Rushing yards: ASU 224, UA 87. First downs: ASU 23, UA 11.

But the Arizona Stadium scoreboard told a much different story. UA quarterback Jim Krohn threw a pair of touchdown passes in the second quarter – a 10-yard pass to Beyer and a 4-yard throw to flanker Tim Holmes – to give the Wildcats an unexpected 14-3 halftime lead.

Though ASU was 7-3 coming into the game, it had been beaten earlier that season by inferior opponents such as Stanford and Washington State – and quarterback Mark Malone (1977-79) said some Sun Devil players were concerned that history was about to repeat itself.

"I remember the disappointments early in the year after having gotten off to a pretty good start," he said, "and being down in that football game (to UA) was just like, 'God, are we going to finish this thing off by losing to our archrivals in the state?'"

But McIntyre said his guys knew they were capable of rallying. "It was the first year we went to the Pac-10, and we kind of had a bull's-eye on our back because we were the only team that beat (1978 national champions) USC all year," he said. "Everyone was on us, especially UA.

"But I don't feel we ever got in a game that we couldn't come back. We just kept plugging at it and playing. We kept trying to find a weakness or something. And we started capitalizing on their mistakes (in the second half)."

The Devils found their offense in the third quarter. Malone's 4-yard TD pass to DeFrance followed by a 54-yard strike from running back Alvin Moore to wideout Bernard Henry – coupled with a pair of failed two-point conversion attempts – gave ASU a 15-14 lead going into the final period.

Zivic misses

The Cats and Devils traded field goals in the fourth quarter. UA kicker Bill Zivic's 34-yarder cut the Devils' lead to a single point, 18-17, with less than eight minutes to go.

The Wildcats got the ball back in the final minutes and again wound up in field-goal range for Zivic, who lined up for a last-second 45-yard attempt that would have given UA its first win over ASU in four seasons.

"They completed a couple passes that drove them down within field-goal range, and I know as a defensive unit, we were just cringing," said Padjen (1976-79). "I remember (Zivic) kicking that ball, and I thought, 'Oh my God, we're just going to get our butts handed to us the following week.' Even though it was the last game of the season, it was just a bad thing to have to end the season on that."

McIntyre said he and Al Harris knew what they had to do. "(Zivic) was known for kicking far, and we said that if we don't block this, we're going to lose the game," he said. "And I remember Al Harris and I got through (the UA line), and I remember diving for the ball and us almost hitting each other."

But neither McIntyre nor Harris was able to get a finger on the ball as it sailed toward the uprights. "We're just lying there, and we both had disgust on our face, like, 'Damn, we just lost this game,'" McIntyre said.

"And then we looked to the sideline, and no one on UA's side was cheering. We looked at the referee, and he was showing a motion (that the kick had missed) to the left. And we could not believe it."

Zivic's miss took the air out of Arizona Stadium, and it allowed the Devils to exhale. "I think the word is pandemonium," Padjen said. "We were all just going crazy in the locker room."

Brandon said Zivic's expression following his missed attempt has been etched in his mind.

"It was blank. His eyes were just big, and it was a big, blank expression," he said. "I still can see that to this day. It's something you'll never forget. It was just a blank stare, like nothing was there.

"Zivic was a big-time kicker in the state of Arizona. He was never the same after that."

To this day, Beyer, who worked with Zivic in Tucson after their playing days were over, has never brought up that play. "I've seen him over the years and I've never talked to him about it," he said. "It's just something that I always felt that he was not interested in talking about.

"It was just a bitter defeat against those guys because we lost all four years against them. It was just sad to not share a victory over ASU as a player with all my teammates."

The win propelled the Devils to the Garden State Bowl, where they defeated Rutgers, 34-18.

Disaster averted

The special-teams gods were definitely smiling on the Sun Devils in the '78 Duel.

ASU quarterback Mike Pagel (1978-81) didn't start against UA that year, but he was called upon in an important situation late in the game. "We had the ball deep in our territory late in the game, and it was pouring, raining like crazy, and the field was really sloppy," he said. "And our punter had gotten hurt early in the game, so I got pressed into punting again, which I did a lot in my freshman year."

Pagel knew it wasn't crucial to get off a long punt; he just needed to make sure it didn't get blocked. "The snap comes back high, and I literally have to jump and catch it one-handed," he said. "And because it had been ingrained in me, 'Get if off, get if off,' I took one step. I slipped, the ball hit me in the shin, and it ended up being something like a whopping 18-yard punt.

The punt actually traveled just 14 yards. And all UA needed was a field goal to win. "So they get the ball in our territory with about two minutes to go in the game," Pagel said. "And fortunately for us and unfortunately for them, their kicker slipped on his plant foot and shanked (the field goal) and missed it badly. Talk about going from being the potential goat of the game to getting a reprieve."

Pagel said Kush approached him after the game to discuss his less-than-stellar punt. "Frank Kush came up to me, he grabbed me on the shoulders, he looked me right in the eye and asked me if I was Polish or something. And we all know Frank was Polish," he said. "I looked him right in the eye and said, 'No, Frank, I'm one step below: I'm Czechoslovakian.' And he lost it. He thought that was the funniest thing he'd ever heard. And it's true. I'm half Czech; my mother was full Czech.

"But being an 18-year-old punter who could've been the cause of us ending that winning streak we had against them, it didn't sit with me very well at the time until after the game."

Pagel was much more fortunate than another ASU punter would be against UA in a crunch-time kicking situation nine years later.

Wildcat fans pummel Devils' bus

It's fair to say that the UA faithful did not take the heartbreaking loss to ASU very well.

"We were in the parking lot and we were leaving, and I guess some fans got in front of our bus and threw some stuff at our bus," McIntyre said. "And we thought, 'These people are nuts.' It was that crazy. It was the first time I'd ever seen somebody get really violent over something like that. And we waited and we actually had to have police drive us out.

"I played in the NFL for several years, and I'd have to say the Raiders fans are probably that stupid, too. (UA fans) were actually throwing beer bottles. The law had not passed to not have glass in the stadium yet. Whatever they had in their hands, they would throw it – full beer bottles, empty beer bottles, beer cans, food, ice chests."

Did the ASU players respond to the UA fans? "Oh, no, no, you did not taunt when you played for Frank," McIntyre said with a laugh. "We didn't do that. We didn't want to meet his wrath come Monday if we did."

Frustrated Frank's finale

While the players were reveling in their escape from Tucson – both inside and outside the stadium – Kush was not.

"Frank was not happy," Padjen said. "A win is a win, but I know Frank wasn't happy with that performance. We were happy and everything else, but I remember Frank telling us we played like jackasses.

"The locker room was celebrating, but it was a very short celebration. Even though we won, he was still not happy with us. The ride back on the bus was not one where we were screwing around and celebrating."

But a win is a win – and the victory in the 1978 Duel in the Desert was Kush's last against Arizona.

Players remember Kush's tough love

A legal controversy erupted the following fall when a former player alleged that he was hit by Kush and filed a lawsuit. While a jury later cleared Kush of that charge, the school determined that the longtime coach interfered with an internal investigation and fired him in October 1979.

Kush's career at the ASU helm included 176 wins, seven bowl game appearances, six bowl victories, nine conference championships (two in the Border Conference and seven in the WAC), the Walter Camp Coach of the Year Award in 1975 and, perhaps most importantly, a 16-5 record against UA, including a nine-game winning streak from 1965-73.

Padjen said his father, who was a rugged Utah coal miner, wanted him to go to ASU after meeting Kush. "Frank had that tough, marine, drill sergeant-type persona about him, and that was one thing my father liked," he said. "He said, 'If you want to be accomplished and go to the pros, I recommend you go somewhere where someone's going to be tough on you and get the best out of you.'

"Kids going into college – sometimes they need a little bit of tough love, and Frank presented that. If you don't do things the way Frank expects you to, he makes you accountable. I was used to that from my father."

Looking back, Al Harris is amazed that he survived the boot camp that was Arizona State football under Frank Kush. "I love Frank. I don't know how I made it through four years with Frank because he was so tough, but to me, he made me who I was," he said.

Kush acknowledged that he was as hard on his players as any coach in the country, and he learned that approach from his dad, whom he called "a tough son of a buck," as well as his high school coaches who instilled discipline in him at an early age.

"The game not only makes a great contribution to them individually and athletically, but I think from the standpoint of personal discipline, socially, and academics," he said. "And the greatest thing I learned is that to be successful academically (includes) basic characteristics. I had a notebook on every damn thing from every book I read, whether it was math, science or whatever it may be. I acquired that from my high school coaches."

And if he had to do it all over again? "I'd work them the same way that I always worked them," Kush said. "I love to see people be successful. My biggest problem was every time I recruited a kid, I thought he was going to be great. Well, you know, some kids have limited ability. But I learned that getting the maximum amount out of that individual was the biggest thing. You can control it as a coach at the collegiate level and high school level, in my opinion. (At the professional level) they'd tell you to go to hell."

Kush's impact on the rivalry

Al Harris said none of the head coaches who succeeded Kush at ASU have truly appreciated the rivalry with Arizona like he did.

"If you look at Frank's record versus UA, they didn't take it the same way that Frank took it. Frank really built that up," he said. "He built that thing into a rivalry, and I think it branched into other sports like basketball, track and baseball.

"If you look at our athletics program back then, we were at our apex. That was our heyday. Our wrestling team was outstanding. You name it, almost every major sport at ASU at that time had very strong programs, and UA was that way, too."

ASU wide receiver John Mistler (1977-80) agreed that Kush understood the Duel in the Desert like no one else. "No one that I was around could put as much emphasis on it as Frank Kush," he said. "He had been in that rivalry for 21 years, and he coached in it before that with Dan Devine. That's kind of what helped build ASU – the stature of him starting to win.

"It used to be a dominant game (for UA) in which ASU would get beat 5-10 years in a row, and Frank helped turn it around. It was his signature game. There were a lot of times in the WAC when that *was* the bowl game; you didn't get to go anywhere else."

Kush-less Devils in "turmoil"

Mark Malone said the rumors swirling around Kush's potential dismissal had the Devils in disarray for most of 1979.

"There was turmoil on the roster," he said. "Some people wanted change. Some of the younger guys who certainly hadn't adjusted to Frank Kush's coaching style wanted to see him leave. You had coaches that were taking sides. It was just a pretty big mess. The entire season seemed to be that way, to be honest."

When Kush was let go following ASU's fifth game of the '79 season, defensive coordinator Bob Owens was promoted to interim head coach.

"I don't think he handled it very well, honestly," Padjen said of Owens. "The whole atmosphere changed from having Frank running the team to Bob Owens. Bob was the linebacker coach and my direct coach, but as far as the head coach was concerned, he couldn't hold a candle to Frank. And it showed, too, because we floundered in the rest of the games that were played in '79. There were a lot of distractions."

ASU did manage to win six games that year but lost two of three leading up to the UA game in Tempe.

Cats make good with second chance

For perhaps the first time since Frank Kush's arrival in Tempe, UA's football program was enjoying more stability than Arizona State's. Unfortunately for the Wildcats, under Tony Mason, that didn't exactly translate to on-field success, as they were just 5-4-1 before their trip up north in '79.

But UA was playing for more than just pride; a bowl bid was a very real possibility if the Cats could upend their rivals for the first time since 1974.

"Usually, when you go to any type of bowl game, you'll get a bowl ring and you'll get a watch," Brandon said. "I remember what Mason told us all week long: If you want rings and you want watches, you need to win this game to get to a bowl game."

Thanks to a touchdown pass by Krohn and a pair of touchdown runs by running back Hubert Oliver, Arizona jumped out to a 24-10 lead in the '79 Duel – only to see ASU battle back to tie the score in the fourth quarter via a 6-yard quarterback keeper by Malone followed by a 30-yard run by sophomore running back Robert Weathers.

But just like in the '78 game, UA would have a chance to win on a last-second kick – this time by barefooted kicker Brent Weber, whom Mason decided to let attempt the game-winner in place of Zivic, who had made a 34-yard field goal in the second quarter.

"I remember (Mason) put his arms around (Weber) and said, 'What do you want for Christmas?' because they played the Fiesta Bowl on Christmas day back then," said UA safety Mike Woodford (1979-81). "Mason knew if they won that game that we were going to the Fiesta Bowl."

But just like in the '78 game, the last-second kick sailed wide – only this time, the Wildcats got a do-over.

"He missed a field goal with like five seconds left," Brandon said. "I remember I had turned my back, and I remember the (ASU) crowd yelling because he missed it. But then I turned around and I saw the flag."

Though officials didn't specify which player committed infractions in those days, Mistler said it was ASU defensive end Ron Brown who was flagged for a roughing-the-kicker penalty, which gave Weber a second chance, this time from just 27 yards out.

"He got to kick it again, and he made it," Brandon said.

The second-chance opportunity catapulted the Cats to their first bowl game in 31 years, though they lost in the Fiesta Bowl to Pittsburgh, 16-10.

Mark Malone said the way ASU lost to UA was symbolic of the overall season. "I remember thinking we might have gone into this thing thinking that it wasn't that important or just sleepwalking through this thing, and we got our butts kicked a little bit, but we had the chance to come back and maybe win the football game," he said. "But that's just the way the season goes:

The guy misses the field goal, you rough the guy, he gets another chance and he makes it."

Mistler said that, prior to Kush's ouster, the Devils had the same focus and drive to beat the Wildcats that they'd always had – but that all changed when Owens took over.

"It was a laser focus on UA. We talked about it every week. And then we went to Bob Owens, who was trying to prove himself as a head coach, and it was just turmoil. Nothing was what it used to be," he said. "We did what we did, which was come from behind, but we couldn't finish it at the end. It kind of felt like we had lost a lot. We just weren't focused."

New beginnings in Tucson and Tempe

For the first time since 1952, ASU and UA introduced new head coaches in the same year.

In Tucson, Mason was let go after the '79 season, as the NCAA learned of illegal operations under his watch, including a "slush fund" for payments to players on the roster. The investigation would eventually lead to UA being banned from postseason play in 1983 and '84.

Before the 1980 season, the Wildcats brought back Larry Smith, who served as Jim Young's defensive coordinator at Arizona and became incensed over his belief that Frank Kush ran up the score against UA on at least one occasion.

"When he came in, he had some pretty good talent to work with," Woodford said. "He had kind of a clean slate."

Among that talent was linebacker and future two-time All-American Ricky Hunley (1980-83). "Tony Mason recruited me and signed me, and Larry came in and re-recruited me and re-signed me," he said. "I was also drafted by the (Pittsburgh) Pirates of baseball, and I turned them down because I had a commitment to play football.

"I loved playing for Coach Smith. He was an awesome, awesome person. He was everything to us. A lot of us would get (to college) with no fathers in the home, and he was Dad, he was

Coach. He kept us on the straight and narrow, and he helped build character in young men."

And Coach Smith drove into his players from day one the importance of beating the Sun Devils. "That was one of the main goals from the beginning, from the first day you walk into the building: Beat ASU," Hunley said.

Up north, ASU replaced Kush with Darryl Rogers, who had spent 1976-79 as head coach at Michigan State, where the Spartans were co-Big Ten champions in '78.

Pagel said there was a sizable difference between the approaches of Kush and Rogers. "Coach Kush saw everything, and you worried about him constantly jumping on your case, whereas Darryl was the opposite," he said. "When Darryl came in, he had to call us all together as a team after a couple days of spring ball and told us all basically to stop worrying about making mistakes and go play football. He was very motivating but not a guy who was going to scream and yell and get in your face all the time. The game was different with him. With Frank, you were always on edge, and Darryl told us to relax and go play. But I liked playing for them both."

Rogers said he wasn't familiar with the rivalry when he took over the Sun Devils – partly because he lived across the country before his move to Arizona and partly because of Kush's domination of the Wildcats, which seemed to create a national perception that ASU's biggest games were against other teams.

"My thought when I first came was the rivalry with USC (was more important), because USC was the leader of the Pac-10 at the time, and I had seen Arizona State play at a great fever pitch against USC," he said. "I had never seen Arizona State play UA; I had never seen any of the rivalry within the state because I wasn't in the state.

"When I came out to Arizona, I had learned that, yeah, it's a rivalry because it's in-state. But they had so much success against UA that it wasn't quite the same rivalry."

Rogers remembers what one of his players, linebacker and Scottsdale native Joey Lumpkin, told him during pregame warmups before the 1980 Duel. "He said, 'Look at those guys over there, Coach. They think they got a chance,'" he said. "And I kind of laughed and I said, 'Don't they?' And he said, 'Nah.'"

And Lumpkin was right – at least on that particular day. "The first year we played UA, our kids played exceptionally well," Rogers said. "I don't think we'd ever played as well when I was there as we did the first year we played them."

Back to the past

In ASU's first full season without Kush at the helm, the Devils put on a very Kush-era-like performance against the Wildcats at Arizona Stadium, avenging the '79 loss to UA with a 44-7 rout.

The Devils' defense and special teams put on a display for an ABC television audience during a rare day game. ASU linebacker Vernon Maxwell notched 16 tackles, a sack, a fumble recovery and a blocked punt return for a touchdown that put the Devils up 14-0 in the first quarter. Safety Mike Richardson followed with a 35-yard interception return for a score that put the Devils ahead 21-0.

On the offensive end, Pagel shredded a UA defense that was missing Hunley due to injury, throwing a pair of first-half touchdown passes, one to Mistler and one to tight end Ron Wetzel. ASU led 31-0 at halftime and was in control throughout.

Brandon put the Wildcats' loss into the proper perspective.

"They kicked our ass," he said. "They just put all their scout-team guys in at the end of the game."

In a so-so season for both teams – ASU finished with a 7-4 record while UA went 5-6 – Pagel said everything went right that day for the Devils. "We were clicking so well offensively and defensively that it seemed like total chaos in what they were trying to do against us defensively and offensively, and we just came out and dominated them right from the beginning of the game," he said. "And then, from what I understand, they actually turned the game off national (television) and went to another game because it was such a blowout."

Mistler said the Devils expected more of a challenge from a hyped Wildcat defense. "We went down there and they were on the field right when we walked in (for practice), and they were just yappin'. It was unbelievable," he said. "They were a big team that year. They had all these big safeties and linebackers, and their defense was really touted and all of these things. It seemed like they were very intimidating, but we took it all in stride.

"We got up the next day and we just took it to them right at the beginning of the game, and it was just a total rout. We were totally focused. That year before, there were just too many people and issues around the program after Frank left.

"I'll never forget that ride back (to Tempe). That was probably one of the sweetest rides I ever had."

Devils settle in, Ricky comes to play

By the middle of the 1981 season, it had become evident that the Sun Devils could remain a formidable force in the West, even without the man who had coached them ever since they were rebranded as Arizona State University.

With Rogers in charge, the Devils were enjoying their best Pac-10 season in three tries with an 8-2 overall record and a 4-2 conference mark leading up to their late-November encounter with the Cats, who were 6-4 in Smith's second season and had found some success of their own, knocking off USC and a John Elway-led Stanford team in back-to-back games.

Even though he didn't play in the '80 Duel, Ricky Hunley said ASU's total dominance of UA in that game stuck in his craw. "They just beat the dog crap out of us," he said. "You name it, they had an all-star team, and they just beat us up and down the field.

"I just had a whole new sense of urgency when it came to playing Arizona State. People just rub your face in it."

Joining Hunley in '81 was his brother and fellow linebacker, LaMonte Hunley, who said Ricky's decision to play at Arizona influenced him to do the same.

"We get along very well, and the thing is, hell yeah, we loved playing side by side with each other," LaMonte Hunley said. "We were very competitive towards one another as far as getting there first and making the tackle. I'd get to the ball or he'd get to the ball, and he'd try to hold the person so the other could get a piece, so to speak.

"We were kind of like Siamese twins as far as playing and enjoying the game. Since we were 4 or 5 years of age (all the way up) to our college career, we always were together."

Desert downpour

Many football players will forget the details of the games they played in 10, 20, 30 years ago.

But there's one detail that everyone who participated in the 1981 Duel in the Desert in Tempe remembers: It rained. A lot.

In fact, the official Sun Devil Athletics guide from that game called it a "torrential rainstorm."

And much like the playing conditions, the '81 Duel was a sloppy affair. The teams traded 10 turnovers, including nine interceptions – four by ASU and five by UA.

Pagel threw four interceptions in that game, but he didn't blame the weather for those mistakes. "They had a much better game plan against us in '81. They came out with a lot more fire," he said. "We were a much better football team talent-wise than they were, but defensively, they had a pretty good game plan and they got after us pretty good."

Pagel, however, did have a very good first half. After UA took the lead with a touchdown pass from quarterback Tom Tunnicliffe to tight end Bill Cook, Pagel answered with three first-half touchdown passes, including two to split end Bernard Henry, to give ASU a 21-6 halftime lead.

The Devils didn't mount much offense in the messy, rainy, turnover-plagued second half, but they held on. The Wildcats cut the lead to 21-13 in the third quarter on a 1-yard run by running back Brian Holland, but a field goal by ASU freshman kicker Luis

Zendejas in the fourth put the game away, with the Devils finishing off a 24-13 win.

"We won because we were more talented and made a few more plays," Pagel said.

LaMonte Hunley remembers a dropped second-half pass that could have reversed UA's fortunes that day. "We got the ball back and we were driving down to the 10-yard line. Tom Tunnicliffe throws the ball to one of his tight ends, and the ball hits him in the hands and he drops the ball," he said. "That could've won the game for us."

Not that Hunley is still bitter about it. "It was a muddy game (and the rain) was coming down. But he still should've caught the damn ball," he said.

Restricting Ricky

Pagel said one of ASU's game plans on offense in '81 was to contain Ricky Hunley, who was named to the All-Pac-10 team in each of his final three collegiate seasons.

"What made him effective was he was so darn big and he could run so well," he said. "But what we did is we took advantage of his speed by starting away from him and cutting back to where he was.

"We had seven very talented running backs – three fullbacks and four tailbacks – so we could just throw fresh running backs at people over and over and over again, and whichever of the seven was hot was who we were going to give the ball to. And we had a talented, experienced line that made adjustments on the fly all the time.

"He could hit a running back with a lot of velocity, and that seemed to jack their team up. And we did a very good job of locking him up and not allowing him to get those big hits that would psych them up."

Ricky Hunley can still recall the dejection of leaving the soaking-wet, muddy Sun Devil Stadium field that day. "It was just a sad, sad feeling to leave their place the way they won the game and the way we played. And we had a chance to win the game," he said. "It was two seasons, back to back, that I lost to Arizona State."

But he said the loss inspired him and the rest of the team to work harder in practice, in the weight room and on the field. "One of the qualities of a Wildcat is we had to be poised under pressure, because we were facing a lot of pressure to win games that we were supposed to win," he said. "We had to out-physical people and be the bully on the block."

The win gave Arizona State its 16th victory in its last 19 meetings with its rival from the Old Pueblo – and the downpour that took place during the 1981 Duel in the Desert was unquestionably symbolic of the way the Devils had poured it on against the Wildcats during those years.

But much to the dismay of ASU fans – and to the immense pleasure of UA players, students and alumni – an unlikely and often bizarre nine-year Sun Devil drought was right around the corner.

Members of the 1899 Tempe Normal School football team sit on the steps of Old Main with the Territorial Cup, which they earned for winning that season's Arizona Territorial Football League. As of 2001, the cup is awarded to the annual winner of the ASU-UA football game.
(Credit: Arizona State University)

Wilford "Whizzer" White of Arizona State College (left) and Moose Crum of The University of Arizona compete for the football in the 1947 Duel in the Desert. (Credit: University of Arizona Library Special Collections)

"The Cactus Comet" Art Luppino scores a touchdown vs. Arizona State College in the 1954 Duel in the Desert. Luppino led the NCAA in rushing yards in 1954 and '55. (Credit: 1955 "Desert" Yearbook, The University of Arizona)

Vandals from The University of Arizona burned "No 200" into the grass of the brand-new Sun Devil Stadium in protest of the upcoming statewide vote that would turn Arizona State College into Arizona State University in 1958. (Credit: Arizona State University Archives & Special Collections)

ASU players carry head coach Frank Kush off the field after the Sun Devils defeat UA 20-17 at Arizona Stadium in Tucson in 1966. Kush went 16-5 in his career vs. the Wildcats. (Credit: Sun Devil Athletics Media Relations)

ASU players celebrate a touchdown in the so-called Ultimatum Bowl against
UA in 1968. The Sun Devils won the game, 30-7, in Tucson.
(Credit: Sun Devil Athletics Media Relations)

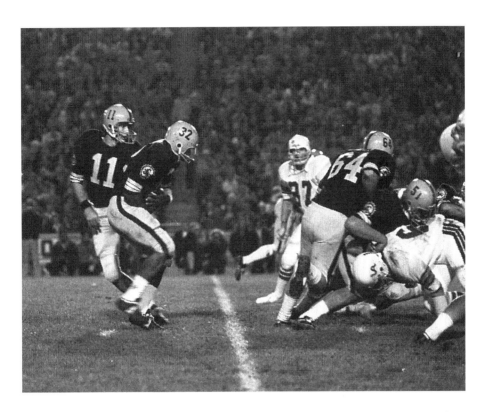

ASU quarterback Danny White (11) hands off to tailback Ben Malone in the 1973 Duel in the Desert in Tempe. The Sun Devils won the game, 55-19, as part of an 11-1 season. (Credit: Sun Devil Athletics Media Relations)

ASU wide receiver John Jefferson makes what many consider the greatest play in Sun Devil football history in the 1975 game versus UA at Sun Devil Stadium. The play cut the Wildcats' lead to 14-10 right before halftime, and the Devils went on to win, 24-21, in a game in which both schools were highly ranked nationally. (Credit: Sun Devil Athletics Media Relations)

UA wide receiver Jay Dobyns celebrates kicker Max Zendejas' game-winning field goal against ASU at Sun Devil Stadium in 1983. UA won, 17-15, in what was Zendejas' first of two game-winning kicks against the Devils. His last-second kick in 1985 knocked ASU out of what would have been its first-ever Rose Bowl. (Credit: Jay Dobyns)

UA defensive back Chuck Cecil intercepts an ASU pass and returns it 106 yards for a touchdown as part of the Wildcats' 34-17 win over the previously undefeated and Rose Bowl-bound Sun Devils at Arizona Stadium in 1986. (Credit: *Arizona Daily Star*)

ASU head coach Larry Marmie is carried off the field by his players after the Sun Devils end "The Streak" in 1991 by defeating the Wildcats 37-14 at Sun Devil Stadium. (Credit: Sun Devil Athletics Media Relations)

ASU quarterback Jake Plummer (16) and wide receiver Keith Poole celebrate a touchdown during the Sun Devils' 56-14 win over the Wildcats at Arizona Stadium in 1996. The '96 squad was the second ASU team to advance to the Rose Bowl.

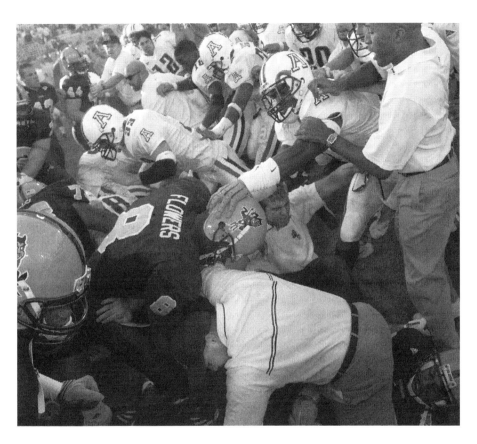

UA and ASU players get into a confrontation on the middle of the field after Wildcat players begin to dance and stomp on the Sun Devil "Sparky" logo following UA's 34-21 victory in Tempe in 2001. The incident canceled what would have been the first-ever on-field presentation of the Territorial Cup. (Credit: *Arizona Daily Star*)

UA quarterback celebrates with the Territorial Cup following UA's 31-10 win over ASU at Arizona Stadium in 2008. The win earned the Wildcats their first bowl bid in ten seasons. (Credit: Morgan Bellinger, *Arizona State Press*)

UA head coach Mike Stoops celebrates as he heads off Sun Devil Stadium following the Wildcats' 20-17 win over ASU on a last-second field goal by kicker Alex Zendejas. (Credit: *Arizona Daily Star*)

ASU defensive end James Brooks blocks Alex Zendejas' extra-point attempt that would have given UA a one-point lead with less than 30 seconds to play in the 2011 Duel in the Desert at Arizona Stadium. Brooks blocked another Zendejas extra-point attempt in the game's second overtime to give the Sun Devils a 30-29 win. (Credit: Sun Devil Athletics Media Relations)

UA wide receiver Gino Crump flies the school flag after the Wildcats' 31-27 win over ASU in the 2011 Duel in the Desert at Sun Devil Stadium. (Credit: Bruce Yeung)

ASU head coach Todd Graham and fans celebrate with the replica Territorial Cup after the Sun Devils defeat the Wildcats 41-34 in the 2012 Duel in the Desert in Tucson. (Credit: Sun Devil Athletics Media Relations)

CHAPTER 5

The Streak

To the impartial observer, the results of the Duels that took place from 1982-90 comprise a fascinating case study, not only in the history of college football but in all of sports.

In those nine seasons, Arizona State's record was almost always better than or comparable to Arizona's. And more often than not, ASU seemed to have superior talent.

But year after perplexing year, the Wildcats found a way to defeat the Sun Devils in an era that would become known at both schools as The Streak.

UA's "golden period"

Hansen said The Streak was due in part to a series of Wildcat squads placing a greater emphasis on the rivalry than the Sun Devils did. "No. 1, they made it their priority, and they weren't afraid to say it," he said. "ASU thought they had moved to a higher level than simply being a rival of Arizona's. But when you walked into Larry Smith's office at McKale Center, the first thing you saw on the wall was a list of goals for the programs. No. 1 said, 'Have fun.' No. 2 said, 'Win the Rose Bowl.' And No. 3 said, 'Beat the Sun Devils.'"

Hansen said Smith had a chip on his shoulder from losing to Frank Kush as Jim Young's assistant, and he did an excellent job of playing up the city versus city element of the rivalry.

"Part of it is obviously the inferiority complex to some degree of Tucson versus Phoenix, and that if you beat the big school in the big city, you can make it a good season, even if you didn't have a real good record. Smith totally embraced that," Hansen said. "When he was an assistant at Arizona in the '70s, they lost to ASU, 55-19, and he thought Frank Kush ran (the score) up on him, and that just stuck with him.

"When he became the head coach in 1980, he was on a crusade against ASU, and he talked about it all the time. ASU beat him in Tucson his first year (as head coach), 44-7, and again, he thought they ran it up on him and rubbed his nose in it. That intensified his effort to get back at them, and the players talked about it. Even if USC was No. 1 or if they played Notre Dame like they did, ASU was the game of the year."

Smith's intense attitude toward Arizona State was transferred to his players in an era that Hansen called Arizona's "golden period" of the rivalry.

The Streak left Sun Devil fans dumbfounded and exasperated. "You have to remember the history. Frank Kush dominated UA for, what, 25 years?" said *Arizona Republic* columnist and ASU alum Scott Bordow. "ASU was used to dominating UA in football. Then UA turns the tables, and ASU just cannot beat them in those nine years."

ASU play-by-play man Tim Healey, who moved to the Valley in 1983, said it felt as though he came to town at the wrong time. "There were times when I felt like I was personally responsible for the Sun Devils' struggles in the rivalry," he said. "I moved here in the second of those years, and I did not see an ASU victory in the rivalry game until 1991.

"It seems like, in so many of the games, I can almost condense it down to one play or one moment that I might remember as being the seminal moment of that particular game."

While Wildcat fans remember those game-changing plays as heroic, clutch moments, Healey said Sun Devil fans obviously saw them a bit differently. "Not in every year of that nine-year stretch, but a couple of them, it seemed like there were a lot of plays that Wildcat fans would probably describe as their team making a big play, and Sun Devil fans would probably say that it was a fluke type of play that went against Arizona State that would enable Arizona to come away with those wins," he said.

The Streak began in Arizona Stadium in a game that ASU needed to win in order to advance to what would have been the biggest bowl game in program history.

1982

ASU's record:	9-1 (5-1 Pac-10)
UA's record:	5-4-1 (3-3-1)
Final score:	UA 28, ASU 18

ASU was undefeated and had a chance to clinch its first-ever Rose Bowl berth by defeating Washington in the 10th game of the season. The Devils came up just short, losing to the Huskies in Tempe, 17-13.

But they got a second chance: Defeat a mediocre Arizona squad and they would still come up roses.

"We played Washington and we lost, so Washington was (supposed to go) to the Rose Bowl," said ASU quarterback Todd Hons (1981-83). "But the next week, we had a bye and Washington State beat them, so that put us back in there."

The Wildcats also knew perfectly well what was on the line for the Sun Devils.

"What I remember leading up to that game was ASU had already inked in their appointment to the Rose Bowl," said UA wide receiver Jay Dobyns (1981-84). "I remember pregame, their fans were shaking roses at us."

Color scheme

Hons remembers some pregame uniform confusion in '82 that he still suspects might have been a result of some gamesmanship on UA's part.

"They told us to bring our maroon jerseys for some reason, and they were going to wear their white uniforms, which never happened. You always wore your home jerseys with your dark colors," he said.

UA wanted to wear its white uniforms for the ASU game "because their superstitious coach, Larry Smith, hoped to capture the karma the all-whites produced in '82 road upsets over No. 8 Notre Dame and over John Elway's final Stanford team," Hansen wrote in the *Daily Star*.

Hons wasn't too fond of Smith's decision, which came as a last-minute surprise to the Devils. "That was kind of stupid, and whether that had any bearing (on the game's outcome) or if it's just another way to get our mind off the game or something, you never know," he said. "That's a coaching thing with Larry Smith, and you've got to give him credit."

UA linebacker John Kaiser (1982-83) also recalled the color controversy that year. "There were a lot of head games between the two teams," he said.

Tunnicliffe's time

The '82 Duel came down to a pair of big plays on offense and a pair on defense for the Wildcats.

On the offensive end, Tunnicliffe set the tone early by connecting with Holland for a 92-yard score to put the Wildcats ahead,

7-0, against the Devils, who were near the top of the NCAA rankings in most defensive categories that season. Tunnicliffe did it again in the second half with a 65-yard TD strike to wide receiver and Phoenix native Brad Anderson.

"I had the best seat in the house for two of the greatest plays in the Arizona-Arizona State rivalry," Dobyns said. "On Brian Holland's 92-yard catch and run, I made a block on that play that kind of cut a guy down that had an angle (on Holland). Brian – we called him H-Bomb in college – there were very few people that were going to catch that dude. And then, there was a great tip and run by Brad Anderson where he outran (cornerback) Mario Montgomery to the corner."

Holland's 1-yard run in the third quarter gave the Wildcats a very improbable 26-0 lead going into the fourth quarter.

Hons said the Sun Devil defense may have gambled more than necessary in that game. "We lived and died by the blitz that year," he said. "Our defense was No. 1 in the nation, and we usually sent eight people (after the quarterback) on just about every play. And that's how we kind of died that night: on the blitz.

"They had two huge plays that went for touchdowns that were kind of demoralizing that set the tone for them, and we were playing catch-up. We never gave up a 92-yard (touchdown to a) running back out of the backfield straight up the middle. That never happened all year. But I would never blame them because we would never have been in that situation (to get to the Rose Bowl) if it wasn't for them. It was defense that carried us that year."

Remarkably, UA's defense outclassed ASU's that night, as nose guard Joe Drake notched not one but two safeties, one at the beginning of the third quarter and another in the fourth to complete the Wildcats' scoring.

"Joe Drake was always being double-teamed, and that's probably why I got so many tackles," Ricky Hunley said. "He took those two guys and just knocked them back and got the safety. That electrified the whole team when Joe Drake made that safety (in the third quarter).

"We really, really, really wanted that game. We still had a little taste in our mouth from that last loss our previous year, and we were playing at home, too. Our fans were awesome. Just awesome."

ASU running back Darryl Clack (1982-85) was tackled by Drake on the first UA safety. He said the Devils, who missed out on the Rose Bowl that year but won their fifth Fiesta Bowl by defeating Oklahoma, may have been caught a bit off guard by the intensity of the Wildcat players and fans (a sellout crowd of 58,515) that evening.

"We were prepared and everything, but we just got surprised," he said. "And I think through that surprise, it kind of threw us off a little bit, and we had to just kind of regroup ourselves.

"Once they had that momentum, it was kind of hard to take that momentum away, especially in a high-impact game like it was, because it was an opportunity to go to the Rose Bowl. They may have seen it as an opportunity to kick us out of the Rose Bowl, so it kind of played both ways."

LaMonte Hunley said the '82 upset was a culmination of the preparation that Smith and his coaching staff put in before the season along with Smith's three-tiered to-do list. "Those goals were set in stone every year that I played under Coach Smith," he said.

Clack scored a pair of late touchdowns to make the score less lopsided. But the '82 game put the Sun Devils, who had become used to nothing less than domination in the rivalry, on notice: The Wildcats were no longer content to be their annual punching bag.

"The 1982 game, which doesn't get a lot of run, was just epic. The Sun Devils came in as the best defensive team in the country, or close to that with their revolutionary everybody-blitzing defense," Hansen said. "And Arizona just kicked their pants.

"The noise in that stadium was just thunderous. The old press box there was shaking. That game was such a big deal, and it was the first game of The Streak."

Hansen said he was making his way to Smith's office the day after the game when he saw the 320-pound Drake in the hallway. "I asked him, 'What did you do last night to celebrate?'" he said.

Drake explained to Hansen that he and his teammates got together at Dirtbag's, a popular Tucson bar and grill, and saw several UA students walk by with the Arizona Stadium goalposts they had torn down to celebrate the win.

"They were parading them around campus, and I guess (Drake) was at Dirtbag's at about 2 in the morning, and somebody carried the goalposts by," Hansen said.

It was a perfect illustration of what was a major turning point in the Duel in the Desert: After two-plus decades of ASU domination, Arizona had moved the goalposts in the rivalry.

1983

ASU's record:	6-3-1 (3-2-1 Pac-10)
UA's record:	6-3-1 (3-3-1 Pac-10)
Final score:	UA 17, ASU 15

A pair of talented and coveted placekickers from Chino, Calif., Luis Zendejas (1981-84) and Max Zendejas (1982-85) decided to go to school in Tempe and Tucson, respectively, for similar reasons.

Luis chose ASU because of the opportunity and the coaching staff. "Places like USC were averaging three field goals a year; ASU was averaging three field goals a game," he said. "And Darryl Rogers was the coach and a great person. I think it was just the visit to Arizona and Tempe – it was really a very, very nice visit."

During his senior year in high school, Max went to Tempe to watch his brother kick in his first Duel in 1981. "At the time, I had a lot of offers, and I just wanted to get out of California. I didn't really think I was going to end up at UA because ASU had such a great team," he said.

"But eventually, when I went to visit the UA in Tucson, there were some people who showed me around, and I had a great time and decided to come to Tucson."

Max didn't really understand the importance of the rivalry with ASU until the week of his first Duel in '82. "But by the time we got to ASU, there was a lot of buildup," he said. "It was pretty fun, especially playing against my own brother."

Other than the games they played against each other, Luis said he and Max always cheered each other on. "We always looked at each other's stats and always wished each other the best against other teams," he said.

And while Luis set multiple NCAA kicking records in 1983 and nailed three field goals in the '83 Duel in Tempe, Max saw fit to steal his brother's glory.

"Atomic" coin-flip confrontation

The '83 Duel was a nail-biter, but Hons said the game's intensity began even before the opening kickoff.

"I was team captain, and it meant a lot because we could've been 7-3-1 and gotten into a bowl game," he said. "We came out for the opening coin flip (at midfield) and we had our four captains, and they brought up their captains plus all their seniors, which I think was a tradition they did a lot. They had 20-30 guys jumping around. So then our whole team came up behind us, and then their whole team came up behind them, just on the coin toss.

"It was pretty intense. I was like, 'Yeah, hey, we're ready.' I knew it was going to be a good one because just on the coin toss, both teams were jumping up and down. It was pretty cool."

Dobyns also remembers the emotions in the air before kickoff. "There was a big team-to-team confrontation at the coin toss," he said. "Having won the year before and having stolen the Rose Bowl (from ASU), the energy there was just atomic."

Wildcats jump ahead again

Since UA was on probation in 1983 for infractions that occurred under Tony Mason, the Wildcats knew they weren't going to a bowl game that season.

"We knew during the time that we were on probation that the ASU game, in our opinion, was our bowl game, even though we (would have been) bowl-eligible," said UA defensive back Randy Robbins (1980-83), who went on to have a nine-year NFL career. "It was kind of like a double-meaning game for us."

UA opened the Duel as if it was playing in a bowl game, gaining a double-digit lead thanks to a 2-yard TD run by fullback Chris Brewer and a 4-yard TD pass from Tunnicliffe to running back-wide receiver Vance Johnson, who went on to star with the Denver Broncos from 1985-95. In between the scores was a 33-yard field goal by Luis Zendejas, who added a 23-yard kick in the second quarter to make the score 14-6 UA at the half.

With his third and final field goal of the day – a 36-yarder that cut Arizona's lead to 14-9 in the third quarter – Luis broke the NCAA record for points scored by a kicker in a single season (112), and he matched the record for most made field goals in a season (28).

The Devils' defense held the Wildcats in check after those early scores, and Hons' 21-yard TD pass to tailback Mike Crawford gave ASU its first lead, 15-14 – though it could not convert on what would have been a critical two-point conversion.

When ASU had the ball first-and-10 at its 20-yard line and leading by one point with less than six minutes to go, Robbins said he and the rest of the defense knew they had to hold firm. "We knew if we needed a field goal, Max was good," he said, "and I remember we talked about it on the field: We can't let them score, and at minimum, we need a field goal to win this game."

The Wildcat defense hung tough and got the offense the ball back with just under five minutes to play. "I think we just wanted it more," Robbins said. "Our incentive was that it was our bowl game, and we knew we just had to get it close for Max."

"I wouldn't want it any other way"

When they got the ball back, Tunnicliffe and the UA offense grinded out a tough 35 yards against ASU's defense, and on third-and-1 from the Sun Devil 28 with three seconds remaining, they called a timeout to bring on Max Zendejas to attempt the game-winner.

Ricky Hunley said many of the UA players were praying on the sidelines that the kick would be good. But he said they all had confidence in Max, who had already made a number of game-winning field goals in his career. "Oh yeah, I had no doubt in my mind that he was going to make that field goal," he said. "No doubt."

Neither did Max, who said he thrived on – and even desired – that kind of pressure. "It was one of those things that I craved it, I wanted it, and when I got the opportunity, there was no way of missing," he said. "I enjoyed the competition. I was one of those guys that I wouldn't want it any other way. I didn't want us to score a touchdown; I wanted to hit that field goal."

Max took full advantage of the opportunity he was given that year, nailing the field goal and giving UA just its second victory at Sun Devil Stadium since 1961.

"It was bedlam," Robbins said. "I mean, we were jumping around. We were excited. To us, that was our bowl game.

"The thing that I remember is how quiet the fans were. I think everyone was in shock. The whole stadium was probably in shock after that game."

Kaiser said he relished the negative energy from the ASU fans. "Just walking into that stadium, you love being booed by those people, and then having them just completely shut up at the end of the game, it's a rush as a visiting player," he said. "I really enjoyed being booed going into a game and then just making the fans be quiet.

"In the locker room afterwards, Coach Smith and his emotion, him having tears in his eyes about beating them – that's how passionate he was. That's what you remember."

Before they went to the locker room, Dobyns said, Smith had the team remain on the field to celebrate with the UA fans who had made the trip. "I remember one of my favorite things about that game is the Arizona players didn't leave the field," he said. "They had all the Arizona fans bunched up in one part of the stadium, and it was just like this massive celebration between players, coaches and fans in that little corner of the stadium that nobody wanted to end. It was just such a high."

Max said he didn't want the party to end, either. "It was incredible. And then afterwards, I couldn't leave the locker room. It took hours and hours before I could go home," he said.

As happy as he and his brother were for each other's success, Luis still considers whether he should have done something a little differently during that game.

"Max and I don't talk about it, but I really didn't want it to come down to a field goal," he said. "When it came down to that, I (wonder) if I should've told him to miss it. But you want the best for him as much as he wanted it for us."

Rogers had another encounter with Max Zendejas several years later when he coached the Detroit Lions. "We lined up to play the Green Bay Packers in a (players') strike year, and he's kicking along the sidelines (for the Packers), and they line up to kick a field goal to win the game. And I'm looking and I'm thinking, 'You mean to tell me the kid's going to beat me again?'" he said with a laugh.

Only this time, Max missed his last-second attempt. "But I thought that was amazing. You see kids in different places," Rogers said. "He had a very strong leg and he was a good kicker."

In on the ground floor

The '83 win over the Devils was Ricky Hunley's last as a Wildcat, and UA's victory in Tempe gave the program its first two-game winning streak against ASU in over 20 years.

"On that day, the best team won," he said. "You don't win games as individuals; you win those as teams. And those were team wins.

"That was just a special time for me: Growing up, becoming a man, going away from home, making new friends. My brother's my best friend, without a doubt. Very few people can say they played their high school and college career side by side with their brother."

The Territorial Cup resurfaces

Another major development in the rivalry came in 1983 with the reemergence of the Territorial Cup, which had gone missing some time shortly after the first-ever Duel in the Desert.

The cup was found by chance in a closet at the First Congregational Church in Tempe, much to the bewilderment of Spindler and university officials. "How it ends up in the church basement is anybody's guess," he said. "There's nothing in (historical documents) that says anything about how it got there."

And though it had finally been located, it would be another 18 years before the cup – which remained the property of Tempe Normal/ASTC/ASC/ASU throughout all those years – would be awarded to the winner of the annual ASU-UA football game.

"The cup was returned to the ASU Alumni Association, and it was displayed at Mariposa Hall, which at that time was the headquarters for the alumni association," Spindler said. "We knew where it came from and that it was important. We didn't know that it was the nation's oldest intercollegiate rivalry trophy. So it was kind of an interesting discovery."

1984

ASU's record:	5-5 (3-3 Pac-10)
UA's record:	6-4 (4-2)
Final score:	UA 16, ASU 10

Neither team had anything left to play for after the 1983 Duel. UA was still on probation, and ASU's record wasn't good enough for a bowl game.

But back-to-back victories over ASU enhanced Smith's recruiting efforts at UA, and he made beating the Devils a big part of his pitch to potential Wildcats.

"Larry Smith emphasized on my recruiting trip that beating Arizona State was a big thing," said UA tight end and California native Glenn Howell (1983-85). "I knew about rivalries, but Coach Smith when he came to visit me said, 'We're going to beat Arizona State.'

"And when I got there, the players were like, 'I hate Arizona State.' I come in there for spring ball in January and they're all talking about how they're going to kick Arizona State's ass, and when you go to Phoenix, watch your back. We had a thing in our locker room (that displayed) how many days until we beat Arizona State."

Tucson "conspiracy theory"

In '84, the Sun Devils' new starting quarterback, Jeff van Raaphorst (1983-86), was looking forward to the challenge of making his Duel debut in the hostile confines of Arizona Stadium – though one of the things he remembers most about that game was what he thought might have been another act of gamesmanship on behalf of the Wildcats.

"In '84, I remember in the middle of the first quarter, on a third-and-5 or something down on their 15-yard line, I was looking over (to the sidelines) to get a play. And the coaches have their headsets off and are staring at each other, and they're looking around because our phones went dead," he said. "It was kind of like, 'Great timing,' and everybody's thinking conspiracy theory. We ended up throwing an incomplete pass or something, and then we called timeout."

In the interest of fairness, the officials eventually made UA turn its phones off until the situation was corrected. "But it's just one of those deals. Everybody chalks it up to playing on the road," van Raaphorst said.

Defense dominates again

For the second straight Duel, both teams found points very difficult to come by. After a 32-yard field goal in the first quarter by Max Zendejas, van Raaphorst threw for what would be ASU's only score of the game – a 44-yard touchdown pass to wide receiver Doug Allen – to give the Devils a 7-3 halftime lead.

"He had the mechanics of a good quarterback, and to be honest with you, he was extremely calm," said Clack of van Raaphorst. "I never saw an incident with him when he wasn't under control. He knew everything that was taking place in the game and made the right choices in the game, and that's really what you look for in a quarterback, because he's the leader."

Van Raaphorst's counterpart, UA quarterback and fellow Californian Alfred Jenkins, opened the second-half scoring with a 23-yard TD strike to split end Joe Horton, giving Arizona a 10-7 advantage.

"Alfred was tremendously athletic," Dobyns said. "Alfred was a quarterback, but he could have played tight end, he could have played defensive end, linebacker, strong safety, running back – that's how athletic he was."

Howell said he was called upon to block some of ASU's talented linebackers and defensive backs in that game, including Eric Allen, who would go on to be a six-time Pro-Bowler with the Eagles.

"Our offensive line was pretty good – we had Charlie Dickey and some guys that were really pivotal in that offensive line," he said. "But they had great defensive backs, so tight ends had to come out and block on those guys."

Howell was matched up against future NFL linebacker Brian Noble early and often. "He was supposed to be all-world and everything, and the tight ends had to control him from the outside," he said. "We had to make sure we could block this guy. He was a bitch (to block). He knew who I was, and he said, 'You can't block me,' and we were battling all the time. Me and him had a battle all game."

All broken up

Dobyns, who knew the '84 Duel would be his last, played with a lot of pain for most of the contest following a devastating tackle early in the game.

"About halfway through the first quarter, I caught a pass over the middle, and (ASU linebacker) Jimmy Williams just freaking knocked the dog snot out of me, and I broke a couple ribs," he said. "I remember how painful that was, how bad that hurt on the sidelines, and I remember just aching and not being able to breathe."

But watching the rest of the game from the sidelines simply wasn't an option for the man whom the *Tucson Citizen* ranked No. 1 on its Arizona Wildcats Offensive Badass List. "I knew my ribs were broken, and I lifted my shirt up, they wrapped a big bandage around my waist, and I just remember refusing not to play," he said. "This is potentially the last time I might wear shoulder pads and a helmet, it's against ASU, it's in my stadium – I'll be damned if I'm not playing."

Dobyns went on to make some crucial catches in the game that led to UA points. "That was a pretty cool game because, for a career, I went over 100 catches in that game," he said. "There was some sense of personal achievement there."

Late pick seals it

Luis Zendejas kicked a 52-yard field goal to tie the score at 10-10 going into the fourth quarter, but Max quickly matched it with a 52-yarder of his own, then hit again from 32 yards out to give Arizona a 16-10 advantage.

But after the Devils blocked a punt that gave them the ball near midfield with just over three minutes to play, the stage was set perfectly for van Raaphorst and Arizona State: A late touchdown drive and Luis Zendejas extra point would win the game, end Arizona's two-game rivalry run and deal Wildcat fans the same heartbreak on their field that Devil diehards experienced a year earlier.

But freaky things tend to happen in the Duel in the Desert – and they seemed to come in bunches during The Streak.

On that final possession, van Raaphorst and Clack moved ASU to the UA 22. "You feel good because you're moving the ball," van Raaphorst said. "And then you go to throw, you get hit as you throw the ball, and the ball flutters up and goes right to them."

Sure enough, on second-and-5 with 1:30 to play, van Raaphorst was hit by Wildcat linebacker Steve Boadway as he threw, sending the ball straight up in the air and eventually into the arms of fellow linebacker Craig Vesling, who was lying on the ground as he brought it in. Game over.

"That kind of seems to be what transpired a lot in that game," said van Raaphorst of his experience against UA. "Those close games, you leave those up to chance, and those usually have gone against the more talented team."

Rogers said things like that tend to happen in rivalry games. "It's amazing how one play changes things, but they got it, and that's all that counts," he said. "There's nothing you can complain about. I'll tell you what: An outstanding play by certain players makes it happen.

"But that's why they're rivalries. That's why you can't really tell the favorite."

And at that point, Luis Zendejas said the Devils were beginning to feel like every single break in the rivalry was going the way of the Wildcats. "I just know that every time, something fluky came out of it, from a field goal to a bad snap or a punt over our heads. It was always something," he said.

And like his brother a year earlier, LaMonte Hunley was able to go out on top against ASU.

"The biggest thing in that game was knowing that, first and foremost, that was my last game playing on a collegiate level, and secondly, playing against ASU in our hometown and in front of our fans there," he said. "In that game, all of our seniors walk out collectively as captains for the coin flip, and that by itself just motivates you to get the game started.

"I didn't want to come off the field at all. I didn't want it to end at all, and playing with my brothers that were out there, (defensive tackle) David Wood and (linebacker) Byron Evans, people of that capacity. It was my last time getting in that huddle and calling the signals and being part of this rivalry."

They meet again

The '84 Duel was also the last collegiate contest for Dobyns, but it was not the last time he squared off with a Sun Devil on the gridiron.

"Years later, I'm coaching youth football in Tucson, and my team goes to play for the state championship in our division in Phoenix," he said. "And we're warming up and the other team's warming up, and I'm watching them, and I'm watching this (coach for the other team).

"And I say, 'I know this guy.' And I go up and say, 'Man, where do I know you from?' It was Jeff van Raaphorst."

It turned out that Dobyns and van Raaphorst were the offensive coordinators for their respective youth squads. "We were both laughing about stuff that happened in the games," he said. "He was a really good dude and obviously a key member in the history of Arizona State football. And just seeing him 20-plus years after the game and talking to him just as a man, that was really cool."

And on that day, the Sun Devil got the best of the Wildcat. "They just whipped our ass," Dobyns said. "The funny thing was we were very friendly before the game, but with that rivalry and knowing he was calling the plays on his side, I so wanted to beat his ass. I so wanted to walk across that field and shake his hand and say, 'I got you again.' But they had a really good team, he was a great coach, and I walked across the field and shook hands and tried to be a humble and gracious loser."

1985

ASU's record:	8-2 (5-1 Pac-10)
UA's record:	7-3 (4-2)
Final score:	UA 16, ASU 13

Before the '85 season, Rogers moved on to coach the Lions in the NFL, and ASU replaced him with Tulsa head coach John

Cooper, who came in with an immediate understanding of the passion behind the rivalry.

"I had a feel. I coached at Oregon State, and of course Oregon State-Oregon is a pretty bitter rivalry, and then I went down to UCLA, and it doesn't get much bigger than playing USC in the Coliseum," he said. "The biggest one I ever coached in was, of course, Ohio State-Michigan (Cooper went to Ohio State after ASU).

"But hey, the Arizona-Arizona State game is one of the great games. It's one of the great spectacles in college football."

Van Raaphorst said it took some time for him to adjust from Rogers to Cooper. "Darryl Rogers was very much a coach's coach, a head coach administrator, and Coop was, too, but I think Darryl was more knowledgeable about what we were trying to do than John," he said. "Cooper would kind of hand off (duties) to everybody, where Rogers was pretty involved in the schemes.

"From a player's perspective, I liked playing for Darryl a lot more. Darryl let you play, where Cooper, he and his assistants wanted things done almost robotic."

But similar to Kush, van Raaphorst said, Cooper was effective in giving certain players a kick in the butt when necessary. "Cooper brought in a couple guys – the weight coach and some other guys – and they would yell and scream, and that was just their nature," he said. "I didn't particularly like that, but it certainly seemed to work with a lot of people because (they were) more old school."

A second chance

Despite an early-season loss to UCLA, the Devils were faced with the same scenario as two years earlier: Beat the Wildcats to earn a trip to Pasadena.

"If I'm not mistaken, UCLA got upset Saturday afternoon (17-13 at USC)," Cooper said, "and if we beat Arizona at home that night, we'd go to the Rose Bowl. And ASU had never been to the Rose Bowl."

Because of that result, van Raaphorst said the coaching staff made a last-minute decision to take a more conservative approach toward the UA game. "I believe UCLA had just lost, so all we needed was a tie (to go to the Rose Bowl)," he said. "Before the game, I got called in to the pregame with the coaches, and I remember the coaches saying, 'OK, we're going to go more conservative and go with different (passing) routes and different combinations.' So, the feeling in the pregame was, 'OK, we just need to tie.'"

Van Raaphorst wasn't a fan of that approach, and he believed the team should've maintained its original, more aggressive game plan. "That's where I think you're better off putting your foot on the throttle and just going," he said.

ASU's student section a "tidal wave"

UA offensive guard and Tucson native Doug Penner (1985-88), who worked as a soda vendor at Arizona Stadium in his high school days, was surprised by how jacked up the ASU fans were for the game.

"When we got off the bus, they were throwing stuff at us," he said. "It was just a crazy environment. People were so fired up.

"I'll never forget right before the game. We're out on the field just kind of walking around getting ready for the game, and suddenly, the student section opened up. And I tell you, it was like a tidal wave of students that ran into the stadium, and they just started screaming at us."

Arizona clearly wasn't prepared for the noise when the game began, either. "The very first play of the game, they kicked to us, we got the ball, and Alfred Jenkins gets under center, and he had to call a timeout," Penner said. "He just wasn't ready, and we had to burn a timeout right then, and (the fans) erupted. They went nuts."

Devils jump in front, then falter

In front of their home crowd, the Sun Devils' conservative approach worked for the game's first three quarters, as they took a 13-3 lead into the fourth quarter, with the lone touchdown of the game coming on a 7-yard pass from van Raaphorst to fullback Vince Amoia in the third.

But it was a special-teams play that got the Wildcats back in the game. With ASU up by 10 points late in the third, cornerback Anthony Parker was hit hard by Evans on a punt return deep in Sun Devil territory. The ball came loose and bounced backwards into the ASU end zone, where it was recovered by UA safety Don Be'Ans.

All of a sudden, it was another nail-biter: ASU 13, UA 10, with all the momentum squarely in favor of the Wildcats, who had recently grown accustomed to winning close games against the Devils.

With nothing going right for the Wildcats on offense – they managed just 186 yards of total offense to the Sun Devils' 362 – Evans (1983-86) said he knew UA needed a big play in a hurry. "You always have a sense that you can make a play," he said. "It was 13-3 at the time, but being a player, you never really panic.

"I can recall that our offense was sputtering a little bit. I recall being on the punt team, and (UA punter) Ruben Rodriguez was probably one of the best punters in the conference. He got a lot of hang time (on the punt), and I wasn't very fast, so it had to have a lot of hang time with Anthony Parker being one of the best return guys.

"And I just said, 'This is the time that I'm going to make a play,' and I just spoke it into fruition. I put my head in front of the ball, made a play and got the ball out."

Larry Marmie, ASU's defensive coordinator under Cooper, remembers the momentum shift that resulted from the fumble. "Up until that point, defensively we felt like we were in total control of the game," he said. "But instead of being 13-3 with us having the football, it becomes 13-10, and now it's obviously a different ballgame."

Mad Max does it again

Luis Zendejas had graduated a year earlier, but his brother remained in Tucson as a senior in '85 to torment the Sun Devils one last time.

With less than six minutes to play, the Wildcats had managed just enough offense to get Max Zendejas in position to tie the game.

"One of those Zendejas kids lined up to kick a 52-yard field goal," Cooper recalled. "And right before the ball snapped, I think their left guard flinched – and, well, you know what the penalty is, don't you? False start to move it back 5 yards."

The penalty set up a 57-yard field goal try, out of the range of most college kickers. But this was Max Zendejas, who recalled the penalized lineman apologizing to him after Max made the 52-yarder that didn't count.

"He came up to me and he said, 'Man, Max, I'm sorry. You hit that one good.' And I said, 'You know what? I'm glad you did that, because I wanted to break the record (for UA's longest field goal),'" he said. "Most kickers are going to say, 'Damn it, I already made this field goal. Now I have to do it again.' But I was thanking the lineman because I got the one chance to break the record the last game of my career here, and that was the last record I wanted to break at UA."

Bottom line: Max Zendejas simply didn't miss against ASU. His 57-yarder, which actually tied Arizona's school record, also tied the score late in the fourth quarter.

ASU plays not to lose - and loses

ASU wasn't panicked after Max's kick. After all, the Devils needed only a tie to advance to Pasadena.

"If we run out of the clock, we tie the game, and that puts us in the Rose Bowl," Cooper said. "But there was a tradition at Arizona State that you didn't play for a tie."

So the Devils kept trying to move the ball through the air. But after an incomplete pass on second-and-8, van Raaphorst went back to pass on third down and was hit by Wildcat defensive tackle Stan Mataele before he could get rid of the ball. The ball popped loose, and UA recovered deep in ASU territory. The Wildcats proceeded to run three straight running plays to set up a 32-yard game-winner by Max Zendejas.

"I remember us lining up for that kick and telling (the ASU players), 'It's over. Do you know who's kicking this ball?'" Howell said. "We knew that he was kicking that ball through."

Howell, of course, was right. Max nailed the kick and knocked the Sun Devils out of the Rose Bowl. Again.

"Max was solid. He was just a guy who exudes confidence, and he was probably the best kicker in the country," Howell said. "I was just (telling the ASU players), 'It's over. You guys aren't going anywhere.' It's always great knocking them out."

Given the chance, Cooper said he would probably do things differently on ASU's final possession.

"I've got to be honest: That was pretty stupid on my part," he said. "And they very intelligently ran three plays, put the ball in the middle of the field and kicked the field goal, and they beat us and knocked us out of going to the Rose Bowl."

But van Raaphorst said it never should have come down to that, and he wishes that the coaching staff hadn't decided to play not to lose up until ASU's final possession.

"There's an old adage in football: If it's good enough to practice during the week, it's good enough to call on Saturday. If the play looks good and you go through the process, then call the dang thing," he said.

"But the coaches – not (quarterbacks coach) Mike Martz, but the other coaches – clearly took their foot off the throttle in that one. They were thinking, 'Let's play conservative.'"

ASU offensive guard Randall McDaniel (1984-87), who was a 1987 All-American and starred in the NFL from 1988-2001, said the loss fell squarely on the players' shoulders. "I think there may have been some time in the game that, being young, you feel like you should be going after it (more)," he said. "But it's still our job to go out and execute the plays. If we don't execute, the only person you can look at in the mirror is yourself.

"I never blame the coaches. They're not out on the field with us. It comes down to us executing, and we didn't execute in that game."

Marmie said that if any members on the new coaching staff didn't comprehend the importance of the Duel in the Desert before the 1985 game, they did after that season.

"That game stands out in my mind," he said, "and I think probably from then on, maybe the guys that were new to this rivalry certainly had an understanding about what it was after that."

Evans, who was All-Pac-10 in 1985 and the Pac-10 Defensive Player of the year in '86, said Arizona simply did what it needed to do in '85 to beat ASU for the fourth straight time – something that hadn't been accomplished since the Wildcats defeated the then-Bulldogs in 11 consecutive games from 1932-48.

"They had some really good players, but I think our players just stepped up and just came together and played, and that's when you win – when you play as a team," he said. "I think our players – Alfred Jenkins, (tailback) David Adams, and (split end) Jon Horton, and (linebackers) Craig Vesling and Cliff Thorpe coming up the outside – they just stepped up. We just had a little bit better game, and it came together at the right time."

Rose Bowl or no Rose Bowl, Evans doesn't buy the idea that ASU would have been satisfied with a tie in that game. "They were always playing to win," he said. "We just stayed in the game, believed in the game and made plays. That was the difference."

A bowl milestone

For the first time ever, both schools earned a bowl bid in the same season. The Wildcats were invited back to the Sun Bowl for the first time since the infamous Ultimatum Bowl of '68, and they tied Georgia, 13-13. And while the Devils missed out on the Rose Bowl, they did receive an invite to the Holiday Bowl, where they suffered another heartbreaking loss on a last-second field goal, falling to Arkansas, 18-17.

The following season, ASU took care of business by clinching its Rose Bowl berth before its showdown with UA. But that didn't mean the Wildcats weren't eager to inflict some pain on the Devils en route to Pasadena.

1986

ASU's record:	9-0-1 (5-0-1 Pac-10)
UA's record:	7-2 (4-2)
Final score:	UA 34, ASU 17

ASU seemed to learn a lesson from two of its more recent losses to UA: Make sure you secure a Rose Bowl bid *before* the Duel in the Desert.

In '86, the Sun Devils were enjoying an undefeated season – their only blemish being a 21-21 tie with Washington State – and had already punched their ticket to face Michigan in the bowl game deemed The Granddaddy of Them All.

"I tell you, the '86 Rose Bowl team, in my opinion, was the No. 1 team in college football that year. We should've been national champions," Cooper said. "You go position by position – most of those guys played in the NFL. We had a hell of a football team."

The only drawback to locking up the Rose Bowl, even if Sun Devil fans would consider it unforgivable: Maybe – just maybe – Arizona State was taking its archrival a tad lightly that year.

"There are some things you do the same way every time, but (before) that game, I remember Coach Cooper took us to a nicer hotel," van Raaphorst said. "And I don't know why, but the night before the game, I look down and there are guys in the Jacuzzi. And you just kind of shake your head and go, 'Why? We've never been in a nice hotel.'

"I remember telling Martz and (offensive coordinator Jim) Colletto, 'This is ridiculous. We've never stayed in a nice hotel. What are we doing?'"

But van Raaphorst admitted that, despite the Devils' losing streak against the Wildcats, beating UA wasn't the biggest thing on his team's mind that season. "Our goal going into this season – and I know this is going to be sacrilegious to come people – but our goals were not to beat UA, No. 1," he said. "Our first goal was a national championship, goal No. 2 was a Pac-10 championship and No. 3 was UA."

Chuck, the walk-on from California

Under Smith's guidance, the Wildcats had won seven games with two games to go in '86, as a matchup with Stanford would follow the ASU game.

One of UA's unlikely defensive leaders that season was a walk-on from La Mesa, Calif. "I was about 130-some-odd pounds coming out of high school, so I wasn't a really high recruit," said Wildcat strong safety Chuck Cecil (1984-87). "I got a chance to go to a couple of Ivy League schools and Colorado State, but Arizona was really the only Pac-10 school that recruited me, and that was the allure, basically."

When Cecil finally decided on Arizona, Smith was fresh out of scholarships, which meant he would have to make the team as a walk-on if he wanted to be a Wildcat. "He said, 'Chuck, I hate to tell you this, but we don't have any scholarships left,'" he said. "I still had scholarship offers from several schools, but I decided that I'd rather go to UA than take a scholarship somewhere else."

Arizona nose guard Dana Wells (1985-88), who had starred at Phoenix Brophy Prep, said it was Cecil's toughness and intelligence that made the walk-on a team leader and, eventually, the defensive coordinator for the Tennessee Titans and secondary coach for the St. Louis Rams. "Chuck's a very intelligent guy, for one. Book smarts, street smarts – whatever you want to call it, he has a very high intelligence," he said "He could read the offensive schemes and understand what's going on. That's probably why he's gotten where he is at the coaching level. And fear wasn't an option. He wouldn't lose, and he'd knock them out before they knocked him out."

Like many Wildcats and Sun Devils in the 1980s, Cecil came from out of state and wasn't very familiar with the rivalry at first - but once he got a taste of it, he said it became embedded in his blood.

Cecil made his first big mark on the rivalry with an interception in the '85 Duel at Sun Devil Stadium. "That was my first visit to Tempe, and it kind of put the exclamation point on it for me about my feelings for the Sun Devils, because it was very apparent to me that they felt the same way about us," he said. "It was kind of, 'Game on,' you know?

"You always get up for each game, but I think that the endorphins might run a little higher for a game like that, absolutely. You might get a little more revved up for it."

And Cecil said Arizona was champing at the bit to end ASU's undefeated run in '86. "If you're not confident that you can beat the other team going in, you're already defeated," he said. "You look at it now – they had a long list of NFL-caliber players, and talent-wise, they were unbelievable.

"But you know what? It was ASU-UA. That was the thing all week (in practice): It doesn't matter if they hadn't won a game or if they'd won them all. It's a one-game season, basically. Everything else doesn't matter. All bets are off. And we felt very good about our chances."

DeBowed

Buoyed by a noisy sellout crowd of 58,000-plus in front of a national TV audience on CBS, the Wildcats jumped all over the Devils early in 1986.

Jenkins connected on an 18-yard touchdown pass to Adams midway through the first quarter, and tailback Art Greathouse scored on a 5-yard run in the second quarter to give UA a 14-0 lead.

Van Raaphorst stopped the bleeding by throwing a 7-yard TD pass to split end Chris Garrett, and a Sun Devil field goal in the final seconds of the half made the score UA 14, ASU 10 at halftime.

In the second half, it was two amazing plays by undersized Wildcat defensive backs that made the difference. The first one took place in the third quarter.

"There was one play in that game that doesn't get the credit it's due, and that was (by defensive back) James DeBow," Penner said. "It was fourth down on our own 2-yard line, and ASU decided to kick a field goal. So they kicked it, but we were offsides."

The penalty, which was actually called on UA for too many men on the field, moved the ball down to the Wildcat 1-yard line. "So then Cooper takes points off the board, and they say they're going to go for (a touchdown)," Penner said. "And they were lined up in this big, heavy formation."

The formation included McDaniel, an offensive lineman, lined up at the fullback position. "They had this guy, (fullback) Channing Williams, who was about 240 pounds, playing running back," Penner said. "And they went off-tackle right to us, and James DeBow stepped up from the corner and got right on Channing Williams and kept him out of the end zone."

The 195-pound DeBow won the one-on-one matchup with the bigger Williams, standing him up three feet from the end zone before his teammates joined in to push Williams backwards and send the Arizona fans into a frenzy. "Everybody piled on, and it was unbelievable," Penner said. "That kind of just set the tone for the day."

The stop gave UA the ball with the lead intact. And following a 6-yard TD run by running back Chris McLemore and a 28-yard field goal, the Wildcats led 24-10 in the fourth quarter.

106 yards

Many Sun Devils consider a pass from an ASU quarterback that was caught in the back of the end zone – John Jefferson's touchdown grab in the '75 win over UA – to be the greatest moment in the history of the rivalry.

Appropriately enough, many Wildcats consider another pass from an ASU quarterback that was caught in the back of the end zone to be their all-time favorite Duel moment.

On third-and-goal from the UA 5-yard line in the fourth quarter, van Raaphorst rolled to his right and threw across his body to the left, looking for receiver Aaron Cox in the back of the end zone.

Instead, he found Cecil, who didn't hesitate to run the ball out of the end zone, returning it 106 yards the other way for a touchdown. The gassed Cecil collapsed in the north end zone after his sprint across the field.

The play put the Wildcats ahead of the Rose Bowl-bound Sun Devils by 21 points, reignited the Arizona Stadium crowd and smashed ASU's hopes of an undefeated campaign.

Here's how van Raaphorst remembers Tucson's most talked-about play:

"The play I threw to Chuck was actually a play I didn't like that was in there. If you watch that play, I come out, look left and (the tight end) is covered; there's a guy running with him. And then from there, it turns into a scramble. You're trying to find a guy. It's a one-on-one, and everybody's shaking.

"I'm rolling right, I throw that ball, trying to find Aaron Cox as he's working along the end-zone line. He had changed directions and was trying to work back to me.

"And then I throw it and, you know, Chuck makes history and makes a lot of money, because he looks fast running (106) yards."

And here's how Cecil remembers it:

"It was at the end of a long (ASU) drive. I was exhausted when they snapped the ball, and I don't know if it was eight, nine, 10 plays, but they started at their end of the field, and it was a pretty good drive, if I remember correctly.

"It's just funny because it's something that I had seen them do on film several times, and when he rolled out, it was an educated guess where he was going to throw it, and I was right. I just caught it and started running. I didn't even think about downing it (in the end zone); I caught it and then saw an open field and just started running. I almost didn't make it to the end zone, I was so tired. I was (already) gassed when they snapped the ball.

"The amazing part of it is, if you watch it, Brent Wood, our linebacker, he actually tips it – I mean, he barely touched it with the tip of his fingers. I always kid him because he's kind of short, and if he'd been an inch taller, I never would have gotten that one."

Van Raaphorst, who also grew up near San Diego, said he was already familiar with Cecil from their high school days. "I remember one of the big interceptions I threw in high school was to Chuck," he said. "I threw this ball and I thought for sure it was going to get caught, and Chuck picked it up and ran down the sidelines.

"People back home still talk about (the 1986 interception). It made Chuck look faster than he was, that's for sure, because he caught it at the right angle."

Naturally, the interception, which has been replayed early and often in Tucson – most recently in a pregame video shown before the 2010 Duel at Arizona Stadium – impacted the two men's lives in very different ways.

"It just makes me happy, and it's almost surreal to this day just to watch it and go, 'Gosh, that was me,'" Cecil said. "That's really all I get from it. I'm happy it was against the Sun Devils."

Cecil, who was a 1987 All-American and would play seven seasons in the NFL, said the pick was probably his No. 1 moment as a football player. "If there was a one-play highlight of my football career, that one's a pretty good one, I guess," he said.

Van Raaphorst said he can laugh about the moment now – which is important considering how often he's reminded of it, including one recent morning at work.

"I manage a sales team, and a couple of (employees) I have are in the Tucson area, and one of our guys is a big football fan," he said. "He went down to the (UA) sports information department and he had gotten a copy of that play."

Van Raaphorst had asked his group to put together a sales presentation for that morning. "We had our whole team there and some other people, and I gave them access to PowerPoint and stuff," he said. "And I'm looking down at my notes and I hear (the announcer say), 'Van Raaphorst drops back to pass.' And I think, 'Oh, no.'"

Van Raaphorst's sales team had decided to razz him by playing the video of the Cecil interception, with Verne Lundquist providing commentary on CBS. "Of course, UA sports and information was more than happy to provide that," van Raaphorst said. "But it was good. I don't like the memory, but it's funny. Unfortunately, in life, you remember the negatives more than the positives. So that was the one rub.

"But you know what? There's a lot of serious stuff out there in the world, and you know, it's a football game, and you've got to keep it somewhat in perspective."

Cats win fifth straight Duel

Van Raaphorst eventually did connect with Cox for a fourth-quarter touchdown, but it was way too little and too late. At that point, the 17-point margin of victory was Arizona's largest during what had become an extremely improbable five-game winning streak over Arizona State.

Cecil said he could understand how complacency might have been a contributing factor to the Devils' defeat. "I can't speak for them, but if I put myself in their shoes, I could see how they might be a little overconfident, maybe," he said. "Here's the thing: That team that they had, the players that they put on the field, were as good a team as you got in college. I mean, they were really, really good and really talented. It wasn't one guy. It wasn't a couple guys. They had 15 guys that were good NFL players. So for them to be overconfident – sure, why wouldn't they be? But we kind of used that for our own motivation."

Looking back, Cooper admits that ASU prematurely basked in the glory of its Rose Bowl berth. "I will agree. There's no question," he said. "We were going to the Rose Bowl for the first time ever. If anything, I think we celebrated too early."

But regardless of the reason, Marmie said the Wildcats earned the win. "I think it would not be fair to Arizona for us to even act like that was part of the problem, because we were totally outplayed in that football game," he said. "We were outplayed, outcoached – about everything you can put into that game or talk about from our standpoint, it was very negative in terms of how we performed in that game. It was a total nightmare, I think, for all of us."

Arizona lost to Stanford the following week but then won its bowl game for the first time, defeating North Carolina in the Aloha Bowl, 30-21. The win bumped the Wildcats up to No. 11 in the final Associated Press poll of the season.

Five weeks later, ASU rebounded from its Duel defeat to upend Michigan, 22-15, for a victory in its Rose Bowl debut. The Devils finished No. 4 in the final AP poll, and their fans were able to celebrate a historic season. But the players and coaches still wonder what might have been if not for the loss to the Cats.

"We went and pretty much handled Michigan," Cooper said, "and Penn St. played Miami the next night for the national championship (in the Fiesta Bowl), and I thought we could've beaten either one of them.

"We had a heck of a coaching staff. Goodness gracious, we had Mike Martz (who later led the St. Louis Rams to the Super Bowl), Colletto, Bill Young, Tom Freeman. And we had great players."

Van Raaphorst said he considers the '86 season a success, especially because his team remains the only one in school history to have won a Rose Bowl. But part of him still laments losing to UA – a team he never beat in his collegiate career.

"We had juniors and seniors – Randall McDaniel, Aaron Cox, Bruce Hill, (nose guard) Dan Saleaumua, (linebacker) Scott Stephen, Eric Allen, Anthony Parker – all those guys played long, long NFL careers, and yet we end up losing," he said.

"So I think that was the disappointing part. Knowing you have more talent and not putting it together on that night was very disappointing. And me throwing the ball to Chuck certainly didn't help."

Smith heads to the Coast

Smith's overall success at Arizona, not to mention his five wins against extremely talented ASU teams, caught the attention of USC, which lured him away from Tucson after the '86 season.

Many players expressed disappointment and feelings of abandonment after Smith's departure, which was to be expected considering just how important he had become in many of their lives.

UA offensive lineman Steve Justice (1982-85) said Smith, who passed away in 2008, was a father figure to a lot of guys on the team. "Larry Smith was a fantastic coach. He loved his players," he said. "When he died in 2008, I went to his funeral, and not only were UA people there, but USC and Missouri people were there. He touched a lot of people."

Smith moved back to Tucson following the end of his coaching career, and he lived out the rest of his life there. "It was kind of cool that when I played football there, his wife was involved and his kids were on the sidelines. We were doing jump rope and aerobics with his wife and assistants," Justice said. "It was a very cool family atmosphere. I wish he never went to USC and left Arizona."

Dobyns also has fond memories of the tough but tender man who spearheaded The Streak. "Coach Smith would be the first guy to put his foot in your ass and the first guy to put his arm around your shoulder," he said.

Tomey takes over

It wasn't an easy task for UA administrators to find a coach who shared Smith's ability to build a rapport with his players – not to mention his ability to beat Arizona State. But Dick Tomey, who coached at Hawaii from 1977-86, was up to the task.

Arizona offensive tackle John Fina (1988-91), who graduated from Salpointe Catholic High School in Tucson, said Tomey did a great job of picking up the pieces after Smith's very sudden departure. "Larry Smith left in the dark of the night over New Year's, and I think a lot of Larry's guys felt betrayed," he said. "And Dick wrapped his arms around those guys and said, 'Hey, you're my guys now. Things aren't going to be the same, but you're my guys.' And I think that set the tone for Dick Tomey down in Tucson.

"He was passionate about the game. He was passionate about the University of Arizona. He opened his home to the players and their families. He was a very warm, welcoming guy, and you could always go up and talk to him in his office, and you could always approach him on the field. He wasn't a pushover; he wasn't going to tell you what you wanted to hear all the time. But he damn sure was there for you."

Penner said there were some growing pains in Tucson upon Tomey's arrival in '87. "I call it the locker combination year: We were 4-4-3," he said. "We had a good team, but at first, a lot of the guys didn't buy into the program. He completely changed the offense around, and that really kind of set some guys the wrong way.

"But he did have a good coaching staff. He surrounded himself with some great coaches like Ron McBride, the offensive line coach who's like a father to me to this day, (secondary coach) Duane Akina and (defensive coordinator) Larry MacDuff – just some really good football coaches."

Of course, the players whom Tomey inherited from Smith, along with UA fans and longtime Tucsonans, let him know that he needed to continue the Wildcats' success against the Devils to which they had recently grown accustomed.

"Obviously in the Frank Kush years, ASU had their way with UA, and that created a lot of frustration," Tomey said. "Early on, we did a training camp so our younger players would get a flavor for it. We would have some of our former players come in and talk to the guys about the rivalry."

1987

ASU's record:	6-4 (3-3 Pac-10)
UA's record:	4-4-2 (2-3-1)
Final score:	UA 24, ASU 24

Cecil was a captain on the '87 Wildcat squad, and he took it upon himself to get the players fired up in front of the fans at Sun Devil Stadium before the game began.

"I led the pregame stretch there, and the entire student section was filled. They were there in force," he said. "So I basically had the entire team turn (to them), do our jumping jacks and spell some really creative words to the ASU student section."

The Sun Devil students didn't take kindly to this display. "After we broke the team stretch, the secondary drills were on the sidelines. And I mean to tell you, I did not stand still. There were oranges and ice and all sorts of stuff coming down on the field," Cecil said. "It was anarchy."

A mediocre '87

The Sun Devils were having a mediocre season following the graduation of some of their top players, including Clack and van Raaphorst. But once again, Arizona State had a better overall and conference record than Arizona as well as another shot at UA in front of its home crowd.

And the early portion of the game went according to plan for the Devils. Led by new starting QB Daniel Ford, ASU opened up a 14-0 first-quarter lead. Arizona responded with a short touchdown run by QB Ronnie Veal and a pair of field goals by kicker Gary Coston, including a 51-yarder, to trim the margin to 14-13 at the half.

Williams, the man who was stuffed by DeBow at the goal line a year earlier, opened the third-quarter scoring with a 59-yard run that extended the Devils' lead to 21-13. But the Wildcats evened the score later in the quarter with a 53-yard run by running back Alonzo Washington and a two-point conversion by Greathouse.

ASU's defense clamped down in the fourth, and Alan Zendejas – the brother of Luis and Max – kicked a 40-yard field goal to put the Devils ahead, 24-21, with less than three minutes to play.

And after Eric Allen picked off a Veal pass on fourth down with 1:21 to go – a play that actually hurt ASU's field position, as an incomplete pass would have allowed the Devils to take over possession in Wildcat territory – it seemed as though ASU would finally get the UA monkey off its back.

Instead, the interception set up perhaps the most bizarre sequence of events in rivalry history.

"All they had to do was punt the ball"

UA kicker Doug Pfaff (1987-89) watched the '87 game from the sidelines, but he has a perfect memory of the atmosphere in Sun Devil Stadium when it appeared that ASU would finally get back on top in the rivalry.

"It was funny because the fans are pretty close to the sidelines, and they were all talking trash to UA. It really looked like The Streak was going to end," he said. "We had won five straight going into that game, and they had us beat pretty much the whole game.

"It was 24-21 with just seconds remaining, and all they had to do was punt the ball."

ASU punter Mike Schuh, who was selected to the All-Pac-10 team in 1985, was called on to punt on a fourth-and-3 from the Sun Devil 38-yard line.

Cecil was determined to block the punt because UA would have almost no time to drive the field if Schuh was able to get it away cleanly. "He had some sort of record number of punts without a block. He'd never had a punt blocked in his entire career," he said. "But the punt before that one, I came through (the offensive line) and got through pretty clean, and I actually got part of the ball – just the very tip of the ball with my fingers, and you could barely tell. But I did turn to the punter and tell him that, 'Oh, by the way, I'm going to get the next one.'"

Cecil didn't get to Schuh's punt, but his words after the previous kick just might have gotten into the punter's head. "I came through clean, and honestly, I don't know if I would've blocked it, but I think I would've been close again," he said.

But Cecil didn't get the opportunity to block the kick; Schuh dropped the ball before it made contact with his leg.

"When he muffed it, I actually went down to pick it up and try to run it in, but as I went down and it was almost in my hand, he kicked it on the ground and kicked it into the line," Cecil said. "And basically, I turned around, it bounced off somebody, and it came right back to me."

Cecil's recovery of Schuh's muffed punt, combined with the penalty that Schuh was assessed for illegally kicking the ball on the ground, unbelievably gave UA possession at the ASU 13-yard line with just 13 seconds to play.

"I'm not saying (my previous comments were) the reason he muffed it, but then they come to the next one and all he has to do is punt the ball," Cecil said. "If he punts the ball, the game is over."

UA beats ASU, 24-24

A 2008 documentary detailed the 1968 football game between Harvard and Yale that ended in a tie due to 16 unanswered Harvard points in the game's final minutes. Since the outcome thrilled Harvard fans and stunned Yale supporters, the name of the documentary was "Harvard Beats Yale 29-29."

If one were to make a documentary of the '87 Duel, it could be called "Arizona beats Arizona State 24-24," because after Coston's 30-yard field goal gave the Wildcats an improbable tie – that year's Duel is still the only one that has ended without a winner, and it will most likely will remain that way since college football now uses overtime to decide games that are tied at the end of regulation – the prevailing feeling in Sun Devil Stadium that evening was that, unofficially, UA had won and ASU had lost.

"We were elated, absolutely," Cecil said. "You can't say it was just as sweet as a victory, but it was about as close as you can possibly get, because really and truly, we had lost the game three or four times, and they kept bailing us out.

"First of all, if Eric Allen would not have intercepted the ball on fourth down (late in the fourth quarter), they would have won the game, because he basically turned it into a punt for us, whereas if he would've knocked it down, they would've taken the ball in our territory. There were a handful of very minor little things that somehow, some way, happened in our favor."

Penner said the Wildcats were definitely charmed that evening. "To be quite honest with you, they should've won that game," he said. "They had the game won, there's no doubt about it. And they lined up for the punt, and when the punter bobbled the snap, it was like, 'You've got to be kidding.'"

Tomey also felt like his team had just won the game. "I remember John Cooper and I met across the field after the game, and John Cooper and I have been longtime friends. The way I was feeling and the way he was feeling (was much different)," he said. "Clearly, there was a sense of euphoria or relief on our part because it felt like much more than just a tie. We had consecutive wins in the series, and that kept The Streak alive."

The scoreboard may have shown a 24-24 tie, but Bordow said the fans filed out of Sun Devil Stadium that day feeling as though UA had just won its sixth straight Duel. "It felt like UA won," he said. "Every ASU fan left the stadium feeling like they lost the game."

Healey said the muff symbolized the Devils' fortunes during The Streak better than any other play in any Duel from 1982-1990. "It just seemed like most of those close games had a play or two that a Sun Devil fan would probably say was a fluke play and a Wildcat fan would probably say was a big play by their team," he said. "But it seemed like those plays always went against Arizona State in that nine-year stretch."

McDaniel said the Devils always seemed to find a way to shoot themselves in the foot during the Wildcats' run. "We have a chance to win one, and what do we do? We give it back to them," he said. "I don't know what it was. We always found a way to screw it up and give it back."

And for McDaniel, a tie was worse than a loss. "They didn't have a tiebreaker back then. I would rather win or lose and know that's going to happen," he said. "I would've liked to play it out like they do now (with overtime periods). At least that way, you know who wins or loses. That's the one that stings a little bit."

Cooper doesn't recall a lot from the '87 game, which was his last against UA as ASU's head coach. But he sure remembers the muffed punt.

"If our punter punts the ball – if he kicks a 10-yard punt – we win the game," he said. "But he drops it."

Cooper goes to Ohio State

After three winning seasons, a pair of bowl victories (including a 33-28 win over Air Force in the Freedom Bowl to end the '87 season) and, of course, the Devils' one and only Rose Bowl win, Cooper decided to accept a job as head coach at perennial college football powerhouse Ohio State.

But Cooper said he sometimes thinks about what might have been had he stuck around. "I had three great years out there, and I've got to be honest: There are times when I look back and I wonder why the heck I ever left," he said. "Let me say this: I had some really, really good players when I coached there. Gosh almighty: Randall McDaniel, Danny Saleaumua, Eric Allen, Anthony Parker – a bunch of those guys went on (to the NFL).

"People ask me how good we were. Trace Armstrong, who played 14 years in the National Football League, was a backup defensive tackle on our team. That's how good we were."

And while Cooper didn't have much success in the Duel in the Desert, he thought highly of the two head coaches he battled.

"I have great respect for Larry, and I've known Dick forever," he said. "I didn't have a real good record versus Arizona (0-2-1), but nobody had more respect for Larry Smith and Dick Tomey than I did. They did things the right way."

Marmie moves up

In Cooper's absence, ASU decided to hire from within, promoting Marmie from defensive coordinator to head coach.

As an assistant, Marmie appreciated both the magnitude of the rivalry and the frustration that had built up among Sun Devil fans over the previous six seasons.

"Of course, before I came the head coach in '88, I was a part of it for three years, so I had experienced the game and everything that went in with the game as an assistant coach, and I already had an idea of how this game affected the state of Arizona and the people in the state, even if they weren't an Arizona or Arizona State graduate," he said. "Regardless of how you approached it with your players, they knew that it wasn't just another game."

Much like the Wildcats must have felt during most of the Frank Kush era, Marmie said it was difficult to consider the Duel in the Desert much of a duel at all during the 1980s. "I hate to say this, but the unfortunate thing was in the certain period of time there, I don't know whether you can call it a rivalry or not because we didn't win," he said.

And Marmie knew something had to change in the week leading up to the Duel in order to get over that hump, which had become as much a mental hurdle as a physical one for the Sun Devils. "The thing that we tried to remain constant with was we were going to win the game based on how we prepared for the game – not what the people on the outside had to say about it, but how well we prepared and how well we executed when game day rolled around," he said.

ASU running back Bruce Perkins (1988-89) said Marmie's preparation for the UA game was superior to Cooper's. "Marmie approached it with more of a sense of urgency. He wanted us to recognize that it's a very important game that will follow us the rest of our lives – you would always know whether you beat or didn't beat UA, and you'd be able to tell your grandchildren and share those moments with your grandkids," he said.

"He approached it by having some alumni come back and speak to us about the importance of us going out and playing Sun Devil football, and be winners and win with class. And that was our approach: Just go out and play 60 minutes of football. He really worked us that week just to make sure that we went out and played a good, solid, hard ballgame."

Tomey's "adopted" rivalry

Fina said Tomey had fully embraced the rivalry by the end of his first full season in Tucson.

"Dick Tomey was very clear: He adopted that rivalry, no ifs, ands or buts," he said. "He knew, and you could see in his face and his delivery of the preparation of the season going into training camps that you can divide the season into three different parts: the first five games, the second five games and the last game, which is more important than everything else, and that was the game versus ASU.

"Dick made it very clear going in that, when we got 10 games in, whether we were 10-0 or 0-10, we can salvage the season or put the cherry on top by crushing the Scum Devils from that horrid city up north that's actually well below our feet in elevation. We're in a much more beautiful location, we're a far better school, and that's why I was there. And we dominated the series."

1988

ASU's record:	6-4 (3-3 Pac-10)
UA's record:	6-4 (4-3)
Final score:	UA 28, ASU 18

Reminiscent of Jay Dobyns, who overcame broken ribs to finish a game against the Devils, Wells shook off an excruciating injury early in the '88 Duel to stay on the field in his final game as a Wildcat.

"I got my ankle blown out in the first quarter, but I played on it the whole game," he said. "I was pretty much a non-factor the rest of the game. I played on one leg. The ankle was pretty much worthless. I had it wrapped all up. That was something that really hurt me for 3-4 months, through the (NFL) combine and everything.

"But yeah, I played. And as it relates to the rivalry, we got a win and I finished out my career never losing to them."

Hail to the Cats

ASU was coming off a 50-0 loss to Larry Smith's USC squad heading into its matchup with UA in Tucson. But for the second straight season, the Devils jumped out to a lead, as quarterback Paul Justin connected with tight end Ryan McReynolds for an 8-yard first-quarter score.

The Cats and Devils traded leads in the second quarter. Arizona found the end zone via a 47-yard Veal pass to flanker Derek Hill and a 10-yard run by Washington, while Perkins scored on a 44-yard run and Justin found McReynolds for his second touchdown of the game to put ASU ahead, 18-14, with just 34 seconds to play before halftime.

But that was more than enough time for the Wildcats to make the Sun Devils feel, once again, that they had stepped into the Twilight Zone.

On the final play of the half, Veal threw up a pass from midfield in the hopes that a UA receiver would bring it down in the end zone. The ball came down 5 yards short of the goal line, where Hill snatched it from a cluster of Cats and Devils before darting into the end zone for a 55-yard score.

"I remember the pass was to (split end) Melvin Smith," Tomey said, "and Hill grabbed it out of his hands and ran it into the end zone. It was a great throw by Ronnie and quite a way to go into the locker room at halftime."

The halftime score: Wildcats 21, shell-shocked Sun Devils 18. Just another devastating but familiar blow for ASU.

"Certainly, when you look at most Hail Marys, regardless of what level of competition it is, something unusual has to happen on that play for it to succeed," Marmie said. "I think it did change the momentum of the game. Obviously, we still had a half to play, and a lot of things enter in (to the outcome). But when I think about that game in particular, that's what comes to my mind."

Perkins, who finished just short of 100 rushing yards in the game, agreed that the play was a killer. "That really put a dagger in us as far as maintaining momentum, because it was going back and forth for a while," he said.

ASU didn't score in the second half, and UA added a fourth-quarter score – another Washington TD run – to ice the victory.

"That Hail Mary pass, I think, really changed the outcome of the game," Tomey said. "They were beating us in the first half, and it was a close game going into halftime, and we hit that Hail Mary pass, which was just kind of a fluke.

"What I really remember was us dominating ASU in the second half. We continued to play ball control, and Alonzo Washington had a great game in the second half. Our defense just dominated, and our offense played solid. But it was just a total different outcome in the second half, and I think it was because of that Hail Mary."

Fina said Hill's grab put Arizona back on track. "I think the first half wasn't very pretty for the Cats. It just seemed like it was going to be another one of those tooth-and-nail games," he said. "But if you have one hallmark play that gives you inspiration you can point to – just by having that alone, you definitely can build on that, and whatever small lead you have, you can just draw from that, no matter what kind of onslaught comes at you."

1989

ASU's record:	6-3-1 (3-2-1 Pac-10)
UA's record:	6-4 (4-3 Pac-10)
Final score:	UA 28, ASU 10

Marmie was determined to keep trying new things – or old things, in the case of a Frank Kush tactic - until his team found a way to get over the hump in the Duel.

"There were banners of the previous seven years with the scores (of the ASU-UA games) on the practice field, and they'd pipe in the Arizona fight song into the locker room two weeks straight," said ASU linebacker Brett Wallerstedt (1989-92). "It was almost a very obvious effort to try to do anything and everything possible to add some motivation to the game."

But Wallerstedt said those efforts may have been counterproductive. "A lot of times, it may have added pressure and affected on-field performance in a negative way," he said.

UA implemented some motivational tactics of its own in '89. Penner, who was a graduate assistant with the Wildcats that season, made sure that a quote by ASU's quarterback was read by every Arizona player before the game.

"Earlier in that week, Paul Justin guaranteed a victory," he said. "Well, I got a hold of that quote and I made no less than 1,000 copies, and I pasted them all over McKale Center – every locker, every coach's locker, every door, every meeting room, every door outside of McKale Center. I went as far as to post them around the student union. I spent two hours walking around and putting these everywhere. When we gave the players the scouting report, I put that on top. They saw it: This guy guaranteed a victory."

UA defensive back Heath Bray (1988-92) said Tomey rallied his team to beat ASU that year in a fashion reminiscent of Jim Young. "We were in the hotel (in Tempe) and we had this team meeting, and we were getting ready to go to the stadium," he said. "And Coach Tomey's talking to us, and he says, 'Wait a minute. I've got something I want to show you.'

"And the lights go out, and a big video screen goes on. And it's (ASU's) starting center, and he just starts talking crap and he starts calling out (UA) players. He called out (linebackers) Zeno Alexander and Chris Singleton.

"And (Tomey) said, 'If they want to play smash-mouth football, let's go.' And then he turned on the lights, and he looked at us and said, 'Let's go.'

"And holy (expletive), did that room go nuts. I mean, completely nuts. There's an old adage as a football coach: You don't let your team get too excited. But for some reason, it was exactly opposite with ASU. We never got tired."

The team was so pumped up, according to Penner, that several Wildcats who were expected to sit out the game due to injury were determined to get on the field.

"Glenn Parker, our offensive tackle, played on a broken bone in his leg that game," he said. "He was hopping around, but he gutted it out."

"The Screaming Bananas"

This is how Bray remembers the chain of events in the hour before the '89 Duel at Sun Devil Stadium:

"We come out and (the Sun Devils were) warming up in their nasty-ass mustard and rust colors," he said. "It was the first time I really got a look at it, and I thought, 'God, they're awful.' It was just funny.

"And then they go in their locker room, we go in ours, and it was kind of solemn in there. And (linebacker) Donnie Salum, who's one of my really good friends, gets up and just starts going ape crazy – I mean yelling, screaming, slamming his helmet down on this table that was full of Gatorade. The table exploded and cut Coach McBride in the face.

"Everyone looks at each other, and there was just this rush. And everyone came together in the middle of the room, and I mean, you could cut the electricity with a knife.

"And we go out in the tunnel, and the fans are throwing crap at us. It's the first time in my life I've ever had stuff thrown at me. And we come out, and those idiots come out in all mustard."

In another effort to change things up specifically for the UA game, Marmie had decided to mix up ASU's uniforms a little: He had the team remove its traditional home uniforms before the game and retake the field entirely in Sun Devil gold just before kickoff.

But Fina said he remembers the uniforms being more of a banana color. "It wasn't that rich gold color; it was that horrible, flat, banana yellow," he said. "They came running out head to toe in banana yellow."

Bray, who referred to the Devils as "The Screaming Bananas" for that game, said the '89 Duel in the Desert was over right then and there. "I mean, we won the game before the ball was kicked off," he said. "They were so awful. I mean, we were physically laughing at them. It was just pitiful, and we were like, 'We're going to kick their ass.' And then we went to literally kicking their ass the whole game."

Perkins said the players didn't know anything about the color change until they put on their uniforms right before the game. "To my knowledge, we were all kind of surprised that we were going to go out with all-yellow uniforms," he said. "We really didn't care too much about the uniforms at the time because we were pretty much focused on trying to go out and execute more so than worrying about our uniforms.

"But as we stepped back and at the end of the year, we were looking back and thinking, 'Damn, why did we go out in these uniforms?' So it really didn't hit us until after the game. It was like, 'Man, we had these banana uniforms.'"

Marmie admitted that, in retrospect, the uniform switcheroo may have been a mistake. "It wasn't something we talked to the players about during the week. That was basically a decision I made that might give us some sort of a special lift, to go into the locker room and come back out at home," he said. "Sometimes you do things and you're hopeful that it might be something that gives you something a little bit extra. But looking back at it now, I probably wouldn't do that again, and obviously it didn't pay off. It didn't make any difference, and I probably should've known that at the time."

Cats dominate second half

ASU led the so-called Banana Bowl at halftime, 10-7, but UA scored 21 unanswered points in the second half thanks to a pair of 1-yard touchdown runs by running back David Eldridge and a 3-yard TD rush by tailback Michael Bates.

The Wildcats were also boosted by a pair of forced fumbles in the second half that they recovered – one by defensive tackle Reggie Johnson, who stripped Justin in the third quarter, and another by cornerback Darryll Lewis, who pried the ball away from Devils tailback David Winsley deep in UA territory later in the third.

Tomey said the defense came up big in the second half. "I just think Darryll Lewis made so many plays in his career that were huge plays. I remember that play that he stripped (Justin), and I remember the one Reggie did, as well," Tomey said. "Those were huge. Those changed that game completely."

The win catapulted the Cats to their first bowl game under Tomey – a 17-10 win over North Carolina State at the first-ever Copper Bowl, which was played at Arizona Stadium.

Fina and the rest of the offensive line helped UA gain 285 yards rushing to ASU's 43 in the '89 game, and he said the Wildcats' 18-point win – their largest margin of victory during The Streak – wasn't indicative of their domination.

"We physically just took it to them offensively," he said. "Some of the early Dick Tomey years were (about) finding an offensive identity for us, and just to have that success offensively and really just wearing them out was the most satisfying aspect of that game. We didn't beat them by 35 or even 28 points, but we had the satisfaction of manhandling them."

Whether it was the uniforms, a lack of execution or both, Perkins said his Devils just weren't up to the challenge that night. "Just the way we came out with the uniforms and we didn't perform and play like we should've played – it was disappointing," he said.

1990

ASU's record:	4-5 (2-4 Pac-10)
UA's record:	6-4 (4-4)
Final score:	UA 21, ASU 17

Fina said the Sun Devils' sub-.500 record didn't reflect the talent that their 1990 team possessed.

"That was a skilled team that ASU had," he said. "They were a better football team than I think we were."

Particularly on defense, the Devils were loaded with talented players who would make a big impact in the NFL, including linebacker and five-time Pro Bowler Darren Woodson, defensive end Shante Carver, who played alongside Woodson with the Dallas Cowboys, and defensive back Phillippi Sparks, who spent eight seasons with the New York Giants.

Records aside, Sparks (1990-91) said the '90 Duel was another example of ASU entering the game as the more talented squad. "Being a defensive player, we were whooping their butt. There's no way in heck we should've lost that game," Sparks said.

And it wasn't the first time during The Streak that ASU led late in the game. This time, the Devils had a 17-14 advantage in the fourth quarter.

"I thought that was another game that was certainly much more competitive a game that we had opportunities to win," Marmie said. "And there were two big plays in that game."

The first of those two plays came with just under 10 minutes left, when ASU running back Leonard Russell lost a fumble that was caused by a hit from Arizona linebacker Jimmie Hopkins near midfield. UA recovered the ball and ate up nearly seven minutes of clock on its ensuing possession before a 1-yard Greathouse touchdown run gave the Wildcats a 21-17 advantage with just over three minutes remaining.

The second play came after Justin had led ASU, which needed a touchdown to win, deep into UA territory on just five plays in the game's final two minutes.

"I kind of felt like, 'Oh boy, we're in trouble. They're really on the march here,'" Fina said. "This is that moment when a quarterback – in this case, ASU's quarterback – is feeling like he's going to be the hero, and on the sideline, you always have the trepidation of, 'Oh, come on, guys, we need something.'"

With 40 seconds to play and the Devils with the ball at the Wildcat 24-yard line, UA came up with the play Fina was hoping for, as Justin's pass was intercepted by strong safety Bobby Roland at the 5-yard line.

Roland probably should've fallen to the ground as soon as he caught the ball, but instead he attempted to make an unnecessary return on the interception, much to the trepidation of the Wildcat players and coaches on the sideline. "We were just like, 'Don't fumble, Bobby! Don't fumble!'" Bray said. "All of us were saying that in between just screaming our heads off."

Tomey wanted Roland to take a knee because he knew that, even though the breaks had been going UA's way, freaky things tend to happen in this rivalry. "We were all telling him, 'Just get down!' he said. "We just needed to run out the clock."

Roland was eventually tackled just short of the 20-yard line, where he held on to the ball to extend The Streak to nine games. "That was a heck of a game. That was a battle. ASU played really well," Tomey said. "It could have gone either way, for sure."

Fina said he enjoyed the gritty nature of the 1990 contest – and, of course, he enjoyed stealing another game from the Sun Devils. "It was a very good, hard-fought game played pretty darn well," he said. "And then Bobby Roland with that pick – you just get that nice jubilation with the ending, which is better than just running the clock out.

"Even if it was a game against Oklahoma, Michigan or some other school, it'd be a great game. But because it's the rivalry, those single events have a much more salient place in your memory."

Wallerstedt recalled the devastation that the ASU seniors felt after losing another game to UA, as the outgoing 1990 Sun Devil class was one of many from that era that never tasted victory against the Wildcats.

"I vividly remember standing on the bench next to (safety) Nathan LaDuke – as a senior, he'd never beaten Arizona – and just having that feeling that, 'Hey, something's got to go our way,'" he said. "There had been a lot of quirky endings, a lot of big plays that swung and ultimately were the deciding factor in Arizona State not winning.

"So I'm just standing next to Nathan, and we're watching our offense take the ball down the field (in the fourth quarter) in big chunks and moving the ball pretty easily against their defense. And then, seeing a receiver go into the end zone and thinking (it was) the winning touchdown but it turning into an interception – that was pretty frustrating."

Reexamining The Streak

There are plenty of explanations from Wildcats and Sun Devils who participated in The Streak as to how and why UA managed to compile an 8-0-1 record against ASU from 1982-90.

Hons said it's possible that UA just wanted those games more, especially during the seasons when the Wildcats were ineligible for postseason play due to either NCAA probation or having a record that simply wasn't bowl-worthy.

"Honestly, I think maybe it meant more to them because they weren't going anywhere," he said. "I just think that was part of it, although I know I wanted to win every time.

"It also could've been coaching. They had some good coaches with Larry Smith and Dick Tomey, so it could've been that. But year to year, it changes, I guess, and if you've got a lot more wins and you're doing better than them, maybe they have a lot more to play for, because at least they can say they beat us."

Fina said the roles that Smith and Tomey played in The Streak can't be overstated. "Without offending anyone, I think we were better coached," he said. "I think we might have been a little more motivated by the rivalry. I think we might have been a little more in touch with it.

"I wasn't in their locker room, but we certainly played with more emotion, I think, during those years. We played more with a chip on our shoulder, like it was our season or it was more important."

Kaiser said Smith and Tomey did an excellent job of relaying the rivalry's importance to their players. "I don't know how it was with previous coaching staffs, but Coach Smith really drove home the point of disliking ASU, and I think Coach Tomey carried that over," he said. "Coach Tomey had a lot of players that had that driven in their minds already, and I think that carried over from class to class how important it was."

Rogers, who coached ASU at the beginning of The Streak, said he made an error in not emphasizing the UA game as much as he should have. "(The Wildcats) pointed at the Arizona State game. They pointed at it, and we didn't," he said. "I would say that was a miscalculation, basically because of the fact that we had won so many in a row. And now when they play, it seems like it's considered and understood that this is a big game.

"They had a great streak in the '80s, and it started against me. But they did a good job, yes they did."

Perkins said The Streak had crept into the minds of many of his Sun Devil teammates by the late 1980s. "I think it was just more the hype and the mental aspect," he said. "A lot of players, particularly young players, get caught up in the numbers game and who won the most games as opposed to going out and actually putting that aside and executing.

"In my mind and in my experience, football is 10 percent physical and 90 percent mental, and if you can get past the mental aspect of The Streak and just go on pure talent and executing your assignments flawlessly, I think the outcome could have come out a little bit more in ASU's favor. But I think The Streak just got in players' heads, and they just didn't perform. They made key mistakes down the stretch, and it really cost us the ballgames."

As The Streak went on, Tomey said UA's self-assurance going into each ASU game continued to grow. "I think any time you have a long run, there's obviously confidence," he said. "There's also pressure, but there's a feeling that, you know, we can do this, and when it gets right down to the end, we're going to make a play."

That mindset goes completely the opposite direction for the team on the losing end, according to Tomey, who was on the flip side of that coin when he was a UCLA assistant coach in the '70s. "There is a feeling subconsciously on the other side – I know there was with UCLA – that if UCLA would be ahead and USC started a run, it'd be, 'Oh, here we go again,'" he said.

"Whichever side you're on in a streak, you have to overcome that. The guy who tends to think things haven't gone well for us, you have to understand that's just one game, and you have to believe you can overcome it. And if you're the team that's had the streak, you have to make plays; it's not going to happen for you just because it's happened before."

Wells said ASU had a tendency to tighten up toward the end of some of those games. "To be totally honest, as The Streak got going, it's like they were playing not to lose," he said. "I guess you can maybe see that in some people's eyes when the game kicked off. And I think as the stakes got bigger and The Streak got longer, they might have tightened up even more."

Many ASU fans lamented what they believed was a string of bad luck during UA's nine-game run. Marmie refused to suggest that luck was the deciding factor, but he admitted that the timing of some of the biggest plays in those games was especially detrimental.

"I would hesitate to call them fluky plays because people will say that you're kind of making an excuse," he said. "Sometimes you can have a play like that happen in a game and it won't affect (the outcome) like it did. But it affected it as far as how much how much time was left in the game and where it was. That same play wouldn't have had the same influence on the game (if it happened) in the first quarter.

"I would say, more than fluky, there were some really unusual things that happened in several of those games. But some of those things were the result of what we did, and some of them were a result of what UA did."

Whether it was 100 percent skill or a mixture of talent and good fortune, Tomey was proud to be a part of an amazing era of Arizona football.

"Certainly, we believed we could do well, but we also had a lot of respect for ASU's coaches and players, and we knew we had our share of good fortune in The Streak," he said. "But it was something UA people took a lot of pride in, because when Kush was there, he had the extended streak (against UA)."

Hansen said the magnitude of The Streak in Tucson was enormous. "In the whole decade of the '80s, I thought those UA-ASU football games surpassed everything (former UA basketball coach) Lute Olson did, except for when he went to the Final Four in 1988," he said. "Those UA-ASU football games gave the town a feeling of being a winner as much as what Lute did."

When asked what an undefeated record in his career against Arizona State means to him, Cecil said it's on his list of things for which he's most thankful.

"There's God, my wife, my daughter and beating ASU," he said.

1991

ASU's record:	5-5 (3-4 Pac-10)
UA's record:	4-6 (3-4)
Final score:	ASU 37, UA 14

One of the big differences between the 1991 Duel in the Desert and the previous nine was that the Sun Devils were in the same position the Wildcats had often found themselves in during The Streak. They had nothing to play for at the end of the season other than the satisfaction of beating their rival.

ASU was just a .500 team in '91, and with that, Marmie knew he was about to be replaced. But he likes to think that ASU's pre-game prep was a little sharper and its overall team health was a bit better before his final Duel.

"I think we basically tried to prepare things hopefully better than we did in some of those other weeks," he said, "and I think we had some consistency in some areas that we hadn't had before. We had some consistency with our quarterback that year, Bret Powers, and in some of those earlier years, we had some injuries and things that caused us to be not as consistent."

In fact, it was the Wildcats who were hurting the most before the '91 game at Sun Devil Stadium. "That was a tough year for us. We just lost so many players to injury. Our defense was decimated," Tomey said. "It was also a year that we came back and won a couple of big games at the end of the year (including a 31-14 win over USC a week earlier). But in the time that our staff was together, both at Hawaii and Arizona, that was the worst season we had."

Bray remembers how depleted UA's roster was in '91. "I played four different positions during that season," he said. "At one time, we had 17 starters that missed at least one ballgame. It was pretty bad."

So was the loss that the Wildcats suffered to the Sun Devils on the night of Nov. 23, 1991 – one that was more lopsided on the scoreboard than any of the victories that UA enjoyed during The Streak.

Devils due

If the Sun Devils weren't able to match the Wildcats' intensity before and during their previous nine matchups, they certainly did in '91. Just ask Heath Bray.

"Michael Bates was a teammate of mine, and Mario, his little brother, was (ASU's) running back," he said. "And Mario had been at a party at my house once."

Mario Bates, a Tucson native who went on to play seven seasons in the NFL, instantly became reacquainted with Bray on the field that night. "Early in the game, I come off the corner, and it's a pass play," Bray said. "Mario blocks me. I turn and look, and it's incomplete.

"And right as the ball goes over my head, Mario hits me in the back of the knees. And I'm like, 'Bro, what the hell are you doing?' And he's just, 'F you! F you! Get back to your huddle!'

"And I'm thinking, 'This is the ASU game, that's for sure.'"

That's not to say that the Wildcats didn't throw some nastiness right back at the Devils, as noted by ASU cornerback Kevin

Miniefield (1989-92), a dual-sport star who was recruited by UA's football and basketball staffs. "It was their secondary coach, Duane Akina, who recruited me to play (football)," he said. "I heard on the sidelines all these vulgarities coming at me from the sidelines. (At first) I was thinking it was a player. But it was him."

The Wildcats may have been able to dish it out from the sidelines that night, but not on the field. After the Devils took an early 10-0 lead, wide receiver Eric Guliford, who caught ASU's first touchdown of the game from Powers, returned an Arizona punt 68 yards for a score late in the first quarter to make it 17-0.

And while its defense stonewalled injury-plagued UA, allowing just 155 yards of total offense for the game, ASU added a field goal in the second quarter to take a 20-0 halftime lead.

"I remember at halftime we were pretty down, trying to find some momentum, trying to figure out what would work," said Arizona tight end Barry Julian (1988-92). "Our offense was sputtering, and you always think, 'Yeah, we can pull this out. Let's get on a roll.'"

But unlike the Duels from 1982-90, the Devils didn't leave the door open for a Wildcat comeback. ASU added another field goal in the third quarter, and early in the fourth, a 4-yard TD run by fullback Kelvin Fisher followed by 2-yard score from Powers to tight end Bob Brasher gave the Sun Devils a 37-0 lead in front of 73,000 maroon-and-gold-clad fans whose reward for enduring an excruciating near-decade of losses to the Wildcats had finally arrived.

Miniefield said it was a night to remember. "The game we beat them here, the first time we broke The Streak, that was probably the best, most exciting, most memorable game I've been a part of here at ASU," he said. "There are different moments in that rivalry, but that defined it for me."

Rubbing it in?

Larry Smith became irate when he believed Frank Kush ran up the score on UA in a 1970s contest. Tomey had a similar reaction to a play that ASU ran in the fourth quarter of the '91 Duel when, with the game out of reach, Marmie decided to call a fake punt with the Devils deep in their own territory.

"We pulled out every trick play and everything else known to man, and we just about used all of them," said ASU strong safety Jean Boyd (1991-93). "But I think the exclamation point for me was, we were up 37-0 in the fourth quarter and the game's in the bag, and myself and Phillippi Sparks didn't take a lot to convince (Marmie) to run that fake punt on our own 10-yard line.

"It's not like we were at midfield. And the fact that he did it was, I thought, an exclamation point on what it meant to snap that losing streak."

Sparks recalled the details of the play. "This was a play for our punt team, and I was on one end, Jean was on the other end, and our punter had an opportunity to throw it to either one of us," he said. "So, to make a long story short, here we are, we both do our assignments, we turn around, and (the punter) throws Jean the ball."

Boyd made the catch and took it all the way for a touchdown – and even though the play didn't count because of a penalty, it didn't decrease Tomey's level of irritation. "I watched the replay since then many times, and to see Coach Tomey – the reaction to that happening and the words that came out of his mouth told you everything you needed to know about it," Boyd said.

But Marmie said the fake punt was absolutely not an attempt to run up the score and embarrass Arizona. "Here's the reason, and I talked to Coach Tomey even after it happened: They were a terrific punt-block unit. They were very good on special teams; they always were," he said. "My thinking was that, I know they're coming after this kick, and I'm going to take my chances with calling the fake where we may have a chance to get a first down and not let them have a touchdown. That was the whole thought about it in my mind. Plus, it was something we had worked on all year. We worked it every week. I guess (in the past) I didn't have enough guts to call it.

"I have a tremendous amount of respect for Dick Tomey as a person and as a coach, and I would hope that during my coaching career that I would never do anything that would be totally embarrassing to someone else."

Marmie said his decision was validated when the Sun Devils did decide to punt following the penalty. "You know what happened on the next play? They blocked the punt (and returned it) for a touchdown," he said.

"They put it on us"

Tomey gave the Devils kudos for their performance that night. "ASU played great. They deserved the win," he said. "At the end of a game like that, it just reminds you of how big a game that is, because there's no feeling like losing to your rival. In the case of that game, we were all very emotional about the loss. But they beat us handily, for sure."

Fina, whose '91 Duel was his last, said the Wildcats were as pumped for that game as they were for any that they played under Tomey; they were just beaten by a better team. "If you couldn't get excited and understand how important that game was by listening to Dick Tomey speak, as well as being surrounded by the fans and the school, you've got a problem. You didn't have a pulse. You didn't have a heart in your chest. You got angry when that game started coming up," he said.

"I didn't go to a lot of bowl games at UA, and I played in few pretty big games, but the closest I ever felt in college to a pro game or a Super Bowl, two of which I was in (with the Buffalo Bills) – the closest feeling you could get was the locker room before the UA-ASU game. Just that fever pitch, that excitement, that adrenaline flow – that's the closest I ever got in college. But my senior year, we weren't very healthy, and they put it on us."

According to Miniefield, falling short against the Wildcats for a 10th straight season simply wasn't an option.

"We were just going to do anything we needed to do to win the game and come out on top," he said. "I remember just playing at an emotionally high level."

Boyd, who experienced the rivalry for the first time that season and joined ASU's athletic department in 1995, understood the collective sigh of relief in Tempe when the game ended.

"Our fans rushed the field. You had thousands of fans on the field after the game," Boyd said. "I had a young lady that ran onto the field and kissed me smack on the lips. And I said, 'Wow, this is big.'

"All that was surreal. Being part of ASU since then, working at ASU – certainly in that Rose Bowl year (in 1996) there were games that were huge, and the atmosphere was remarkable. But that '91 game was as charged up as any of those were."

Marmie's moment

The '91 Duel was Marmie's last game as ASU's coach, but he went out in style, as his players carried him off the field that evening.

"Obviously, I was only a (head) coach in college for those four years, so that was a great win because of the situation that a lot of us were in," he said. "For the players that had never beaten them, and for the fans and everybody involved, I think it was something that everybody felt a part of. Everybody had been waiting for this to happen, or maybe some people were wondering *if* it was going to happen. It ranks very high on my list."

Wallerstedt regrets that he and his teammates didn't have more overall success during Marmie's tenure. "He's a great defensive coach, a great defensive mind, and I think it's a thing where, if we win a couple more bowl games here and there, he's the coach there for an extended period of time," he said. "You wanted to work hard for him because he was just passionate about the game. "He was just an honest guy, a guy who did things the right way, a guy who stressed academics and expected you to put forth 100 percent effort at all times. He treated the top players the same as the second-stringers. There was no favoritism going on, and he expected your best at all times."

Marmie appreciated the success that ASU enjoyed against UA under Frank Kush for two-plus decades, which is one of the reasons that the '91 victory is still special to him.

"When Coach Kush was there, the worst that happened (in the rivalry) was you win one, they win one. So, for those reasons, in my mind it was a big win," he said. "And for our players, just to see them and their reactions and their responses to that kind of win are things that stay with you for the rest of your life."

CHAPTER 6

Tomey Vs. Snyder

After the Sun Devils dismissed Larry Marmie, they brought in Bruce Snyder, whom they lured away from fellow Pac-10 school California.

ASU tailback Kevin Galbreath (1990-92) said he preferred Snyder and his run-first style to Marmie, who had the pass-oriented Mike Martz run the offense. "He went back to a running offense. I loved the fact that two backs would get 10-20 carries a game," he said.

Dan Cozzetto, whom Snyder brought with him from Cal to be his offensive coordinator at Arizona State, said Snyder left it up to his lieutenants to educate his players about the Duel. "He put it on the staff. He was the type of guy that he was going to treat the players a little bit differently than he was going to treat the coaches, and it was on us to get it done," he said.

"I heard all about (the rivalry) from Jeff van Raaphorst and all those guys, and from everybody involved in the game. Our biggest deal was we had established a philosophy with Bruce of one game at a time. But you've just got to understand that Bruce and Dick (Tomey), they went after each other in recruiting and everything."

Operation Desert Swarm

While ASU was undergoing yet another rebuilding job since the departure of Frank Kush 13 years earlier, UA was humming right along under Tomey, thanks in large part to a number of talented athletes on a defense that came to be known as Desert Swarm, a variation of Operation Desert Storm, the American military campaign that was launched against Saddam Hussein's Iraq less than two years earlier.

Arizona defensive tackle Jimmy Hoffman (1991-94) said the nickname came from something that Coach MacDuff would always tell his defense to do. "He'd always say, 'Swarm to the ball.' That was his thing," he said.

The Wildcats saw many of their defensive players from the early '90s eventually go pro, including linebacker Sean Harris, defensive back Mike Scurlock, safety Brandon Sanders, defensive back Tony Bouie, linebacker Brant Boyer, two-time All-American nose guard Rob Waldrop and, perhaps the most heralded Arizona football player in the last 25 years, defensive lineman Tedy Bruschi, a two-time All-American and eventual three-time Super Bowl champion as a linebacker with the New England Patriots.

"He was fun to play with, and I had Rob on the other side of me, so I lucked out," said Hoffman of playing alongside Bruschi and Waldrop. "My thing was I knew they were going to do their job, so if I don't do what I'm supposed to do, I'm going to stick out."

Scurlock (1991-94) said MacDuff always squeezed the maximum amount of effort and skill out of the talent he had. "He did an awesome job of getting everybody to perform at a high level, and that was one thing that was required for us, and it became habit," he said. "He wanted to see 11 guys around the football. He wanted to see you coming into the picture when he watched video."

26 Counter

In the 1992 Duel in the Desert, the script that had been written during The Streak was flipped. Arizona appeared to have the superior team – and for most of the game, it had the upper hand on the scoreboard.

The only points in the first three quarters of the game came from the foot of Wildcat kicker Steve McLaughlin, who booted a 48-yard field goal in the second quarter and a 47-yarder in the third to give UA a 6-0 lead going into the final period.

The 16th-ranked Wildcats and their Desert Swarm D had been so dominant throughout the game that the Sun Devils didn't even reach 100 yards of total offense until the fourth quarter. And with an injury-depleted backfield, the little-used Galbreath was called upon to carry the load.

But in this low-scoring contest, all it took was one play to turn it all around. On a first-and-10 from the ASU 49-yard line, Cozzetto called a play on which Sun Devil quarterback Grady Benton handed the football to Galbreath, who ran to the right side of the line. After a modest 5-yard gain, Galbreath looked like he was about to be brought down by a pair of UA defenders.

But Galbreath broke through the Desert Swarm's grip, then stormed down the right sideline for a 51-yard touchdown. The extra point gave ASU a 7-6 lead in front of an Arizona Stadium crowd that, until then, had seen its team dominate in every facet of the game.

The play that led to the touchdown was called 26 Counter. "I think we ran it about 14-16 times during the game," Cozzetto said, "and Kevin made a hell of a run. That's how we did it. We were just stubborn with the run."

Galbreath still enjoys talking about his defining moment as a Sun Devil. "It was a counter play that was open at first, and then I think the linebacker had me stopped," he said. "I kind of kept my feet going, and you know, I put my hand down. I was going down (to the ground), and I put my hand down to kind of pop myself up. And next thing I know, I'm going down the sidelines."

Galbreath said his run was an example of Rushing 101, which he had the opportunity to teach later in his life. "It's funny: I coached high school football for 7-8 years, and that's some of the techniques I taught my running backs. You always tell your guys to keep their feet going," he said. "Sometimes, the defense may think you're wrapped up, and you're not.

"During the play, I was just running. I didn't realize I was going to break tackles. You always want to."

Tomey coached in 14 games against the Devils, and he can still see the play that did his Cats in that night in Tucson. "I just remember that it was a counter play," he said. "He broke free and we took some bad (tackling) angles. They made all the blocks downfield, and Galbreath did a great job. So that was disappointing."

Boyer (1992-93) still isn't sure how his defense allowed it to happen. "We had done a good job of staying in all our gaps, and I don't remember exactly what happened," he said. "I wasn't fast enough to catch him. That was the turning-point play of the game, and it ended up costing us the game.

"We did a great job up to then, but that's obviously how football goes. We've got to play for 60 minutes, not 59 1/2, right?"

Just short

The Sun Devils maintained the momentum they'd gained from Galbreath's run for most of the fourth quarter, but UA managed to move the ball into ASU territory in the game's final minutes to set up a 57-yard field-goal attempt that would have matched the distance of Max Zendejas' kick in 1985.

And for a brief moment, McLaughlin (1991-94), who grew up in Tucson and enjoyed The Streak when he worked as a soda vendor at Arizona Stadium in the '80s, thought he had won the game.

"It was right on target, and I thought it was good," he said. "I was jumping on the field like it was good. It was right down the middle.

"And it just fell short. It landed, I don't know, just right in front of the goalposts."

Tomey said there was much discussion about whether to allow McLaughlin to attempt the kick in the first place. "That was an iffy situation, but we felt we had some wind with us and we had a shot," he said. "He had the leg."

Before and during the kick, Bray had a bad feeling that what goes around was finally coming around in the rivalry for the Wildcats. "I will tell you, when they went to kick that field goal, I got that shoe-is-on-the-other-foot feeling," he said. "We had beaten them so many times with field goals. It's just the way the ball bounces in that series, because I'll tell you, in my experience, I'd say less than half the time the better team wins.

"When they beat us in '92, we were head-and-shoulders better than them. We had one of the best defenses in the history of college football. We held them to seven points, and they got it on one play."

Cozzetto was proud that his Sun Devils, who finished 6-5 in Snyder's first season, proved that they could match the Wildcats' much-hyped Desert Swarm D. "Our defense held tight. We had guys like Shante Carver and Brett Wallerstedt, so they held their own," he said. "All we had to do was not screw it up on offense and capitalize.

"It was just like pounding a rock. As Bruce would say, you pound that rock until it cracks. It was a special game."

Tomey, whose Cats lost to Baylor, 20-15, in the Sun Bowl to finish the season 6-5-1, gave ASU credit. "We had multiple chances to score that we messed up," he said, "but they did a great job on defense, and it was a defensive struggle.

"We agonized over that one because we played such great team defense the whole game. But it was a good example for the players the rest of my coaching career, because (ASU) just made one play, and that was enough. It just helps you make the point to your players that you've just got to play every play and you can't let down, ever."

And McLaughlin wasn't too hard on himself for his late-game miss. "I mean, 57 (yards) would've tied the school record, so it wasn't like it was a 30-yarder or something," he said. "But it still would've been nice to have made that."

Plummer's mission: Return ASU to national prominence

Idaho has rarely been a top recruiting region for the Sun Devils. But Bruce Snyder must have considered himself fortunate that he happened to have assistants with ties to the state.

"I guess the ultimate reason why (I chose ASU) was he told me face to face that he felt I was the quarterback who could help them win the national title. I hadn't heard that one yet," said Sun Devil quarterback and Boise native Jake Plummer (1993-96) about one of his initial meetings with Snyder. "They were recruiting me pretty hard. They had some pretty strong Idaho ties with Cozzetto and (quarterbacks coach Bobby) Petrino and a bunch of those old coaches that were at the University of Idaho. So they had their eye on me, and once I was able to be contacted by phone, they were the first ones to call me, and that does make an impact when you're being recruited.

"My mom woke me up at 8 with a phone call from them, and Bruce put quite a bit on my shoulders there as a guy who could come in and do something like that. I felt that was worth going to try to do, and we almost did it."

Plummer realized that the Sun Devils were still in rebuilding mode, but he loved the challenge that Snyder laid in front of him: Turn ASU back into the college football powerhouse it was under Frank Kush in the 1970s and John Cooper in the mid-'80s.

"I could've gone to other colleges that had been in national title games or top-10 teams, but ASU was the team that I felt gave me the opportunity to go in and hopefully turn the program around somewhat," he said. "Instead of just being another cog in the wheel, I felt like I could go down there and try to change that place and get it back up to where it should be."

Jake and Brant: Friends off the field, rivals on it

In his first Duel in 1993, the most emotional aspect for Plummer was going against his childhood friend.

"I had a buddy who actually played for UA who I grew up with, Brant Boyer, who played linebacker for them," he said. "We were good buds growing up. He's older than me, but we spent some time in the summers hanging out and getting in trouble as best we could down in Boise.

"On the field, he wanted to kill me, of course. He got me a couple times, but nothing real bad. I was able to keep away from him most of the game, which was pretty good, because he wouldn't have held back at all, I'm sure."

Boyer said his family is still good friends with Plummer's. "I knew him since I was a little kid. We used to dive in golf-ball ponds together, clean them up and sell them for money when we were kids," he said. "He was a heck of an athlete, and I knew he'd get out and cause us some problems (on the field)."

One of Plummer's favorite moments from his first Duel was a rare and often frowned-upon act of sportsmanship with Boyer.

"I remember at halftime, as the teams were leaving the locker room, I ran over and gave him five," he said. "Rarely do you see an ASU player do that with a UA guy. But we set our rivalry aside since we were good friends from way back when we were just kids."

Cecil rallies the Cats

The night before the 1993 game in Tempe, Tomey invited back rivalry hero Chuck Cecil, who was playing for the then-Phoenix Cardinals, to talk to the team.

It was a speech that the '93 Wildcats will never forget.

"I'm getting goosebumps thinking about it right now," said UA safety Tom BoBo (1992-96). "I distinctly remember: We were at ASU before the game, and Chuck Cecil came back and he talked about what it was to be a Wildcat in the rivalry, and he threw down some education on the players who hadn't (played it in before).

"I can almost hear it. The intensity shooting out of his eyes got you so pumped up. That guy is such an intense guy."

UA quarterback Dan White (1993-95; no relation to ASU quarterback Danny White) was one of those players who was about to experience his first Duel that season. "(Cecil) came in and gave us a motivational speech," he said, "and you realize then how emotional and intense it is. That just shows you the intensity that you have to have going into that game, and it's going to be a real battle."

When he was asked whether he remembers what he told the team that night, Cecil laughed. "Yes, I do, but some things are better left unsaid," he said. "That was my first year there playing for the Cardinals, so I was in town, and (Tomey) asked me to come and talk to the guys. And I said, 'Heck yeah, I'd be more than happy to.'

"Believe me: Coach Tomey was very adamant about beating the Sun Devils, as well, and I think Coach Tomey understood how I felt about them and especially what I did my senior year when we played up (in Tempe). And I think that was one of the reasons he wanted me to come back and talk to the guys."

McLaughlin still remembers his favorite part of Cecil's address. "One of the best lines from that speech is, 'When you have them down, you want to reach in, grab their heart, as tiny as it is, and tear it out,'" he said. "The intensity that came out of Cecil was something I've never seen in my life, and it got the whole room going like crazy. It was great."

"The hardest I've ever been hit"

The Desert Swarm-led Wildcats opened the '93 season 7-0 before losing two of their next three – a 20-point road loss to UCLA followed by a 24-20 setback at home to Cal.

But a win over ASU would still get UA to a bowl game that it had never been to, one that the Sun Devils used to dominate: the Fiesta Bowl.

Plummer, who had become the starting QB midway through the season and led ASU to four straight victories before the '93

Duel, knew the Devils also had a chance to play one more game if they could upend the Cats at home. "It held greater importance, not only because it's the rivalry game that you want to win no matter what, but it was also a chance to go to a bowl game," he said.

Plummer said his initiation into the rivalry came in the form of Rob Waldrop. "I remember throwing a ball and his helmet hitting me right in my chest right at the top of my diaphragm there and just absolutely pummeling me," he said. "It was the hardest I've ever been hit, and it was like, 'Oh my God.' That defense was good."

But, like in the '92 game, ASU's D held its own in the first half, as each team scored just once, the Devils on a 1-yard run by Mario Bates and the Wildcats on a 1-yard plunge of their own from 1991 and '93 All-Pac-10 tailback Chuck Levy.

Sun Devil kicker Jon Baker hit a 20-yard field goal in the third quarter to give ASU its only lead of the game, 10-7. But then Arizona's offense woke up, as Dan White threw a touchdown pass on three consecutive possessions – one to wide receiver Richard Dice and two to wide receiver Troy Dickey – to give the Wildcats a commanding 27-10 fourth-quarter lead.

"I think one of his biggest strengths that got overlooked was that he was a tough S.O.B.," said Dice (1993-96) about White. "By no means was he Michael Vick, so he had to stay in the pocket, and if that meant taking a licking to complete a pass, that's what he did.

"For some reason, he was on point for every game against ASU that that guy played. He had a cannon for an arm, and he was tough, man. He took a lot of hits and he always got up, and that's one of the things about being an Arizona Wildcat – we prided ourselves on being tougher than the other team."

Boyer said the Wildcats had prepared all week to limit the rushing opportunities for his buddy, Plummer, who was more than capable of picking up yardage with his feet. "That was one of the main focuses of the week, that he'd get out and run, and we had to stop their running game to have success against them," he said.

And just like during The Streak, the bounces in 1993 went Arizona's way. Levy's fumble in the ASU end zone in the fourth quarter was scooped up by fellow UA tailback Lamar Lovett to give the Wildcats an insurance touchdown, and they would go on to win, 34-20.

"They just beat us. We couldn't control the line of scrimmage," Cozzetto said. "We couldn't block Bruschi, from what I recall."

Boyd still can't stomach the way that his senior season ended. "Losing to those guys in my last ASU game – I have a bitter taste in my mouth I'll never get rid of," he said. "It doesn't matter how many Sun Devil wins I'm around, I'll never get (past) that bitter taste."

Cats win again in Tempe

Thirty-six days later, the Wildcats returned to Sun Devil Stadium to take on Miami – a team they lost to, 8-7, a year earlier following a missed McLaughlin field goal. This time they pummeled the Hurricanes, 29-0, in the Fiesta Bowl to complete a 10-2 season and earn a final top-10 ranking in both national polls.

"I think we just made that our stadium. That's basically all we did. We just took it from them," said Dice of Arizona's back-to-back wins on ASU's field.

Dan White enjoyed seeing Wildcat fans invade Sun Devil Stadium for the Fiesta Bowl on New Year's Day 1994. "Playing up there for the ASU-UA game, it's obviously a majority of ASU fans, but I think to be up there in their stadium and having a majority of them being UA fans – that was fun to be in their home stadium and see it packed with red shirts and play as well as we did," he said.

It might have been UA's first marquee bowl win in its 100-plus-year history, but Dice said the win over the Devils was sweeter. "That was a very gratifying way to end a year, but it's always better to smack ASU around," he said. "The Miami game was great, but it just takes a little bit out of the season when you lose to your rival, and that's just the bottom line."

Boyer said the most amazing aspect of Arizona's '93 season was that most of those Wildcats – especially on defense – were not highly recruited. "They weren't the biggest, they weren't the fastest. Arizona didn't get all the recruits – the blue-chippers, so to speak – but you got a group of guys that came together as a whole team," he said. "(The Fiesta Bowl) was a hell of a win for that program, and it was a hell of a win for all of our guys in the locker room."

High expectations

The Wildcats had plenty of returning starters in 1994, and that, along with their 10-win season in '93, made them preseason national championship favorites in some circles; *Sports Illustrated* ranked Arizona No. 1 before the season began and featured members of the team on its cover.

But perhaps the pressure – or the so-called *Sports Illustrated* cover jinx – got to UA, as it took a step back from '93 by losing three times before the ASU game rolled around.

Hoffman said the hype surrounding the team might have caused some players to lose focus. "It was a screwed-up year for us emotionally," he said. "There was a lot of outside influence. Some of the top players there had agents and stuff who found a way to get to you. I was always trying to avoid that."

But Dice said the Cats were able to refocus in time for their showdown with the Devils in Tucson. "Everybody was still licking their chops for ASU, and we had a good team," he said.

Arizona State had struggles of its own that season, as it carried just a 3-7 record into Arizona Stadium. But, as is often the case, a rivalry win would be good for what ailed that struggling team.

"For us, that (game) was like the season," Plummer said. "And that's why it's the rivalry game – you could lose a lot of games and not have a great year, but you win that one and it changes your whole outlook for the whole offseason and heading into next year."

The '94 Duel was Plummer's first experience in Arizona Stadium's unfriendly confines. "That game, I just remember it was so loud," he said. "The fans were ferocious, and the players down there had nothing nice to say to you."

But for the first three quarters, the visitors weren't very nice to the 19th-ranked Wildcats in front of a national TV audience on ABC. With the Devils trailing 9-3 in the first quarter, a blocked punt that was returned 8 yards by safety Damien Richardson put ASU ahead for the first time, and a 54-yard pass from Plummer to wide receiver Keith Poole, followed by a Baker field goal, gave the Sun Devils a 20-9 advantage.

White grinds out a comeback

After a pair of McLaughlin field goals cut ASU's lead to 20-15 in the third, Plummer scored on his own with a 2-yard run, and Baker's PAT gave the Devils their largest advantage of the game, 27-15, going into the final quarter.

But Dan White, who injured his throwing shoulder in the first half, stayed in the game and grinded out one of the greatest comebacks in rivalry history.

UA tailback Gary Taylor scored from 6 yards out to cut the lead to 27-22 with 10 minutes to play. After the Desert Swarm defense forced ASU to punt, the Wildcats got the ball at their own 40-yard line, and White methodically marched the Cats down the field on a 13-play drive, eventually connecting with tight end Lamar Harris for the go-ahead score with four minutes remaining. A failed two-point conversion attempt made the score UA 28, ASU 27.

Just 6 inches

On ASU's final possession, Plummer led the Devils to midfield in hopes of getting them in range for a game-winning Baker field goal. ASU appeared to be done when Plummer threw an incomplete pass on fourth down, but the Cats were flagged for a 15-yard roughing-the-passer penalty, giving the Devils a first down and new life.

ASU was able to inch 7 yards closer as time ran down, setting up the barefooted Baker for a 47-yard try in front of 58,000 UA fans trying to get into his head.

"I was just walking around going, 'Come on, man, you've got to make this,' because we got down into field-goal range against a pretty good defense," Plummer said.

Poole (1993-96) was confident that the kick would be good. "I thought the game was over because Baker was a pretty money guy," he said.

When the moment came, the snap was good. The hold was good. But the kick sailed just 6 inches wide right.

"Baker was one of those different kickers. He was more of an athlete – a football kind of guy," Poole said. "He was one of those guys that worked his butt off in the weight room. And it was just – you sympathize with the guy.

"I still keep in touch with Baker. That's something that still haunts him. Every time I see him, it's the first thing I think of. I hate to say that, and it's one of those things that we can kind of joke about now, but it still hurts. It hurts him, it hurts us, and it stinks. It's one of those things. If he would've made it, he would've been the hero. But he missed it, and it just stinks that it was (against) UA."

Plummer said Baker is still a good friend of his, as well. "A kicker that kicks barefoot – how could you be mad at a guy like that? I mean, he's out there kicking with no shoe on," he said. "So immediately, I had tons of respect for him because of that. I felt bad for him after that, and it was tough to see a good guy like that miss a field goal to win the game."

ASU offensive tackle Juan Roque (1992-96) remembers how painfully close Baker's kick was to getting inside the right upright. "We're talking inches to the right. If it had been 6 inches to the left, we would've won that game," he said. "That was just a loss that really stung, because we knew we were as good as they were. We knew we could play with them. They had the Desert

Swarm – Bruschi and Jim Hoffman and a bunch of guys that I played with in the NFL. But we hung with them in that game, and it was just heartbreaking."

Beyond the missed field-goal attempt, Roque said the Devils were left to wonder how they let a double-digit lead slip away in the final minutes. "We were just bewildered. How the heck did this happen to us? How did we allow this to happen when we had the game won?" he said. "We were the better team; it wasn't supposed to end this way."

McLaughlin, a '94 All-American who played in his final Duel that year, was asked if he felt bad for his Sun Devil counterpart. "It's hard to feel bad for the other kicker when it's ASU," he said with a laugh. "Baker went on and played for the Cowboys and then jumped around. He was a good kicker, but I remember just hanging on like crazy and hoping we can get the win, and luckily, we did."

Arizona finished 8-4 in '94 after losing to Utah, 16-13, in the Freedom Bowl. But Tomey remembers the narrow rivalry win better than the narrow bowl loss. "It was very emotional, and people's hearts are in their throats on the sidelines," he said. "That's what makes a rivalry like that so wonderful to play in, because it was so emotional."

Roll of the Dice

ASU's 1995 season shared similarities with its '93 campaign: a difficult beginning – including a 77-28 loss at Nebraska en route to a 2-4 record – and then four straight victories as it moved toward its showdown with UA.

And for the first time in years, playing at home against a Wildcat team that was just 5-5, the Devils were the favorites.

For Arizona, the game was as emotionally charged as ever – especially for Dice, who suffered a torn ACL early in the season.

But Bray, who had returned to UA as an assistant coach, said Dice would not be denied the opportunity to compete in the Duel. "I remember when he walked into the staff room. He comes in and says, 'By the way, guys, I'm playing this week.' And he shuts the door and walks out," he said. "And we start laughing. But then Coach Tomey says, 'I wonder if he's serious.'"

Dice hadn't had surgery on his knee to that point, so Bray and Tomey figured Dice's risk of further injury was minimal. "It was his call," Bray said.

Dice said he delayed surgery at the advice of the training staff, which wanted to see whether he could build up muscle in his leg and shorten the recovery process. "Once the week of the ASU game came – there's so much buildup and the stories, and my knee was starting to feel not great but OK. And the light bulb went off in my head: I might be able to play in this game," he said.

"So I went in and dropped the seed in a couple coaches' heads and in the training staff's heads and the doctors' heads. And you know, they were like, 'No, it's just not a good idea.'"

Dice finally persuaded the coaching staff to at least let him suit up for the game. "I think the consensus from the coaches was, 'Yeah, he's cleared, but we're not going to use him,'" he said.

But Dice had made it that far, and he wasn't going to be denied the field against UA's archrival. "I'll never forget: I was in Coach Akina's ear (during the game) saying, 'Let me get in there,'" he said. "I don't think they wanted to tell me that I wasn't going to play; they kept saying, 'Well, we'll just see.'"

But when the Sun Devils took an early 17-7 lead, the Wildcat coaches became a bit more receptive to Dice's pleas. "They kept asking me how I feel, and I said, 'I feel great,' even though my knee was flopping around," he said. "Finally, they put me in on a couple plays. I'll never forget my first play was a run play away from me. I went and lined up, and I tried to explode off the ball - and I just heard a bunch of popping in my knee.

"And I just thought, 'Oh my God, this is no good.' But adrenaline is a pretty powerful thing. Plus, if your mind's set on it, you can work your way through almost anything."

Most athletes would be amazed to see a teammate try to give it a go with a torn ACL. But Dan White wasn't stunned that Dice made his way onto the field. "Knowing Dice, he was a super tough guy, and it was tough to keep him out of any game, let alone that game," he said.

Dice didn't stay in the game for long, but Bray said the impact he made on the game – on the scoreboard and in the momentum category – was invaluable. "He goes in and plays, and I mean, it was the best," he said. "The first catch he made for a first down, and he points to his knee and flips off the crowd. And I'm up in the (coaches') box, and I can't contain myself. I loved every second of it.

"I'm not a guy that would ever promote showboating, but when it comes to those guys, F 'em. I'm telling you right now: All the rules go out the window."

Dice went on to make a 7-yard touchdown catch from White to cut ASU's lead to 17-14 in the second quarter, and he managed to stay in for part of the second half until he made his final catch of the game.

"I just kept begging them to throw it deep to me – at least let me go up and make a play," he said. "I know there was something that I saw (in ASU's defense) that I felt like I could make a play.

"We called a fade (pattern), and I remember looking at Dan, and I was just like, 'Throw it up, let me see if I can go get it.' And that's what happened. He threw it up, I was covered, and I'll never forget: I locked in on the ball, and when I jumped up, everything was popping like the Fourth of July.

"And I caught it and I landed, and I was in so much pain. I knew I came down with the ball, but I didn't know if I came in or out of bounds. I remember I was over there by the ASU cheerleaders, and they were talking so much junk. And once I saw the referee say that it was a catch, I had a few nice words for them. But I couldn't get up right away because my knee was hurting."

That's when Dice decided to let one of the 67,000-plus fans at Sun Devil Stadium know that he was No. 1. "Being a 20-year-old kid with your emotions out of control, I'm walking across the field and looking up into the stands, and I couldn't hear anything, but I was staring at one guy with that brutal orange or whatever color you want to call those colors," he said. "And he looked at me and flipped me off. And I don't know what I was thinking, man, but I returned the favor to him.

"Looking back on it, I can kind of chuckle. It wasn't that bright of a moment in my life. But sometimes, logic gets thrown out in rivalries like that. And they were trying to go to a bowl game, so we figured we'd help them out and beat them, so that way, they couldn't go."

Plummer didn't take offense to the antics, but some of his teammates were exasperated at what Dice was able to accomplish with just one good knee. "It happens. He was feeling it," he said. "I mean, he had one leg, it looked like he can barely run, and we couldn't stop him."

Remember the UA player who told Plummer "I hate your guts" before a game? Yep; it was Richard Dice. "I remember our offensive guys were steaming, like, 'What the hell? Why can't you stop this guy? He's got one leg!' It's just one of those things," Plummer said.

Déjà red and blue

To the Devils' credit, they were able to navigate through the emotion that Dice injected into the game. In the fourth quarter, ASU kicker Robert Nycz hit a 46-yard field goal, and fullback Ryan Wood's 1-yard TD run along with a subsequent two-point conversion from Plummer to tight end Steve Bush gave Arizona State a 28-14 advantage with less than eight minutes to go.

But Dan White and his offense remained confident by remembering UA's late-game comeback in the Duel a year earlier. "We had success in the past in those situations, and we knew what had to be done," he said. "And I think that stays in the back of your mind in a positive manner: We did it before and we can do it again."

Plummer recalled a taboo statement that a former Devil made to him after ASU went up by 14 points. "An ex-player that played on the first Rose Bowl team in '87, he came up to me on the sidelines and said, 'Remember this feeling, Jake. It's the best feeling you'll ever feel,'" he said. "And I was sitting there, and I looked up at the clock and I'm like, 'Oh, (expletive).' And I told everyone to get away from me and started yelling, 'This game's not over! Everyone thinks it is, but this game's not over!'"

Plummer was correct. White led an 11-play drive that took just 1:24 off the clock and concluded with a touchdown pass to wide receiver Cary Taylor to cut ASU's lead in half.

On the Devils' next possession, Plummer went back to pass on third-and-10 deep in ASU territory, but before he could throw, he was hit by defensive tackle Chuck Osborne, and the ball came loose. UA defensive tackle Joe Salave'a recovered and needed to advance the ball just 8 yards for a game-tying touchdown. All of a sudden, it was a brand-new ballgame.

At that point, Roque said the Devils were wondering what else could possibly go wrong. "Any cliché you want to throw in there – whatever could have gone wrong for us in that game went wrong," he said. "We had some breakdowns in the offensive line. I had some breakdowns myself."

Poole said he and his teammates didn't know what hit them. "You know what? It's almost surreal. You're like, 'No, this is not really happening,'" he said. "It's kind of funny because, in rivalry games, stuff like that happens, and it's not supposed to happen, and you freak out and think, 'I can't believe that just happened.' You're thinking, 'Oh my gosh, not again.'

"I think we still had confidence that we could win it, and I think we almost did, but it's still one of those things that, gosh, how did we blow the lead, you know? Everything was going so smooth, and then all of a sudden (it's tied), and it's shocking sometimes. I don't think fans understand it. It was tough."

Prasuhn's precision completes comeback

Unlike the 1994 game, the fate of the '95 Duel rested on the foot of a Wildcat.

After ASU's demoralized offense lost 9 yards on three plays on its next possession, UA got the ball back near midfield. The Wildcats moved down to the Devils' 19-yard line to set up a game-winning 36-yard field-goal attempt for first-year starter and Tucson native Jon Prasuhn (1993-95).

"Growing up in Tucson and pretty much hating ASU, just going into that game – it had a different aura about it," he said. "The way that whole game led up to it, at some point in the fourth quarter I knew it was going to come down to a game-winning field goal, so I started to mentally prepare myself before it came to that point. I just kind of removed myself from everyone else and decided to calm myself down and relax pretty much the whole fourth quarter.

"Thinking back to it and right before I went onto the field, it was almost like an out-of-body experience, because I had really spent that entire last half of the fourth quarter mentally preparing myself and calming myself. I was relaxed. I was so focused beyond anything I'd ever felt in my life. I could feel the pressure, but it was like it was there but it wasn't there, because I was so focused on what I had to do."

When the moment finally came and the ball was snapped, Prasuhn made sure to go through the same motions he always went through on any field-goal try. "I remember trying not to do anything different. I kept my leg down," he said. "I knew it was good before I looked up because our holder had his arms in the air. And then I saw it go through."

One of Prasuhn's most vivid memories is the sound – or lack thereof – inside Sun Devil Stadium immediately after his kick. "The distinct memory I had was the noise going from I don't know how many decibels it was to dead silence," he said. "Our guys were jumping up and down, and Bryan Hand, one of our offensive linemen at the time, immediately grabbed me and picked me up in the air."

The kick put Arizona ahead, 31-28, with 22 seconds left – not enough time for Plummer to mount one of his comebacks for which he would eventually become known.

Bruschi recorded 2.5 sacks of Plummer in the game, which earned him a share of the career NCAA sacks record with 52.

Tomey was impressed with the resilience of his players during that game and throughout the season, especially after of one of their teammates, tight end Damon Terrell, collapsed and died during a team workout at the beginning of the season.

"That was a very, very difficult time for our team," he said. "That seemed like, to me, the greatest comeback of all the ASU wins because that team had experienced that traumatic death of one of our beloved guys and recovered from it, and they were able to win that game. And that was really gratifying."

And despite his completely useless knee, Dice was on top of the world. "I remember that night driving back home from Phoenix, and I was in so much pain, but there wasn't one sliver of doubt in my mind that I didn't do the right thing at the time," he said. "It was so gratifying just sending all those guys out on top. It was an awesome feeling."

After his game-winner, Prasuhn stayed in the Phoenix area and visited a couple bars with Wildcat punter Matt Peyton to celebrate, and he recalled an amusing encounter he had during one of their stops.

"I was in the restroom, and there were a couple ASU (fans) who were at the game talking about, 'Ah, man, I can't believe that game. I can't believe that kicker made that kick,'" he said.

Prasuhn couldn't help but have a little fun with the gentlemen. "Being a pain in the ass, I chimed in and said, 'Oh yeah, I can't believe it, that sucks,' and totally messing with them," he said. "Little did they know they were talking to the guy who made the field goal."

Loss sets stage for Rose Bowl run

The win was Arizona's third straight over ASU after the Devils had finally broken through with back-to-back victories in 1991 and '92.

"The thing about it is it makes me sick, because I think all three of those years, we should've won," Poole said. "I really do think we were the better team, and we played better. But if you think about it, it just makes you sick. One play here, one play there and we had that game."

Roque said the Devils – especially the 1993 freshman class that included himself, Poole, and Plummer – simply hadn't learned to put teams away. "When you look back on it, we did not know how to win yet. We were not there," he said. "Call it complacency, maybe, but it got us and it cost us the game, me included. That was a team effort, and it was a team loss."

Plummer said the '95 loss to UA stung more than almost any other in his collegiate career. "That year, we made a big shift in just players taking over a little bit more and becoming more responsible, and taking pride every day in what you do as a team and looking out for each other," he said. "So that was a really, really hard one that year because we would've gone to a bowl game if we won, and it was at home. And that dude with one leg beat us."

But as miserable a feeling that ASU's players were left with after the Devils' second-straight fourth-quarter collapse against their rivals, it might have been one of the best things that could've happened to the program.

In fact, Roque said the '95 loss "set the tone" for the hard work that the players put in during the months before the 1996 season began. "Believe me: It was a heartbreaking, gut-wrenching, your-soul-ripped-out-of-your-chest type of loss," he said. "And we said there's no way in heck that we're ever going to lose that kind of game again."

Rather than going home at the end of the '95 season, the Devils stuck around campus and spent extra time practicing and building relationships with one another. "A lot of players would usually take trips home during the summertime, and fortunately, we didn't do that," said ASU tailback Terry Battle (1994-96). "We decided we'd stay and really put the work in and leave no doors unturned."

Plummer said the pain he saw in the eyes of his roommate, Ryan Wood, whose final collegiate game was the '95 loss to the Wildcats, was a wakeup call going into his senior season. "And it kind of hit me: Wow, this is going to be it, man. I've got one more year here," he said. "All of us together after that loss, we made the step to working harder and working smarter, and being together and calling each other out instead of the coaches dragging us along and holding our hands.

"To have (the loss to UA) happen at home with what was on the table, it really hurt a lot of guys, and I know that offseason was huge. We definitely banded together and spent a lot of time with coaches, but we also spent a ton of time together working out on the field, working out in the weight room, having barbecues, spending time on the weekends in swimming pools and having parties, and we just banded together as a team. And that was what really made the difference, I think."

Also during that offseason, Snyder, Cozzetto and defensive coordinator Phil Snow came up with a new team motto.

"That's when the ABC's came into play: Always Beat Cats," Cozzetto said. "Whatever they did, I just put that in their brain. Every periodical that went out – everything that went out had that."

Cozzetto even had shirts made for the team that included the ABC motto. "Our backs were up against the wall going into our program's fourth year, and (the feeling was) you'd better get it done or you're going to be out of here," he said.

Roque said the '95 loss and the Devils' offseason work that followed represented a defining moment in Snyder's tenure. "It was then that we said, 'Never again. We're not going to lose again,'" he said.

And they didn't – at least not during the 1996 regular season, and certainly not against the Wildcats.

Undefeated Devils not welcomed in Tucson

There are plenty of ASU squads that would like to claim the mantle of being the best in program history. The '96 team stated one heck of a case by starting the season 10-0, with the most noteworthy wins being a remarkable 19-0 shutout of then-No. 1 Nebraska in Tempe and a double-overtime victory over USC.

But even with a top-five national ranking and a guaranteed Rose Bowl berth, there was no chance that the Devils would be looking past the 5-5 Wildcats – certainly not after what happened in their previous three meetings, and not with the knowledge of what happened to the ASU squad that went to the Rose Bowl 10 years earlier.

"We knew the history. We knew what happened to the '86 team," Roque said. "And to honor them as well as honor Coach Snyder and ourselves, we were not going to let that happen again."

Poole was also aware of what happened to the undefeated 1986 squad en route to the Rose Bowl. "And that's one of those things that made us so nervous going there," he said. "Some things are out of your control, and sometimes it's just their day. It happened in '86, and 10 years later, we're thinking, 'We can't let this happen again.'"

ASU offensive tackle Glen Gable (1994-97) said the bar for the 1996 Duel's intensity was set as soon as the Devils arrived at Arizona Stadium. "They have dorms in their stadium built right into it, and where we exit the bus is right in front of the windows of those dorms," he said. "And somebody had hung some nasty sign about Jake Plummer's mother and stuck it up so we could see it as we got off the bus. So that's how it started. It kind of set the tone."

ASU offensive guard Grey Ruegamer (1995-98) said the setting inside the stadium during the game was pretty much the same as it was outside. "I'm sitting on the far end of the bench, and the crowd's cheering and whatever else," he said, "and there's this old lady that said, 'Hey, 61 (Ruegamer's number), you suck!' And she's just riding my ass."

After Ruegamer decided to send a little trash talk back in her direction, he thought that was the end of it. "But during the game, they hand out these snack-sized power bars to the crowd, and at some point, I get hit in the back with a power bar," he said. "I turn around and (the old lady) is waving her finger at me."

Ruegamer could have let the incident go. But that wouldn't have been fun. "I took a bite out of the bar and I threw it back at her," he said. "The guy in the next section wanted to string me up. That was my first experience in the rivalry."

Poole remembers the lousy treatment that his people received in Tucson during the game. "All my family and friends wore a Keith Poole jersey, and I know they got stuff thrown at them and some pretty bad things said to them," he said. "It's just kind of stupid to me.

"It's kind of stupid if people are worried about coming to Tucson or Tempe because they're worried about (obnoxious fans). And it's not everybody. That's what makes it sad: It's a few people who act drunk and get stupid – probably just a couple students. But it was a nasty game, too."

For the record number of fans at Arizona Stadium who witnessed it, the word "nasty" didn't do the 1996 Duel in the Desert justice.

The Great Tucson Massacre of '96

To the delight and relief of ASU fans, 1996 was no 1986. The Sun Devils dominated the line of scrimmage that night, especially on the ground, as their rushing yards (450) nearly tripled the Wildcats' total offensive yards (170). Battle ran for three touchdowns in the first half, with his third and final score giving ASU a 28-7 lead at halftime.

"I wouldn't say that we expected to manhandle them. But I know the expectations and the bar we had set for ourselves at that point in the season were that we would not go down there and give the game away," Battle said.

Plummer didn't need to throw much in the '96 Duel – he attempted only 19 passes, completing 10 of them – but three of his completions went for touchdowns, including two to Poole, who had 123 receiving yards on just four catches.

One of the rivalry's most famous moments is Poole celebrating one of his TDs with his arms in the air next to UA cornerback and future NFL Pro Bowler Chris McAlister. The moment was captured in a photo that Poole now features on the website for the Phoenix-area gym that he runs.

"For all of us seniors – and it was my senior year, also – we had gone through it and got beaten by stupid situations (in the Duel)," Poole said. "It was our senior year, and it was super important for us."

The Devils didn't dial it back in the second half. Plummer threw two of his three TD passes in the third quarter – one to Poole and another to Bush – to give Arizona State a 42-7 lead.

"We had a real good connection: Plummer to Poole," Plummer said. "It was pretty awesome because (we were) a couple smaller guys that weren't your typical quarterback-receiver duo – kind of skinny and scrappy – and we went into the Pac-10 for many years there and put up some big numbers. I was really lucky to have him while I was playing there."

Needless to say, there would be no late-game UA magic this time.

"I was surprised. I thought the game would be a lot closer," said Wildcat quarterback Keith Smith (1996-99), who scored Arizona's only offensive TD of the game with a 1-yard run in the second quarter. "That was my first time playing in that game. They were pretty much junior- and senior-loaded, and we were a lot younger. Obviously, there are no excuses there, but they had a good team, bottom line.

"It was an experience. I remember waking up the next day and I couldn't move. I was sacked so much, I had scrapes on my legs, and my arms were so bloody. It prepped me for later down the road and made me realize that I would be a better player."

Tomey said the Plummer-led ASU offense simply shredded the UA defense. "All that emotion, all the frustration that Jake had felt all the years – he was a tremendous player," he said. "I got to know him a little bit. He's just a wonderful guy and a tremendous competitor.

"They hammered us. We hoped (we would beat them), but they had a great football team. We felt we could, sure. The overall feeling was that we could find a way. But we didn't. They were a great team."

The Gable-Greer incident

Until 1996, most of the real nastiness in the Duel in the Desert's history had come from the stands in the form of fans taunting players and each other. That all changed in the fourth quarter of the '96 blowout in Tucson.

With a 35-point fourth-quarter lead, ASU was a few yards away from scoring again when Plummer's pass was intercepted by UA safety Mikal Smith, who ran it back 98 yards the other way for a touchdown.

But no one was paying attention to Smith's return, because at least 30 yards behind the play, Gable clipped Wildcat linebacker Daniel Greer from behind, causing severe damage to Greer's knee.

"Obviously, when a quarterback throws an interception, the quarterback is now a defensive player and free game – not protected like he is on offense," Gable said. "I remember seeing Jake get hit by somebody – I don't remember who – and on a split-second decision, I decided I was going to hit one of their guys.

"Looking back, it was a stupid thing to do, and especially I regret him getting hurt; that wasn't my intention. But split-second decisions on the field – you know, you see your quarterback get hit – that's the way we played that year. Nobody was going to hit our guy, and we were protecting each other. Those things factored in half a second before I made that hit."

The way the game had progressed, Roque said it was only a matter of time before something like that occurred. "We weren't being the classiest of guys. We were hitting them late," he said. "In defense of Glen, it was in the heat of the moment. I don't believe he was meaning to injure the guy. But it's the rivalry, and that's how much we hated those guys."

ASU offensive guard Kyle Murphy (1994-97), who was Gable's roommate at the time, agreed that something had to give in that game. "There were already people thrown out, there was a lot of trash talking going on, and quite honestly, I think it was inevitable," he said. "Glen should've never hit Greer. But if it wasn't that, it probably would've been something else that ignited something."

Gable was immediately penalized and thrown out of the game for the hit on Greer. "So I started jogging off the field. This happened right in front of UA's bench, so it was right on their sidelines," he said. "And one of their players came off the bench and hit me in the back as I was about halfway across the field. I never saw him coming.

"But I remember I got knocked onto the ground on my stomach, and I look up at my bench, and our whole bench was starting to run onto the field."

The hit on Greer, followed by the retaliatory hit on Gable, triggered an on-field melee that included a number of Wildcats and Sun Devils coming off the bench to mix it up.

This, of course, was the last thing ASU needed in a lopsided game with the Rose Bowl up next. "I remember the coaches screaming, 'No!' because if you fight, you're suspended for the next game, and the next game was the Rose Bowl," Gable said. "So I think cooler heads prevailed pretty quickly there, and it didn't progress, thankfully.

"I remember my parents were in the stands for that game. My mom and brother were wearing my jersey. They sent a sheriff's officer up to have my parents and brother take off my jersey, and they also escorted them the remainder of the game. It was a pretty hairy situation down there."

It took several minutes, but police and security intervened and finally defused the situation, and a number of additional players were ejected from the game.

Some Wildcat fans weren't soon to forgive and forget the incident. "I had UA people calling my house, threatening me and all kinds of stuff," Gable said. "I actually wrote an apology letter to Daniel and Coach Tomey. I was prompted by Coach Snyder (to write it), but I had no problem with it at all. I felt bad. I didn't want to hurt the guy."

ASU center Kirk Robertson (1992-96) said the hit was uncharacteristic of Gable and was blown a bit out of proportion. "I know Glen personally. He's a good friend of mine and a standup guy," he said. "The guy got hurt on it, and I've had my share of football injuries as well, and it's part of the game.

"That was the style of our play. We weren't going to get backed down. Was it a bad judgment call in the heat of the moment? Was the ball out of the way? Possibly. I don't know. As a referee now, I would've liked to have seen it, because a lot of times, those are legit calls. But I think, you know, you let bygones be bygones."

Playing in his first Duel, ASU defensive lineman and future Pittsburgh Steeler Jeremy Staat (1996-97) said the incident was a wakeup call for him. "I didn't realize the depth of the hatred between the two teams until both benches were clearing out and they had to get the police officers between us," he said.

Cozzetto said Gable was in the game at that point in the fourth quarter only because one of his starting offensive linemen, Pat Thompson, had already been ejected. "Out of respect, I kept (Gable) out of the Rose Bowl," he said. "Somewhere along the line, you've got to draw the line. It ended how it ended, but in the long run, there's a way to play the game, and (it should be) played by treating each other with respect."

When the game finally resumed, the Devils added a pair of short rushing TDs from running back Marlon Farlow to earn a 56-14 win – the most lopsided defeat for any Wildcat team on its home turf in 38 years.

And the already-exasperated UA fans voiced their displeasure in the form of projectiles from the stands.

"I can remember looking back in the stands and seeing Jack Daniel's bottles being thrown onto the field during that little melee," Plummer said. "And it was like, 'Oh, my God, let's get out of here, man. We took out all our aggression for the last few years – those frustrations and those tough losses – we took them all out on them today. Let's get in the bus and get home and get ready for the Rose Bowl.'"

Not to be outdone, the ASU fans who made the trip to the Old Pueblo decided to cause some trouble of their own.

"All my buddies from Tempe came down to that game, and I remember them all storming the field – and that's a terrible thing on your own field – and then they tried to take down the goalposts," BoBo said.

"And then, after that game, I remember we had a party at our house, and everybody from Tempe came down, and they had a bonfire in the backyard. And I just remember my friends – ASU fans – burned the score - ASU 56, UA 14 - on the side of the house.

"And I never forgot that. I didn't like that feeling, man, I'll tell you what."

Tomey had words for Snyder during their midfield meeting at the end of the game, but he said the Gable hit and ensuing on-field chaos prompted him and Snyder to come together and ask players and fans to tone down the rhetoric going forward.

"I think that play, to me, was the impetus for Bruce and I saying to our guys, 'We can't do this,'" he said. "We had to make this more civil with more mutual respect, because that play was unnecessary. It took a guy's knee out."

"My favorite all-time game"

The Devils took their undefeated record and No. 2 national ranking to Pasadena, where they came up just short of a Rose Bowl victory - and possibly a national championship - in a last-minute 20-17 nail-biter against John Cooper-led Ohio State.

But ASU's '96 seniors have nothing but fond memories of their remarkable run – especially the demolition of their rivals that they had waited four seasons to experience.

"That has to be my favorite all-time game, period, I ever played in my life," said Poole, who went on to have a five-year NFL career with the New Orleans Saints and Denver Broncos. "Even in the NFL and high school, that was the most fun I had, and it was the most rewarding.

"I think it didn't matter if it was our only win that year or if we were undefeated – we had to beat them. We couldn't go our four-year career and not beat UA. And to have it happen our senior year made it sweeter, too, because you go out with a bang. That one game made up for the three other games."

Roque dedicated the '96 win over Arizona to the ASU team that had its undefeated dreams dashed in the Duel in Tucson a decade earlier. "That win against UA was just as much for them as it was for us, because it was heartbreaking for them to lose that game the way they did," he said. "That was in the back of our minds when we looked up at the scoreboard in the fourth quarter. We thought, 'This is for the '86 team, as well. This is dedicated to them.'"

Plummer said the undefeated regular-season run, including the 42-point win over the Wildcats, was the Devils' reward for all the hard work they put in before and during the season. "It felt good to at least get one victory against those guys," he said. "My senior year kind of capped off my career there, but the three years prior – really, when you look at them, we didn't go to bowl games, we barely had a winning season, and we lost all three to UA. So we all felt that final year, the class that was together – that was a culmination of frustration coming out that whole year, really. We made it count.

"I didn't care one bit about those dudes down there, the Wildcats. I didn't care one bit about them. I didn't care who we were playing that day. We were a far superior team, we were going to kick whoever's ass was in front of us, and it just so happened to be our rival."

Plummer, who was the 1996 Pac-10 Offensive Player of the Year and played 10 years in the NFL, said the '96 season encapsulated one of the best times of his life. "Just the feeling of being with your buddies, guys you lived with, went to class with, hung out and partied with – and here we are through the years fighting and coming together for that last year to do something pretty special," he said.

"All in all, getting recruited by them, the reason I went there was to do something like that. That's still one of the seasons that's still a benchmark for that program, and it feels good to be a part of that, along with a lot of great football players that came and went during that time. So, looking back, having other colleges I was looking at and wondering whether I should've gone here or there – I mean, geez, I got to play for a national title, I got to play in a great stadium with a lot of great fans and great weather. And all in all, that year was just a lot of fun, man. A lot of fun."

Life without Jake in Tempe; a two-QB system in Tucson

The Devils lost quite a few talented players to graduation before the 1997 season, especially on offense, but they stayed in contention in the conference, thanks in part to the performance of freshman quarterback Ryan Kealy, a graduate of St. Mary's High School in Phoenix.

"Here's a guy who, his freshman year, came out as a (*Sporting News*) Freshman All-American and beat Miami at Miami," said ASU quarterbacks coach John Pettas of Kealy, who led ASU to an 8-2 record and five straight victories before the Devils' tilt with the Wildcats at Sun Devil Stadium.

UA was 5-5 in '97 and had a platoon situation at quarterback, as Keith Smith was splitting time under center with freshman Ortege Jenkins.

"Sharing quarterback time, it's tough," Smith said. "It's a commitment because, playing quarterback, you need to get into a rhythm. Whoever was the hotter guy would probably start the second half and finish the game."

Smith and Jenkins both saw playing time in the '97 Duel, and both prospered.

Didn't get the memo

Tomey and Snyder continued to ask fans to be cordial with one another before and during the '97 game. But some ASU fans chose to ignore that plea.

"Me and (a friend) go to the game, and we're talking on the sidelines pregame," Bray said. "And I swear to God, a full unopened can of Coke comes flying between us and sticks in the ground in front of us.

"And I look up, and there's a guy 15 rows up pointing at himself and saying, 'I threw it! I threw it!' And we go nuts. I go to the back of the bench screaming at him. The only problem was there were about 1,500 people there who all thought I was yelling at them.

"I'd say pandemonium ensued at that point. Stuff came flying out of the stands. It was crazy."

'80s flashback

It was a game that was reminiscent of those during The Streak: UA went into Tempe with a far worse record than ASU yet proceeded to upend its archrival.

"I thought we had a pretty good offensive package, and we did a couple trick plays with O.J. and myself that kind of ignited the offense," Smith said.

Jenkins would often line up as a receiver while Smith was under center, such as when Smith threw a TD pass to running back and tight end Paul Shields to give the Wildcats a 14-0 first-quarter lead.

The Jenkins-Smith package produced throughout the first half, as Jenkins' 40-yard touchdown strike to future NFL wide receiver Dennis Northcutt gave UA a stunning 21-0 lead midway through the second quarter.

To make matters worse for ASU, Kealy left the game in the second quarter with a right knee sprain and didn't return. Junior QB Steve Campbell took his place for the rest of the game – and while he threw a touchdown to wide receiver Ricky Boyer to trim UA's lead to 21-7, Cozzetto said he just wasn't Kealy.

"Steve hadn't played a lot. That changed the whole dimension of the game. We didn't prepare right away for Kealy to go down," he said. "So, advantage them."

Big-time advantage, according to Pettas. "Steve wasn't quite as efficient a thrower as Ryan, and I think that really hurt us," he said. "I think that threw us off offensively to where we couldn't execute the complete game plan we practiced for. That kind of put us in defensive mode."

False stop

Remember those bizarre plays that benefitted the Cats and befuddled the Devils during The Streak? Just for old time's sake, UA threw in one of those late in the second quarter of the '97 Duel.

With Jenkins under center, ASU safety Mitchell Freedman jumped off the line of scrimmage and into the UA backfield before the ball was snapped. Several officials threw flags to signal an offsides penalty, and the Sun Devil defense assumed the play had been blown dead.

But no whistle had blown, and with most ASU players standing still, the play continued. Jenkins took advantage by taking the snap and connecting with uncovered wide receiver Brad Brennan for a 29-yard touchdown.

"That's the play that most people remember from that game," said UA walk-on and 1998 special-teams captain Barrett Baker (1997-98). "ASU jumped offsides and they didn't blow the whistle, and Brad kept running. That was a big one. It was wild."

ASU wide receiver Creig Spann (1996-98) said the play was indicative of the Devils' overall experience during the '97 Duel: No one was sure what just hit them.

"I remember just getting ready for the game, and the whole thought process is that if we can win this game, we could possibly go to the Fiesta Bowl or another big-time bowl game," he said. "But I remember it was just kind of a weird-feeling game. It was kind of tragic how we ended up losing like that."

The Wildcats played conservatively in the second half and didn't score again, but they didn't need to, winning comfortably, 28-16.

Tomey gave a lot of credit to his late offensive coordinator, Homer Smith, for the win. "He did a fabulous job orchestrating that offensive approach to that game," he said. "We scored on a play where we had two quarterbacks in the game at the same time. It was just a tidal wave there in the first half.

"We were glad to win, and that was an incredible game because ASU had a really good team, and I thought the fact that we were able to jump on them at their place was huge."

Just like the Devils' 1996 squad had used previous losses to the Wildcats as a motivational tool, Smith said UA's '97 team pointed to the massacre in Tucson a year earlier as a rallying cry before the season began.

"A lot of those guys on our team that year had played in that game, and we had known what it felt like to lose to them bad, and I think that was motivation for us the next year," he said. "I think that fueled us in the offseason, and we all realized as a group that there's definite room to get better, and when it came to that moment in '97 against them, we were ready to go."

Both teams won bowl games that season - ASU with a 17-7 win over Iowa in the Sun Bowl and UA with a 20-14 victory over New Mexico in the Insight.com Bowl – but the loss to the Wildcats prevented the Devils from enjoying back-to-back 10-win seasons.

"They played better than us in '97. They just kicked our butt," Murphy said. "I'd say they were hungrier. They wanted it so badly because of what happened the previous year. We wanted to win, we practiced hard, and we had a good game plan. But I just think they wanted it so bad, and they weren't going to let anything deter them."

Staat did his part in '97, but it didn't matter to him without the win. "To be honest, you kind of scratch your head. It was kind of a humdinger," he said. "I remember when I got drafted, a couple of scouts said I had a great game – 14 tackles, three sacks, blah, blah, blah – and they asked, 'How do you feel about that game?' And I said, 'It really doesn't matter, 'cause we lost.'

"No matter how good they thought I played, the (feeling) was kind of short-lived just because of the fact that we lost the game. I remember that at the end of the game, I just felt sick. My career against the UA Pussycats was 50-50. I'd much rather have that 100 percent score."

Pat Tillman and the Duel in the Desert

Another Sun Devil who had an outstanding game vs. UA in '97 was linebacker Pat Tillman, the 1997 Pac-10 Defensive Player of the Year and eventual Arizona Cardinals standout.

Staat remembers running several blitzes alongside Tillman in that game. "They used to run a hell of a draw against us, and a couple of times me and Pat met in the middle," he said. "I remember we thought, 'God, is this the only freakin' play they were going to run?' I think they said something like they were going to keep running it until we stop it. And if memory served, I think they ran that play 10-12 times."

Staat, Tillman, and the rest of the ASU defense did well in containing explosive UA halfback and Phoenix native Trung Canidate in that game, holding him to just 62 yards on 22 carries. "Pat was always a gamer. He made plays all over the field," he said. "He played smart football. He knew where he was supposed to be at certain times, and he made the plays he was supposed to."

Staat and Tillman roomed together and became best friends, and they remained that way when they left ASU after the '97 season. Staat was a second-round pick by the Steelers, Tillman a seventh-round pick by the Cardinals.

Tillman famously left behind his successful NFL career to enlist in the U.S. Army following the events of Sept. 11, 2001, and was killed in action in Afghanistan in 2004.

Staat said he voiced a desire to enlist in the Armed Forces before Tillman did. "I was going to try to enlist after 9/11, but Pat actually talked me out of it," he said. "He said, 'You've got three years under your belt in the NFL. You should get your retirement (pension) before you go out and do anything stupid.'"

Staat promised Tillman that he would do just that. "But in the meantime, the year after I went back into the league, Pat went ahead and signed a contract to become an Army Ranger," he said. "I kind of laughed at him and said, 'Dude, you just stole my idea.' Maybe what we had talked about that day kind of set in with him."

In 2003, Staat fulfilled his promise to Tillman. "And about six months later, Pat was killed in Afghanistan," he said. "So I said, 'Forget football.' I retired, and I spent basically about nine months healing up so I could pass the physical to get into the Marine Corps. And then it was all hands on deck, full steam ahead."

Staat served four years as a Marine, and in 2012, he co-led a bicycle ride across the country to raise awareness of a lack of proper health care for U.S. war veterans.

But after all that he has gone through – losing his friend, serving as a machine gunner in Iraq in 2007 and biking across the country – Staat said his feelings toward UA still run deep.

"It's funny, because as time goes on, any time I meet somebody from UA or claims to be a Wildcat, I say, 'OK, I know where you stand now,'" he said. "It kind of grows on you more and more.

"It's also kind of a good thing. Being in the Marine Corps, we see other branches of the military service being kind of under us. It's kind of the same thing with the Wildcats – you just let me know where you stand in the whole chain of mankind. It's kind of at the bottom with the scum suckers."

"Unselfish" Cats have best-ever season

In 1998, Arizona was having one of its best seasons in program history, with a record of 10-1 – its only loss coming to eventual Pac-10 champion UCLA – and a top-10 national ranking.

"We did have some unbelievable talent," Baker said. "When you look at the roster, we had numerous guys that got drafted or went to NFL camps, like Trung and Northcutt. But I know Tomey talked about this a lot: One of the biggest things from that year is that every senior in the program had his best year, and a lot of times, you don't get that."

What set the '98 Wildcats apart, according to Baker, was the team-first focus. "We really did have a very good chemistry," he said. "You think about just my story – I went from a walk-on in the spring of '97, and I think I got maybe three reps that whole spring. To go from a walk on to being named a team captain by your teammates a year and a half later, it shows the unselfishness of the team more than anything else."

Meanwhile, ASU was going through the motions of a challenging 5-5 season in '98 that might have been over before it began.

"You've got to understand something: Before the start of the season, we lost nine starters due to academic problems – all juniors and seniors," Cozzetto said. "We lost a running back, a lot of defensive players – and it became a real big problem between the football staff and the support staff.

"We were playing a lot of different players – a lot of freshmen. They matured, but you can't go in missing that many players the beginning of the season. One of the biggest heartbreakers in my career at Arizona State was watching those players not being able to play."

Coin-toss chaos

Baker said UA fullback Kelvin Eafon, who rushed for 16 touchdowns in 1998, didn't like ASU very much. "Kelvin hated Arizona State with a passion because of the 1996 Glen Gable incident with Daniel Greer," he said.

That's why Eafon decided to make a statement during the '98 pregame coin toss. "We went out to the middle of the field, and most of the time, you just shook hands (with the opposing captains) and this or that. But he was like, 'What the (expletive) are you looking at?' And he just lays into these guys," Baker said.

"And to see the shock on their faces when he lit into them like that – I almost started laughing right then and there. I mean, it caught me off guard because I didn't know what the heck happened. But he lit into these guys for 20 seconds using every word in the book about what he was going to do to them over the course of the game. And finally, the ref pretty much told him that if he didn't shut up, he was going to give him an unsportsmanlike conduct before the game even started."

Eafon didn't get flagged for his tongue-lashing, but Baker said it didn't take him long for him to get a penalty once the game began. "Sure enough, the first play of the game, we go out on kickoff return, and Kelvin did get called for a personal foul for unsportsmanlike conduct for a late hit," he said.

The '98 track meet

Six years after the '92 game, which tied for the lowest-scoring contest in rivalry history, and just a few years removed from

Desert Swarm, the Wildcats and Sun Devils met in Tucson for what would be the highest-scoring Duel of all time.

ASU was missing some of its best athletes, but it still had talent to spare on offense, including future NFL running back J.R. Redmond as well as Kealy and his able receiving corps that included wide receivers Spann and Kenny Mitchell and tight end Todd Heap, a product of Mountain View High School in Mesa.

"Heap was phenomenal. He was like a wide receiver playing tight end," Pettas said. "We monkeyed with the formations and stuff. We matched (our receivers) up with linebackers trying to cover them man to man."

The result: 511 passing yards for Kealy in the '98 Duel – the third-highest total in ASU history at the time – and four touchdown passes. Spann and Mitchell both tallied over 100 receiving yards, and Heap hauled in 84 yards on four receptions while scoring twice in the second half of his first game against Arizona.

Pettas said Kealy's performance was one of the best he's ever seen. "And he did it hurt," he said. "He had a history of bad knees, and during his time there, I think he had six surgeries. But that night was phenomenal. He couldn't miss. He knew where he was going with the ball, and he was hobbling around throwing it."

The Devils were doing their best to play the role of underdog spoiler that had typically been reserved for their southern rivals. They amounted 42 points and 562 yards of total offense on their opponent's home turf.

But it wasn't enough. In a game that saw the lead change hands five times, the Wildcats mustered slightly more offensive firepower that night, largely thanks to Canidate, who like Kealy had one of the best single-game performances in the history of the Duel.

"When Trung saw a crease, he just knew to get north and south," Smith said. "He didn't dance through the line, he wasn't a big guy with moves, but when he planted his foot and went, it was over.

"The blocking scheme we had in our running game was perfect for him. Trung was that home run back. He had a different running style and speed that not a lot of running backs have."

Canidate ran the ball just 18 times that night but amassed 288 yards and scored three long touchdowns. His first, an 80-yard run, gave the Cats a 26-22 halftime lead. His 66-yard score in the third quarter put UA ahead 43-28. And after Heap's second TD reception of the game from Kealy pulled ASU within 43-35 with less than six minutes to play, Canidate scored his final TD on UA's next possession, this time, via a 48-yard run.

"He obviously had great speed," said ASU offensive lineman and fullback Stephen Trejo (1997-2000) of Canidate. "If he got in the open field and made some people miss, he was a home run hitter."

The Devils didn't give up. Kealy connected with wide receiver Lenzie Jackson in the end zone to cut the Wildcats' lead to 50-42. When ASU got the ball back with 49 seconds to go, Kealy quickly got his team down the field once again. "They ended up moving the ball down the field and had a pretty good shot to score a touchdown," Baker said.

But on the last play of the game, from the UA 28-yard line, Kealy had no choice but to throw the ball to the end zone, where his pass to Jackson was broken up, allowing the Wildcats to escape with a win in perhaps the wildest Duel ever.

The win was Arizona's second straight over ASU and its fifth in six years. "That was a crazy game. Todd Heap just had his way with us, but they couldn't stop Trung Canidate," Tomey said. "We played a lot of low-scoring games during our tenure because we had some great defenses, but that certainly was the opposite of that because it was such a back-and-forth game. We had a great team, but it was a very, very tough game, and we were glad to get a win."

The Wildcats and Devils combined for 1,169 yards of total offense that night. "Crazy stuff happens. I think guys step up their games more in that game," said Smith, who once again split time at the QB position with Jenkins.

Smith threw a 72-yard TD pass to Brennan in the first quarter, and Jenkins ran for a 13-yard score in the third. "I felt we were going put up a lot of points. I didn't think 50; I was thinking maybe 40," he said. "But Arizona State had some good talent on that team, too. I really do think that we were the better team, but that was a game that, for whatever reason, we couldn't put them away.

"Kenny Mitchell made one or two catches that were just unbelievable. We knew we'd be able to score a lot of points on them, but we didn't think they'd score that many points on us."

Spann, who played football with Canidate's brother at Phoenix College, said the Wildcats were able to match whatever the Devils did that evening. "I know we battled, even to the last second of the game. We had a chance to win," he said. "It just seemed like whenever we scored, they'd score. It seemed like a long game – maybe because there was just so much offensive production – but I felt like we should've won that game.

"I hated that that was my last game as a Sun Devil. We didn't have a chance to go to a bowl game that year. It just kind of hurt that that was the last game of my career at ASU."

By virtue of losing a tiebreaker to UCLA for the Pac-10 championship, UA came up just short of what would have been its first Rose Bowl appearance. Instead, the Cats went to the Holiday Bowl and defeated Nebraska, 23-20, to end the season with a final ranking of No. 4 in both national polls, their highest season-ending mark in school history.

Tomey said it's difficult to determine whether his '98 team or his '93 squad, which shut out Miami in the Fiesta Bowl, was more talented. "That team was a great team (along with) the team that beat Miami in the bowl game, but record-wise, and in terms of national ranking at the end of the season, that was the best team in the history of the University of Arizona," he said.

And even with all of UA's unprecedented success that season, Baker still treasures the win over ASU as much as any of the Wildcats' other accomplishments.

"Being able to go 2-0 against them for my two years, I can use that for the rest of my life," he said. "That's something I'm very proud of on a team level. Regardless of whether some idiot fan comes up and talks smack now, I can say I never lost to those punks."

Containing Trung in '99

With another 5-5 record, ASU once again needed a win over UA to become bowl-eligible in 1999 - but the Devils hadn't defeated the Wildcats at Sun Devil Stadium since they emphatically ended The Streak in '91.

And even though their record wasn't nearly as impressive that season (6-5) as it was in '98, the Wildcats were trying to play their way into a bowl game of their own.

Smith didn't have to compete with Jenkins for playing time in the '99 Duel, but he was dealing with multiple injuries, including turf toe in both feet. "I remember we were trying to play for a bowl game there, and there was a chance it was going to be my last game in an Arizona jersey," he said. "All those emotions are running pretty good throughout your body in the game, and you just want to put your best on the field and make it a game that fans can remember you by. And it was just a wild game."

The big question was whether ASU would be able to keep Canidate, who finished his career as UA's all-time leading rusher, from running wild for the second straight year.

Trung picked up where he left off to begin the game. After the Devils took a 7-0 lead off a 51-yard pass from Kealy to wide receiver Richard Williams less than four minutes into the game, Canidate tied it with a 1998-like 80-yard TD run with five minutes remaining in the first quarter. Smith then connected with Northcutt on an 80-yard touchdown pass in the second quarter to give the Wildcats a 14-7 edge.

But after Canidate's early score, ASU's defense was finally able to slow down the future St. Louis Ram and Washington Redskin.

"I just remember that we came out and we were physical, and I know we were really physical with Trung that game versus the year before," Trejo said. "I specifically remember Al Williams, our safety, laying a hit on him very early in the game that I think stuck with him and maybe changed a little bit the way the rest of his day went."

Canidate gained the majority of his rushing yards on his early TD run, mustering just 78 yards the rest of the game against an ASU defense that was determined to set the tone.

"I remember they were deep in their (own territory) early in the game, we stuffed them, and they had to punt from deep that set up a score," Trejo said. "And I know we got a few stops late. Even though they were able to score a few points here and there, we were able to let our offense separate."

Kealy goes down again, but Devils come through

Heap and the backfield tandem of Redmond and Delvon Flowers, who both ran for over 100 yards in the '99 Duel, led the Sun Devils' charge the rest of the way.

Flowers' 5-yard TD run tied the score at halftime, and his 38-yard score just 1:19 into the third quarter gave ASU the lead for good, 21-14. Later in the third, Heap, who hauled in seven catches for 170 yards, hooked up with Kealy on a 28-yard touchdown to give the Devils a two-TD advantage that they wouldn't relinquish.

"That was a great game for Delvon. He was a talented guy," Pettas said. "I remember us bring really fired up. It was one of those games that we're not going to lose, come hell or high water. A lot of it is emotion."

On ASU's next-to-last possession of the third quarter, Kealy suffered a right knee injury and was forced to exit the game against UA for the second time in three years. To make matters worse for the Devils, Northcutt returned the subsequent punt 81 yards for a touchdown to trim the lead to 28-20.

In to replace Kealy was John Leonard, who was able to pick up where Kealy left off. With just over eight minutes left in the game, Leonard threw his first career TD pass, a 45-yarder to Richard Williams, who had 149 receiving yards in the game.

And after UA responded with a 12-yard rushing score by Smith, who finished just short of 300 passing yards in his final Duel, Redmond sealed the ASU victory with a 10-yard run to cap an eight play, 90-yard drive with just 1:33 left in the game.

Thanks to the one-two punch of Flowers and Redmond, the Devils actually outrushed Canidate and the Wildcats that day, 226-175. "J.R. Redmond goes down there and ices the game – reaches over the goal line. It was over with. They couldn't tackle him," Cozzetto said.

"I think our momentum just carried us, maybe like the '97 game in reverse, where it seemed like we were a lot more into it than they were. I'm not sure if they had it all together that day. But I know we came firing on all pistons."

It wasn't the year that the Devils had hoped for, but a 6-5 record, including a 42-27 win over the Cats, was good enough for an Aloha Bowl appearance, though they lost, 23-3, to Wake Forest on Christmas Day. "We were pretty good that year; we just had some injuries that kept us from winning games," Cozzetto said. "But that day (against UA) was a good day for us. They were supposed to go in there and whoop our ass."

Like Spann a year earlier, Smith ended his career with a Duel loss that has stuck with him. "It was just unfortunate that my career ended that way, but it is what it is," he said. "I don't really like to talk about that game; I felt like I was a better player than I was on that day."

Tomey said one of the big differences between the Wildcats' 1998 and '99 seasons was a puzzling lack of takeaways by a defense that featured future NFL Pro Bowl linebackers Lance Briggs and Antonio Pierce. In fact, UA didn't cause a single ASU fumble or interception in the '99 game.

"We did a lot of the same things in practice, but we just couldn't create a takeaway, so we just didn't play as good a defense that year than we had (in '98)," he said. "We had some really good talent, but we had trouble stopping people.

"That was a frustrating game and a frustrating season for us. But certainly, ASU played really well and deserved to win. We had a really hard time stopping them."

Synchronized seasons

The 2000 season was a similar one for ASU and UA in more ways than one.

They both had a fantastic first half of the year, and they both followed that up with a lousy second half. And when it was over, both head coaches would be gone.

Trejo said the players knew before the 2000 UA game that Snyder would be let go once the season – which saw the Devils open the year 4-1 but then go 1-4 heading into the Duel – was complete.

But that didn't mean the coach wasn't out to beat the Wildcats one last time. "Snyder had already been fired, so I know he wanted that game in the worst way – just to go out beating the rival, plus we'd be bowl eligible, and I'm sure he wanted to stick it to the administration, just as a parting-shot type of thing," Trejo said.

The Wildcats set fan expectations high in 2000 by winning five of their first six games, but similar to the Sun Devils, they lost their next four contests to head into the ASU game with just a .500 record. That forced Tomey, who grew tired of speculation regarding his job security, to make the decision to resign at the end of the season.

The big difference between the two programs' situations was that UA's players weren't aware of Tomey's decision until after the 2000 Duel.

"It was quite a scene in the locker room after that. It was a blindside," said Arizona tight end and fullback Mike Detwiler (2000-01). "He came in and the first thing he said was, 'I'm done. I'm going to hang it up. I'm not going to let my family be subject to the speculation and the heckling and all that stuff.'

"No one really believed it. It was tough to understand what he was doing, and we kind of sat there with some blank stares. Everyone's kind of looking at Coach Tomey like, 'What? Really? Did you just quit?' It was an awkward scene in that locker room after that game."

There were also some awkward – or certainly confusing – moments for UA on the football field hours earlier.

Devil deception

The first half of the 2000 Duel at Arizona Stadium wasn't particularly entertaining offensively, with both teams bringing their down-the-stretch struggles into the game.

"They were struggling that year. We were struggling that year. It was not a pretty football game," Pettas said. "It was almost just survival of the fittest – who wasn't going to make a mistake."

The lone first-half touchdown came via a 2-yard run by Jenkins in the second quarter. A 25-yard field goal by Wildcat kicker Sean Keel, combined with a pair of field goals from Sun Devil kicker Mike Barth, made the score Arizona 10, ASU 6 at the half.

But early in the third quarter, Snyder decided to liven things up by introducing a bit of trickery into his final Duel in the Desert.

"Here's one thing I remember about all the games I was involved in (at ASU): We made up trick plays all the time, and we put in as many trick plays as we could for UA," Pettas said. "We were going to run 5-6 trick plays, come hell or high water. Coach Snyder would say, 'Run them. I don't care.' That was his motto: Call your trick plays before the other guys call them.

"The kids used to like those, and they knew it was UA week when we (practiced) five trick plays instead of just our normal two. It kind of just turned into a thing every year."

On fourth-and-long from the UA 13-yard line not even three minutes into the third quarter, ASU lined up for what would have been Barth's third field goal of the game, a kick that would have cut the Wildcats' lead to 10-9.

Instead, Barth was handed the ball by holder Griffin Goodman and ran up the middle untouched for the Devils' first touchdown of the game. Barth, who played halfback in high school, remained on the field to kick the extra point – and at that point in the game, he had singlehandedly outscored the Cats, 13-10.

"I remember that fake field goal. It was something we had put in specific for that week, spent time on it all week, and opportunity presented itself," Trejo said. "We called it and (UA) gave us the look we were looking for, and it worked to perfection, just like we drew it up."

Pettas credited special-teams coach Dick Arbuckle for drawing up the successful fake. "We had fake kicks (in our playbook) for a long time and we never used them, and we were sitting on the sideline and thinking, 'We've got to do it,'" he said.

The Wildcats had spent time that week in practice preparing for Snyder's trickery, but it didn't matter. "I remember that fake field goal because we had practiced that situation all week long," said UA defensive back Clay Hardt (2000-03). "And we had a couple guys who didn't execute.

"That was a big turning point in the game. If we had done what we were supposed to do, who knows what ends up happening."

Tomey said those kinds of mishaps on special teams made him want to pull his hair out. "They drive any coach nuts," he said. "The fake field goal was really huge."

Archuleta on the loose

Every member of UA's starting offense in the 2000 Duel remembers one particular ASU defender who gave them fits all day: linebacker and 2000 Pac-10 Defensive Player of the Year Adam Archuleta.

Over a decade later, the first thing that UA running back Clarence Farmer (2000-03) remembers from the 2000 Duel is being drilled by Archuleta. "I took the hardest hit I've ever taken in football, period," he said. "It was going into the south end zone, I think we were around the 3-yard line, and Coach called an inside zone (run). And Adam Archuleta gave me a pretty good shot.

"It was crazy. It didn't take me out of the game, but it was the most physical contact I've ever felt in my life."

Despite the hit, Farmer had a successful Duel debut, rushing 11 times for 82 yards and helping to set up a 14-yard touchdown pass from Jenkins to eventual 10-year NFL tight end Brandon Manumaleuna that allowed UA to regain the lead in the third quarter.

But the Wildcats wouldn't score again, as a Sun Devil defense led by a pair of Chandler natives – Archuleta and future Pro

Bowl linebacker and defensive end Terrell Suggs – took over. The Archuleta hit on Farmer caused the UA freshman to lose the ball, and Suggs' subsequent recovery in the end zone gave ASU a 20-17 lead with six minutes left in the third quarter.

The Devils added 10 more fourth-quarter points via a 3-yard rushing touchdown by tailback Tom Pace and a 48-yard field goal by Barth to earn a 30-17 win and their second straight Duel victory for the first time since 1991-92. Once again, the Sun Devils didn't turn the ball over against the Wildcats, but they forced three turnovers of their own.

"That was a game that was back and forth early, and then the special-teams mistakes got us," Tomey said. "That was a frustrating end to that season."

Tomey leaves lasting mark on players, rivalry

After a career in Tucson in which he became the all-time winningest coach in UA football history and posted an 8-5-1 record against Arizona State, Tomey said it was difficult to say goodbye.

"There were all kinds of emotions after that game, seeing as how it was my last game," Tomey said. "It was an emotional time, because my time at UA was incredible. It was wonderful. The players were incredible. By the time the sun came up the next morning, it (had been) a very emotional night."

While it was a shock, Detwiler said Tomey's postgame announcement didn't breed any long-term resentment from his players. "It's not like he left us for a different job because we weren't as good. We always knew he had things in his personal life that he had to have that were important to him," he said.

Smith said Tomey's tutelage continues to make an impact on his life. "I think Coach Tomey is fantastic. I think he makes you better as a person," he said. "I still find myself quoting him. I coach a freshman team, and I find myself quoting some sayings from Coach Tomey to younger kids."

The most important Tomey-ism that Smith passes on to his players is the coach's positivity. "Coach Tomey always used to say that it's easier to keep believing that good things are going to happen and just move on to the next play," he said. "(He said that) if you think good things, good things start to happen. The next thing you know, you can look up at the scoreboard and you'll get a victory.

"He's somebody that I looked up to and made me a better person through life. I'm passing his knowledge down through me into kids I coach. I felt like he had a personal touch with each and every one of us."

Like Larry Smith before him, McLaughlin said, Tomey was like a father to many Wildcats in the '80s and '90s. "I was lucky enough to have a great dad, but a lot of the players didn't," he said. "I've never played for a guy like him who really cared about his players the way that he did. I mean, yeah, we needed to win the game, and that was the most important thing on the field. But what also was the most important thing was that we graduate from school and get good grades. He took an interest. He really kind of was a father figure and gave us life lessons.

"I've been around so many coaches in this point in my life, and there's no one who was able to do that like Coach Tomey. And that's what sort of separates him from all the other coaches."

Keith Smith, who lives in Thousand Oaks, Calif., said he still meets up with Tomey for lunch whenever he's in the neighborhood. "He's one of those lifelong friends and coaches, and down the road, he just became a better friend to me," he said.

On Oct. 9, 2010, UA athletic director Greg Byrne invited Tomey and his wife back to Arizona Stadium, where he was honored during a halftime ceremony. He received a standing ovation from the Wildcat fans who hadn't forgotten his accomplishments, and he had a chance to share memories with former players at a function the night before the ceremony.

"That was tremendous. People were so welcoming," Tomey said. "It was a memorable occasion for us, and we appreciate it beyond our wildest dreams."

Tomey still thinks fondly of his days coaching in the Duel in the Desert and the men he coached against. "It's a great rivalry. I think it deteriorated at times into something too nasty, but I think Bruce and I tried hard to bring some of the class into the rivalry," he said. "I don't know where it is (today) in regards to that, but I have nothing but respect for what Bruce did, as well as John and Larry."

The late, great Bruce Snyder

ASU's victory over UA in 2000 gave Snyder one more game to coach with the Sun Devils – a 31-17 loss to Boston College in the Aloha Bowl on Christmas Day.

But Snyder didn't take another head coaching job following his release from ASU. His 58 wins are still the second most in ASU history, behind only Frank Kush's 176, and he led the Devils to four bowl games in his final five seasons.

At the age of 69, Snyder passed away in 2009 due to complications from melanoma.

Cozzetto, who spent over a decade under Snyder at ASU and Cal, said he learned more from Snyder than anyone else in the football world. "I had 11 years with him behind closed doors, and I had spent every single morning with him watching practice. He was so very detailed that it could drive you crazy, but I got to the point where my whole success in college football was from the things that he taught me and to never overlook anything," he said. "He wasn't a person that would make quick decisions; he would think things out. He was always a step ahead. He was always looking how to better the program."

Pettas said he didn't get to know Snyder until he was hired at ASU. "I coached 30 years for a lot of different people. He was one of the best coaches I ever worked for," he said. "He was a straight, great, honest man. He was really even-keel, never took things personally and never treated you in that respect. He never said anything to you in a mean way. He never said anything to anyone in a derogatory way, ever. That never came out of Bruce's mouth.

"He was a great guy to work for and a great guy to play for, I'm sure the guys would tell you. We all wish he was still alive today and still working for him."

Poole said Snyder got in touch with him several years ago after his NFL career ended. "He called me up one day and told me he wanted to take me out to eat, and just wanted to talk to me and he missed me," he said. "We did that, and a year and a half later, he was dead.

"He was a great guy. He's the one who recruited me. I was basically a baby, a young kid, and he made us all grow up. He was tough on us - he had tough love - but he taught us good things on and off the football field, and he'll be missed. I think the best decision I ever made in my life was to come here and play for Bruce Snyder and Arizona State."

Plummer said he has Snyder to thank for an incredible collegiate experience. "They had a great group of recruiters, but the head coach, he puts an importance on the players, so he was huge in getting me down there, and he was a great coach," he said. "He put a lot on my shoulders, a lot on my plate, but didn't do it in a way that made me feel a lot of pressure; he did it in a way that encouraged me and let me grow and learn the system and become the player I became my senior year.

"He preached that one at a time, man - one game at a time, one play at a time, and focus on the moment. I know that's something that a lot of these kids miss from some coaches - they're here for two years, the next year they're gone, and you never know what they're thinking. But he really placed an emphasis on being in the moment and taking it one day at a time, and it seems kind of a remedial thing to say, but it really did hold true to us as a team. He was a great coach - always happy, always excited, easy to approach, and everybody was sad when he passed on. We'll miss him, for sure."

Snyder's counterpart in Tucson for nine years respected him as a head coach but even more so as a man. "It's a story in itself, I guess, but I can't overstate what a terrific coach I thought Bruce was, how great a job he did and how I just have nothing but respect for he and his wife, Linda," Tomey said. "I think the fact that he was one of two of the great coaches in the (rivalry) series, he and Larry Smith – to think that they're both gone is very difficult. They'll be remembered by ASU and UA people even more for the people they were than the kind of coaches they were."

Roque said Snyder deserves to be considered among the greatest college football coaches of all time. "I think he was just as good a coach, if not better," he said. "And the people that he touched in his life, he just had such a profound impact on them – his players, his friends.

"He was a father figure to me, and I love him to death. I think about him a lot, and I try to live my life the best I can because that's what Coach would want."

CHAPTER 7

The Return of the Cup

It had been rediscovered almost 20 years earlier, but at the beginning of 2001, the Territorial Cup still hadn't been seen on a football field. In fact, it remained virtually untouched at ASU's university archive center for over a decade after its discovery.

In the Territorial Cup's absence, other awards were given to the annual winner of the Duel in the Desert. Beginning around 1950, the winner received the Victory Bell, which was originally used in an Arizona State dining hall and was eventually mounted on ASU's Memorial Union building in 1956.

"Eventually, it was replaced by a different bell. There have been 2-3 different Victory Bells," Spindler said. "That's another one of those things that early records don't tell us clearly."

After the bell was retired from the field, the UA-ASU winner received the Ben Goo Trophy, a piece of artwork that was donated by Goo, a contemporary artist from Scottsdale. Today, that trophy is given to the athlete who is voted the Duel's most valuable player.

UA was made aware of the cup's re-emergence in the mid-'90s. "In December of 1995, we had the cup on display at Sky Harbor Airport for the upcoming Super Bowl that was played (at Sun Devil Stadium) in January of '96," Spindler said. "And it turned out that two UA alumni staff found it in the airport and said, 'That's the cup we've been looking for.'"

A short time later, Spindler received a call from the Arizona athletic department. "They asked me if I would loan them the cup to be placed on permanent display at the new sports hall of fame at McKale Center," he said. "I politely declined the request and said I didn't think that would be wise."

And that was the end of that – until several years later, when Spindler received a call from ASU vice president Christine Wilkinson, daughter of the legendary Bill Kajikawa. "She said that (ASU president Lattie) Coor has word that, henceforth, the cup will be shared – the winner of the game gets the cup," he said. "And that started a series of meetings and phone conversations between UA and ASU staff about how to do this in a way that celebrated the cup but also protected it for future generations."

Spindler requested that each university president sign a "protocol document" that described who would be responsible for the Territorial Cup when it was in either Tempe or Tucson, as well as how it would be handled and displayed. "They did sign this formal protocol document, and there's a copy in the travel case wherever (the cup) goes," he said.

The schools agreed to begin presenting the Territorial Cup to the winner of the Duel, beginning with the 2001 game at Sun Devil Stadium. But rather than present the actual cup, which was over 100 years old and could be subject to irreparable damage if not handled properly, Spindler insisted on creating a replica for players and coaches to enjoy on the field.

"It was processed because we knew that the teams wanted something to celebrate with, and we thought it would be useful for the cup to be available for celebration, but we knew that the original cup wasn't going to be handled well," he said. "The welds on the arm aren't necessarily as strong as they once were. We had a lot of concerns about the condition.

"So ultimately, an accurate wax casting of the original cup was made by a company here in Tempe. They made the replica that you see at field celebrations and other public events. It's exactly the same size and it has great detail of the features and the engravings that are present on the original. It's a very accurate replica, but it weighs more than the original, and the construction is slightly different from the original."

UA and ASU shared the costs of creating the replica. "It was a nice collaboration between the two universities to ensure the preservation of the original," Spindler said.

The original cup is displayed at the Luhrs Reading Room in ASU's Hayden Library following a Sun Devil win, and in the Jim Click Hall of Champions adjacent to McKale Center after a Wildcat victory.

Koetter calls on Devils to protect the castle

In December of 2000, ASU replaced Bruce Snyder with Dirk Koetter, who had enjoyed a 26-10 record from 1998-2000 as head coach at Boise State, posting back-to-back 10-win seasons in his final two years there.

Sun Devil safety Riccardo Stewart (2000-04) said the new guy had at least one thing in common with Snyder. "Dirk Koetter was a detailed coach," he said. "He was definitely an X's and O's guy. Things weren't just going to slide past him. He was a coach who cared a lot about education, discipline and doing things right."

ASU quarterback Andrew Walter (2000-04) also called Koetter a "detail-oriented" coach who cared about his players, despite what the outside perception of the program may have been during various points of his tenure. "He definitely cared about doing it the right way," he said.

Sun Devil safety Jason Shivers (2001-03) said Koetter immediately bought into the importance of beating the Wildcats. "His first year, he really just wanted to make a statement – that this can win or lose our season depending on the outcome of this game," he said. "It was kind of like staking a claim for (the state of) Arizona."

Walter said Koetter used a dramatic metaphor to emphasize the importance of winning the Territorial Cup. "The metaphor goes like this: At ASU, we need to have a castle mentality," he said. "We're at the heart of a big city, our stadium sits in these cool buttes, and it's a huge university with 50,000-plus students. And his analogy was that we were a castle, and going down to Tucson was a bit like (traveling to) a territory or a fort.

"Every year, he'd use that metaphor to pump us up and that, whether it was in Tempe or down there, to go nuts and unleash fury. We had to withstand the initial barrage, the initial wave, sit in there and defend Tempe and the stadium."

Mackovic slow to win over players, grasp rivalry

In to replace Tomey in Tucson was John Mackovic, who had made previous head coaching stops at Wake Forest, Illinois and, most recently, Texas, where he'd led the Longhorns to back-to-back conference championships in 1995-96.

Detwiler said Mackovic and Tomey had different priorities. "Coach Tomey was there to coach football but, at the same time, was there to kind of mentor young men. He had an open-door policy. You could talk to Coach Tomey about anything, whereas with Coach Mackovic, you couldn't," he said. "He couldn't have cared less about your personal life. He had one agenda, and that was his agenda: to win football games to improve his presence as head coach."

Hardt said Mackovic was much more of an offensive-minded coach than was the defense-first Tomey. The only problem: Mackovic's offensive players at Arizona often struggled to move the ball. "There were just a lot of times that our defense was on the field 90 plays (per game)," he said.

And Farmer said Tomey made a much bigger deal out of beating ASU than Mackovic did. "(Tomey) bleeds red and blue; it was in his aura. He knew everything about the Pac-10 and he understood the magnitude of that game, and that was displayed the week of practice," he said. "With Coach Mackovic, I don't think he understood the magnitude or how UA felt versus ASU. Of course, you have to have a business approach to it, but I don't know if his approach was as deeply rooted as Coach Tomey's."

Hardt said he liked the Tomey coaching staff's strategy of having former players come in the week before the Duel to get the team revved up to beat ASU. "When they got fired, it was just sad, because as the upperclassmen and the older guys, we'd try to relate that to our younger teammates, but they just couldn't grasp it because they never got to experience that passion and history," he said. "When Coach Mackovic came in, it was just like, 'This is the ASU game and this is our rival,' and that was the extent of it."

But the game still meant a lot to the veteran Wildcats on the '01 squad, including Farmer, who had tasted defeat against the Devils on his home turf his freshman year.

"I began to take on the UA tradition fast. I caught a hold to what it meant to UA as a player, which was a pretty important thing as far as my productivity at UA, because when you go to a school, you don't just play at the school; you become part of the tradition and everything at the university and all the school stands for," he said.

Vivid in Farmer's mind before the 2001 Duel was ASU's win on his home field the previous year, which ended with fans from Tempe trying to tear down the goalposts at Arizona Stadium following the Devils' victory.

"I was taught that ever since Pop Warner: You don't let somebody come into your field. You don't let somebody come into your house, disrespect your house, and not do anything about it," he said.

"When we lost the game against ASU my true-freshman year, it was a devastating blow for me, to say the least. It was a game to get us to a bowl game that year, and I lost a head coach that essentially set my role and talked to me and convinced me to come to UA. So I lost a lot my freshman year. And I took it kind of personal."

Farmer's attitude spread among his teammates before, during and definitely after the 2001 showdown at Sun Devil Stadium, leading to an ugly incident that spoiled what was supposed to be the first-ever on-field presentation of the Territorial Cup.

Cats storm Tempe's fortress

The debut seasons for Koetter and Mackovic were winding up the same way the final ones for Snyder and Tomey did. The Sun Devils enjoyed a good start in 2001 (4-2), but that was followed by three straight losses down the stretch, while the Wildcats opened the year 3-0 in nonconference play but then lost six of their first seven games against Pac-10 opponents.

ASU could still reach a bowl game with a home win over UA followed by a victory over UCLA the following week, while the Cats were playing for nothing but pride when the teams met in '01.

"Being a rivalry game, the seniors set a big goal (to win that game), and that really impressed on all of us freshman, and I was lucky enough to play as a true freshman," Shivers said. "For me, the atmosphere was just different."

But it was UA that immediately set the tone that day.

"The biggest play I remember from that game was we were punting down to one of their receivers, and I don't know what made him want to catch the ball, but (UA wide receiver) Bobby Wade went down and plowed him," Farmer said. "I mean, he leveled this guy, and he had to be carried off the field by his teammates. And that, right there, sent a message."

Wade also starred on offense in the '01 game with 11 catches for 157 yards. "At that point in the game, I really felt that everybody on the team, defensively and offensively, we were clicking on all cylinders, and it felt good," Farmer said.

Thanks in large part to a smothering defense that recorded seven sacks on the day – including three by Lance Briggs – Arizona opened up a 20-0 first-quarter lead via a touchdown pass to Wade from quarterback Jason Johnson, a 6-yard QB keeper by

Johnson and a 20-yard TD rush by Farmer, who ran for over 150 yards in the game.

"He might have been one of the best running backs the Pac-10 ever had," Stewart said. "He was a freak. He was an athlete. I remember him in that game for sure. Clarence was big, fast, strong and could run over you. Him and Bobby Wade – they're athletes."

Walter, who split playing time with quarterback Jeff Krohn in the '01 Duel, finally put ASU on the scoreboard with a 19-yard pass to wide receiver Donnie O'Neal early in the second quarter. Flowers then reeled off a 33-yard TD run in the third to cut the UA lead to 20-14.

But the Wildcats quickly reasserted themselves. Late in the third, wide receiver Malosi Leonard caught a 10-yard touchdown pass from Johnson, and less than a minute later, a 13-yard interception return for a score by safety Brandon Nash put Arizona back up by 20. Flowers' second TD run of the day midway through the fourth quarter wasn't enough, and the Wildcats came away with a 34-21 victory over the Devils to ensure that neither team would go bowling that year.

"We obviously weren't that good that year, but we kind of threw everything (at them) for the win," Detwiler said. "And it's not to say that we defied Mackovic, but we kind of didn't really play for him. We just really played for ourselves and for the rivalry. And I thought we were a lot more motivated going into that game."

As the final seconds ticked off the clock, Spindler went down to the field to make the Territorial Cup presentation to the Wildcats. But he never got the opportunity.

"Stomping on Sparky"

The week before the game, Hardt said, Farmer rallied his teammates to try to get them as pumped up as he was to beat the Sun Devils.

"During one of the practices, he says, 'We're going to go up there and we're going to kick their ass, and after we kick their ass, we're going to go to the middle of the field and we're going to sing (our fight song) 'Bear Down' on top of Sparky,'", he said.

Sure enough, that's what the Cats did as the final seconds ticked away. "As soon as we got done winning, we all rushed to the 50-yard line and started singing our song," Hardt said.

The Arizona celebration included some dancing on ASU's midfield logo that depicted Sparky, the long-time Sun Devil mascot. "(ASU) had a couple guys who didn't take kindly to that, ran into our group of guys, and a big-ass brawl started," Hardt said. "It was crazy."

Farmer said the celebration was intended as payback for the ASU fans' actions in Tucson in 2000. "I'm not validating my outburst or my actions at the time, and you can't control your fans. But as far as I can remember at UA, we never stormed anyone's field, we never tore down anyone's goalposts, we never vandalized any person's field," he said. "It was a sign of disrespect, and the only way that I felt that I could validate that was sort of like disrespecting them back – stomping on Sparky.

"Everyone's talking about Sparky this, Sparky that. Well, you know, screw that. I didn't have any regard toward ASU and what they stood for. The game was over, it was out of reach, and we were going to win. That was to send a message to ASU: Don't come to UA and think you're going to run stuff. As long as I have anything to do with it, don't disrespect us like that."

The ensuing fight between UA and ASU players went well beyond a typical postgame shoving contest. Punches were thrown, and the altercation lasted several minutes.

"I got into it once it started happening," Stewart said. "It's hard to really put myself back in those shoes now, but at the time, it was just one of the most disrespectful things anyone could do.

"In my opinion, at that time, that was inviting a fight. That's how you tell someone, 'I want to fight you' – not, 'I just beat you on the scoreboard,' but, 'I'm going to rub it in now.'"

Shivers said the vengeful display was over the line, but he understands the emotion that fueled Farmer and his Wildcat teammates. "I think every player has that moment when they're just caught in the moment and they go a little too overboard and don't really have a chance to think through their decisions," he said. "But yeah, that's very disrespectful in any sport, especially when you work as hard as you do to work as a team and at all the offseason workouts, just like any other team does. That's your mascot; you don't want to be disgraced in that way with people stepping on it or making any gestures towards it."

When asked whether he would act differently if he had the opportunity to do it over again, Farmer was conflicted. "I wouldn't necessarily say I'd do it again, but with me, it was personal," he said. "I wouldn't necessarily say I'd go and stomp on Sparky again.

"I guess it was a combination of frustration, anger, retaliation – a lot of personal emotion I had in me that just came out at the time. I don't have anything against the ASU fans or players. The fans that came down (to Tucson the year before), that wasn't classy, but I don't have anything against the players.

"I played within the whistle. I'm not a dirty player. But the exclamation point at the end was a caption of everything that happened to me at UA prior to that moment."

Detwiler said the decision to stomp on the logo was a poor one, but it was a way for the players to demonstrate their frustration toward Mackovic.

"From a sportsmanship thing, yeah, I think none of us were really proud of it, but we all kind of had some poor attitudes anyway about playing for Mackovic," he said. "So I think we ultimately – excuse my language, but I don't think we gave a (expletive).

"We'd been told by Mackovic that we weren't his players and we were just there for a few years and (we'd be gone) by the time that he got his recruits in there. So we were just kind of selfish, just playing for ourselves and beating our rival, and we couldn't have cared less about the school image at that particular moment.

"But after getting a tongue-lashing from Mackovic and from (Arizona athletic director Jim) Livengood, we understood that was a pretty dumb thing to do. Obviously, it puts a bad name on the sportsmanship between the rivals, and it puts a bad name on the university."

Spindler said UA's actions and the ensuing fight ruined what was supposed to be the first on-field Territorial Cup presentation.

"I'm going out there with the cup, and I see all these helmets flying, and it was the Sparky-stomping incident," he said. "So I was looking for a state trooper to help me with (the cup).

"We turned back, and they never actually had the presentation on the field, which was kind of sad. I think that would have been a very nice, collegial way to celebrate the result of each game."

As a result of the melee, ASU and UA decided to scrap any future plans for an on-field cup ceremony, electing to instead present it in a more discreet fashion going forward.

Devils led by Williams on offense, "frenzy time" on defense

Judging by Arizona's record, Mackovic's rapport with his players hadn't evolved much by 2002.

The Wildcats were again strong in nonconference play, opening the season 3-1, but lost six in a row in the Pac-10 before winning a shootout at Cal the week prior to the Duel in Tucson.

And for the third year in a row, ASU opened the season with promise by going 7-2, including 4-0 in the Pac-10, but then lost three straight conference games by at least 17 points. However, the Sun Devils were still in line for a bowl game, and they could improve their chances of going to a more prominent bowl by paying the Cats back for 2001.

Shivers said his defense couldn't wait to get on the field for the 2002 Duel. "We used to have this saying when we got a team down and we had the momentum. We called it 'frenzy time,'" he said. "Everybody would be on the sidelines and would be saying, 'It's frenzy time! Let's go! Let's go!' It was like (the video game) 'NBA Jam' when you're on fire. Those were the memories from that game."

The first half of the '02 contest was essentially a stalemate, with both teams moving the ball effectively on the ground. UA running back Beau Carr scored both of his team's first-half touchdowns, and Wildcat halfback Mike Bell, who stepped in while

Farmer missed most of the season with a knee injury, paced the running game with 70 yards on 12 carries for the game.

But the UA rushing attack was eventually outdone by ASU's, which was led by tailback Mike Williams. His 5-yard touchdown run in the second quarter gave the Devils a 10-7 lead, and he accounted for all of ASU's 21 second-half points, scoring on rushes of 4, 8 and 4 yards.

Walter said Williams' 40-carry, 162-yard, four-TD game might have been the best he'd been a part of in college. "It makes it easy, I'll tell you, that when you can hand it to a guy who can easily get a first down, especially on third down," he said. "The year before, as a true freshman, he went through some ups and downs, and so to break out in a big game like that (was huge)."

Not to be outdone, the Sun Devil defense ushered in "frenzy time" late in the game. Shivers intercepted Johnson on back-to-back UA possessions in the fourth quarter, with the first leading to Williams' fourth and final touchdown to give ASU a 34-20 lead and the second allowing the Devils to run out the clock.

"I think, coming out of halftime, we really started out to figure out their game plan, and we had some big defensive stops," Shivers said.

Also making his presence known was Suggs, who recorded two of ASU's three sacks and forced a Carr fumble that the Devils recovered in the second quarter.

"No one changed the game like Terrell Suggs. Not even close," Stewart said. "Terrell, hands down, was the best college football player I've ever seen at any position, offense or defense."

Shivers said Suggs had the quickness of a defensive back. "His anticipation before the snap was just tremendous at that time compared to any of the other guys who were getting off the ball who were in the same unit as him," he said. "He was in the backfield before they even knew it."

Home-field advantage?

ASU's '02 win represented the third straight victory by the road team in the Duel – and each time, the away team won by at least

13 points, proving once again that there might not be any such thing as home-field advantage in this rivalry.

"When you go into that game, I don't think anything really matters. I don't think your record matters, I don't think where it's played matters, because the game – it's something all in itself," Hardt said.

But a few distasteful UA fans made sure to remind Shivers after the game that he was in unfriendly territory by spitting on him and members of his family. "My family had my jersey on, and I had two interceptions in that game, so they remembered my jersey and who I was," he said.

The victory in Tucson gave the Devils eight wins on the year – their most in a season since 1997 – and propelled them to the Holiday Bowl in San Diego, where they came up just short, 34-27, against Kansas State.

Mackovic fired amid team turmoil

In terms of on-field performance and off-field friction, the 2003 season could be considered the worst in the history of Arizona football. It was a season in which Mackovic was fired after a 1-4 start amid a backlash from his players, many of whom had demanded his resignation a year earlier.

To this day, Wildcats players are still split on how they feel about Mackovic and what his lasting legacy from his two and a half years at Arizona should be.

One of Mackovic's recruits, wide receiver and future NFL player Syndric Steptoe (2003-06), defended the coach. "Mackovic was more of a treat-you-like-a-professional type of a coach. He'd expected you to do your job, and he wasn't about a lot of babysitting. I think a lot of kids came from where they were who were used to being babysat, and Mackovic wasn't going to do that," he said.

"He expected you to do your job, and if you didn't, he's like, 'What do I have you here for?' I have no bad things to say about him. I thought he was a great man."

Steptoe's college roommate, UA quarterback Kris Heavner (2003-07), who became the starter halfway through the '03 season, echoed Steptoe's sentiments. "I had a really good relationship with Coach Mackovic. I still talk to him to this day," he said. "The position that he was in at UA – a lot of people didn't buy into what he was doing, so they rebelled against it. And when guys don't buy into what you do, it's hard to establish your values and your cores, and that's what kind of got him out the door.

"But I thought he was a great guy. He helped me out in my career, and also personally and academically. He showed me how to do things right, and he was always there for me. I guess he was kind of like a father figure in the short time I was with him."

But Hansen said no one should have been surprised that Mackovic's tenure in Tucson was a failure. "He got fired in Texas, which should've been a big tipoff – if you mess it up in Texas, why do you think you can be successful at Arizona?" he said. "He came here with a haughty attitude, like he was a little bit better than you were and Tucson was a little bit beneath him, and he was a wine-and-cheese guy.

"He made no connection. He couldn't recruit well. He thought he was going be an offensive mastermind, and he recruited three really bad quarterbacks. They had no chance, even though the Pac-10 wasn't great then. I mean, Arizona was just awful."

Farmer was dismissed from the team in '03 following differences between him and the coaching staff, making 2001 – the year he led the Sparky stomp in Tempe – his last game against ASU. He said his dismissal from UA ultimately cost him an opportunity to be a high NFL draft pick.

"I'm not going to say Mackovic was the person who kept me down, but the man had clout," he said. "A lot of people call and ask me about John Mackovic. The real fact of the matter is it's over with, man. I can't do nothing about it. I enjoyed my experiences – my good ones – at UA, and I just keep on moving. It's like Coach Tomey said: Keep my head up."

Taking over for the rest of the '03 season was Mackovic's defensive coordinator, Mike Hankwitz, who was hired before the start of the season. Hankwitz had been a UA assistant coach under Jim Young from 1973-76.

Under Hankwitz, the Wildcats lost four consecutive games to bring their losing streak to eight before finally breaking through with a home victory over Washington. UA was then routed at home by USC prior to the ASU game in Tempe.

However, Heavner said Hankwitz deserves credit for lighting a fire under Arizona's players that had been extinguished under Mackovic. "The ship had sunk and was sinking fast, and he did a good enough job to get us afloat and get us hungry enough to play again," he said.

With all the off-field turmoil in Tucson that year, is it possible that the Wildcats took their focus off the Sun Devils? "No. Gosh, no," Heavner said. "We had (former Wildcats) come back and talk to us about the game, and they made sure, in my mind, that the rivalry was still there.

"ASU's at a different intensity level. They always stressed in our mind how those guys over there were arrogant compared to us, who were blue-collared guys and worked for everything we did, and we took satisfaction in beating those guys. That was kind of given down to me."

The Wildcats may have been hungry heading to Tempe, but Walter and the Devils proved to be more than they could chew on that Friday afternoon.

Devils salvage season with rout

With a 4-7 record and a four-game losing streak, ASU was going through struggles of its own before the '03 Duel. But the energy from the Sun Devil Stadium crowd that day told players from both teams who had yet to experience the rivalry that it was always an important game, no matter the records.

"The atmosphere for the game was something I'd never been a part of. You wouldn't imagine what people say to you out there, fans included," Heavner said. "It was just a different intensity. If you're one step slow that day, you were going to get exploited and you were going to get hurt. And the guys were out to hurt you."

Walter had one of his most proficient games in an ASU uniform that day, throwing for almost 300 yards, three touchdowns and no interceptions.

His final TD toss – an 80-yarder in the fourth quarter to wide receiver and future Miami Dolphins draft pick Derek Hagan, who would become the Pac-10's all-time receptions leader – gave the Devils a 28-7 win, their most lopsided over the Wildcats since the 1996 Tucson massacre.

At the time, Walter – then a junior - was undecided as to whether he would declare for the NFL draft following the season. So, just in case it was his last game as a Sun Devil, he savored the win by taking some pictures with his parents on the field after the game.

"I remember just being disappointed at the result of the season but (feeling) a sense of accomplishment because we beat UA at home, which is what we're supposed to do," he said. "I don't think I took my uniform off for an hour and a half after the game. It was definitely bittersweet, I would say, because we weren't going to a bowl, and that was the last game (of the season)."

Bird's the word

Hardt said the exhaustion that he and his teammates on defense felt after the loss was indicative of the wearying 2003 season.

"I blitzed a lot in that game. We ran maybe three blitzes in a row that I was running, and on the third one, I was just tired as (expletive)," he said.

But in his final Duel, Hardt got in one more shot. After the final whistle, as he left the field and headed into the tunnel toward the locker room, he let the ASU fans know what he thought of them by pulling a Richard Dice and extending his middle finger as he disappeared from view.

"I did a lot of stuff like that," he said with a laugh. "That's just kind of how I felt about them, you know? I have older sisters, and they would almost get in fights in the stands because people are just rowdy and belligerent and rude – and that goes for both sides, whether you're in Tucson or Tempe. That's just how it is. It comes with the territory."

Stoops to a new level

With the program at rock bottom and the recruiting cupboard bare, Arizona announced the hiring of Mike Stoops the day after the '03 loss to ASU. Stoops had previously served under his brother, Bob, as defensive coordinator at Oklahoma.

Heavner, who came back to UA as an assistant coach under Stoops in 2011, said Stoops was much more emotional than Mackovic. "It's not that Coach Stoops wasn't professional, but Coach Mackovic was the guy you'd always see in a suit, whereas Coach Stoops wore his emotions on his sleeve every day," he said. "He just had a certain passion about football. He just loved football in everything he did, and he really showed that to us."

UA linebacker Ronnie Palmer (2004-08) said Stoops, who was a strong safety at Iowa in the early '80s, understood the defensive side of the game in a way few people do. "Coach Stoops was a very passionate coach, loved the game, and he knew everything there was to know about defense," he said. "That's what he brought to Arizona most. He definitely was a very knowledgeable coach."

Since he had been a part of many intense inter- and intrastate rivalries, including Iowa-Iowa State as a player and Oklahoma-Texas as a coach, Stoops didn't need the magnitude of the Duel in the Desert explained to him. But, just in case, the folks in Tempe were happy to do so.

"Like most fans, they're pretty volatile up there and they're going to let you have it. I don't listen to a lot of that stuff, but they're pretty vocal," Stoops said. "I think (all rivalry games are) unique in the fact that they're the game that everyone looks forward to each year. I think (the UA-ASU game), being at the end of the year – it was always kind of neat to have it as the last game."

Koetter's quote "a little bit insulting"

Predictably, the Wildcats struggled through most of Stoops' first season, going 2-8 in their first 10 games - including a 49-9 loss at USC - before the Sun Devils came to town.

But Stoops said he took notice of something that Koetter said during a pregame press conference that got him and his team fired up to face ASU, which was rolling into the Old Pueblo with an 8-2 record.

"Dirk had said something in the media about the team's true colors will show as the game goes on," he said. "I remember the comment very vividly in the paper, and it kind of struck me as being very odd that somebody would say that."

Koetter's exact quote, according to the official Arizona State athletics website, was this:

"I think that in games like this, the team that's favored has to overcome the initial frenzy of the underdog, especially on their home field. I think that as the game goes on, every team, good or bad, returns to their true colors."

Regardless of whether the quote was truly intended as an insult, Stoops got good use out of it. "I don't think he was taking a shot at us, and it may have come out wrong in print, but we certainly used it to our advantage, and that really stuck under our craw a little bit that somebody would say that about us," he said. "I don't think Dirk was trying to be insulting in any way, but we certainly used it as motivation, as bulletin board (material) or whatever. It was a little bit insulting, and we used it to our advantage."

Whether perceived or real, Dirk's slight lit a fire under a UA program that desperately needed a spark.

Kovalcheck, Cats KO Walter, Devils

Arizona has pulled off many upsets over the years against superior Arizona State teams. The 2004 game may have been the most improbable of all of them.

UA quarterback Richard Kovalcheck (2003-05), who was named the starter halfway through the season, said the team played 18th-ranked ASU that day as if it had nothing to lose – unlike earlier in the season, when many players were wound up as tight as could be.

"Going into that game, the last game of the season, it was, 'Let's just go have fun and get after it.' It was a whole different attitude to the team," he said. "Everyone was looser than we had been all season."

The Sun Devils jumped out in front in the first quarter, as tailback Hakim Hill scored on a 1-yard run to give ASU a 10-3 lead. But less than 5 minutes later, early in the second quarter, Kovalcheck found tight end Steve Fleming for a 54-yard touchdown to tie the score.

Kovalcheck said the long TD pass was a momentum-changer that got the partisan Tucson crowd into the game. "I just looked to the left, gave it some air, and he made a great catch and barely made it into the end zone. And that was awesome," he said. "That definitely changed the tide of the game."

ASU took a 17-13 lead later in the quarter on a 24-yard fumble return for a score by defensive tackle Jimmy Verdon, but Arizona went back on top 20-17 with seven seconds left before halftime on a 2-yard TD pass from Kovalcheck to wide receiver Mike Jefferson.

The Cats' first-half point total was remarkable considering that they hadn't scored more than 23 points in a game all year.

"I just remember Richard Kovalcheck and Mike Jefferson having a great game for us. They really stepped up," Steptoe said.

"It was more of a rivalry that year, I would say. It just felt like it, me coming from Texas and going to the Texas-Texas A&M games in my hometown – it kind of felt like that type of atmosphere."

The Wildcats continued to feed off the positive energy from the Arizona Stadium crowd in the second half. With Bell pacing the offense with a 139-yard game on the ground, UA cashed in on a 6-yard TD rush by running back Gilbert Harris in the third quarter, followed by another Kovalcheck-to-Jefferson scoring pass in the fourth, to take a 34-20 lead.

To make matters worse for ASU, Walter, who threw for over 300 yards in the game, had to leave midway through the fourth quarter with a right shoulder injury following a hit on a play that didn't even count because of a UA penalty. "I'm not going to name any particular names, but a particular running back missed a block, and Andrew went down on that right arm," Stewart said.

Backup quarterback Sam Keller was able to complete the drive that Walter had started by hooking up with wide receiver Jamaal Lewis for a 3-yard score that cut Arizona's lead in half.

With less than two minutes left, Keller drove the Devils to the Wildcat 23-yard line in search of a game-tying TD. But on fourth down, wide receiver Matt Miller dropped a perfect pass by Keller that would've given ASU a first down. Arizona took over possession and ran out the clock, allowing Stoops to enjoy his first marquee win as a head coach.

"I think any time in your first year, if you win a game like that against a ranked team, it shows credibility and it gives you credibility," Stoops said. "Certainly, that enhances your ability to go into the offseason with some momentum, and that's what it did.

"It was a great game. It was very exciting for us, and we took a big team picture out in front of the scoreboard after the game. It was the beginning of the rebuilding process for us."

Kovalcheck said the team's relaxed, positive attitude paid huge dividends that day. "It was the last game of the season, so I was just going to play my ass off and have fun," he said. "I don't think it made up for the season, but it definitely set a good tone going into the next season, and it sent off our seniors in the right way."

Keller played well in Walter's place, but the Devils were left to wonder whether they would have been able to complete the comeback if their star quarterback hadn't been knocked out. "Don't get me wrong – Sam Keller came in and played phenomenal. He really did," Stewart said. "But if Andrew had stayed in that game, without a doubt, I thought we would've won that game."

Walter was selected in the third round of the 2005 NFL draft by the Oakland Raiders, but Stewart said the lingering effects from the shoulder injury he suffered against UA caused many teams to pass on him. "I mean, it not only cost us as a team in the game; it cost him, like, millions of dollars," he said.

But Walter isn't as certain that ASU, which completed a nine-win season by defeating Purdue 27-23 in the Sun Bowl, would have won had he not gotten hurt. "I'd like to think we would've had a chance, but with (the amount of) drops and fumbles, it seemed like guys weren't focused," he said.

Indeed, the Sun Devils committed five turnovers in the '04 Duel. "We were playing such a sloppy game that I really don't know if it would've made a difference," Walter said. "I think guys' heads were just in a totally different place – looking forward to a bowl, or maybe had too much turkey the day before. Who knows?

"We felt we were a solid team and could have some momentum to go into a bowl game, and still potentially go to the Holiday Bowl. So it was a frustrating day, which was only compounded with the injury in the fourth quarter."

Koetter challenges Devils to do better

Before the 2005 Duel, Koetter and his staff made sure to refresh the Devils' memories of the previous year's defeat – and, in doing so, he took a page out of Frank Kush's playbook.

"Just watching the game from the year before and seeing that in the training room, and (the coaching staff) playing the UA fight song the entire time we're working out, it got pretty annoying," said ASU safety Zach Catanese (2005-06). "You got to hear that for quite a few hours, not just one day, but every day. It kind of got to you."

Catanese said Koetter threw down the gauntlet to his team before the game. "(He said), 'Are you going to let these guys put an ass-whoopin' on you again? Are you going to take that again this year?'" he said.

But for the first two and a half quarters of the '05 Duel, it seemed as though the Devils *were* going to allow that to happen. The Wildcats opened the game with an odd-looking 20-5 lead thanks to a 7-yard touchdown pass from freshman quarterback Willie Tuitama to tight end Travis Bell, a 1-yard TD run by Mike Bell and two field goals from future NFL Pro Bowl kicker Nick Folk.

UA was just 3-7 heading into the ASU game, but Tuitama (2005-08) said the team picked up steam at the end of the year by winning two straight conference matchups before losing to Washington. And like many freshmen Wildcats before him, he was able to clearly recall the chaotic atmosphere in Tempe during his first rivalry game.

"I just remember it being crazy, especially for me being so young, and it was really one of the biggest games," he said. "I remember the touchdown pass to Travis Bell in the corner, and I remember hearing all those fans go quiet. That was something that I'll probably never forget – going from it being so loud and so many people just talking a lot of noise, and when you score, you hear the crowd just silent. That's something that's kind of hard to believe."

Catanese said Tuitama and the Wildcat offense did a great job of keeping the crowd quiet for most of the game's first 40 minutes. "I remember going into the locker room (at halftime) and Coach Koetter looking around, and he said, 'Hey man, it's going to be a long winter if you guys don't pull your (expletive) together.'"

With a 5-5 record, the Devils knew they had to win the Duel to become bowl-eligible. "I remember sitting there at halftime thinking, 'I want to go to a bowl game. Who cares about what happens in the first half? Let's get it together, let's make some plays and make some things happen, because they're going to get theirs and we're going to get ours,'" Catanese said.

Tuitama's freshman counterpart, ASU quarterback Rudy Carpenter, began the Devils' comeback in the third quarter with an 80-yard drive that was concluded by their first TD of the game, a 7-yard rush by tailback Rudy Burgess.

"Eventually, we kind of figured it out in the second half and we started making plays," said Catanese, who made what was arguably the most important play of the game a few minutes later.

Down goes Willie

Just like Walter the year before, Tuitama was knocked out of the '05 Duel with a shoulder injury following a hit by Catanese in the fourth quarter.

Tuitama said ASU brought an "all-out blitz" on the play. "I just remember coming down on my shoulder, and my shoulder was just hanging there," he said.

To make matters worse for Arizona, the play resulted in Tuitama's only interception of the game. "It's kind of tough, especially being a quarterback. If I was a linebacker or something and I didn't really have to move it that much, I probably would've still played," he said. "But being that I had to throw the ball, it was just something I couldn't do at the time."

Tuitama didn't know the injury would keep him out for the rest of the game until he got back to the sideline. "When you're playing, you still have all that adrenaline going, and then once I got on the sidelines and sat a couple plays, my body cooled down a little bit, and that's when I really started to feel it bad," he said. "I tried to throw the ball around on the sidelines, and I could throw it, but I couldn't throw it the way that I can – nothing to where I'd be able to help the team out in any way."

Catanese remembers the hit and interception a tad more fondly than Tuitama does. "I know some people say it was a cheap shot, but going back and watching the game this year, I watched it and it was pretty legitimate," he said. "Shoot, I was hoping he'd hold on to the ball and I'd get a sack.

"But he saw me coming out of the corner of his eye, and he kind of threw the ball in the middle of the field, and (defensive lineman) DeWayne Hollyfield came in and picked it off. I felt like that was kind of a turning point in the game. I felt a big momentum swing."

The Sun Devils scored two possessions later on a 71-yard punt return for a touchdown by wide receiver Terry Richardson, and Carpenter's two-point conversion to tight end Zach Miller knotted the score at 20-all with just under eight minutes remaining.

"You just know that you're eventually going to have the opportunity to take the game away, so we eventually turned it around and we got a big play," Catanese said. "And I think we saw a different team in the second half versus the first half."

Kovalcheck came in to replace Tuitama, but Steptoe said the Wildcats just weren't the same without their starting quarterback. "He was having a great freshman year, and he had the reins on the offense," he said. "I felt that even though Rich stepped up there and did OK, I think Willie could've done a little bit better.

"Willie was a tough guy. He just had good poise. You'd never seen him get rattled in the pocket. He always came in with his game face and command of the huddle. You could always look in his eyes and tell he was ready to go, and he had a great arm. I felt like he could make any throw on the field."

Minus Tuitama, Arizona didn't score the rest of the day, and in the game's final minutes, ASU was able to both drive the field and run down the clock to set up a potential game-winning 20-yard field-goal attempt by kicker Jesse Ainsworth.

"At that point, the stars were aligning. I was so confident that we were going to do it at that point," Catanese said. "At that point, it was like, 'This is a chip shot. We got this.'"

They did. Ainsworth's kick was good, and the Devils were able to complete the comeback that they'd been unable to finish the previous season, giving them a 23-20 win and a berth in the Insight. com bowl, where they upended Rutgers in a 45-40 shootout.

And just like the Sun Devils in '04 after Walter's exit, Tuitama was left to wonder what might have been. "That was just a bummer for me because it seemed like we had the game, and (it was frustrating) just not being able to go out there and try to help my team," he said. "Even with such a bad season to start, that would've been a huge win for us, just to be able to end strong, especially in a big game like that against your rival, and go into spring (practice). But sometimes that's just the way it goes."

Stoops also lamented the loss in what was his first Duel in hostile territory.

"I remember that pretty vividly. We played well in the first half," he said. "We should've won the game."

UA gets hot, Koetter goes on the hot seat

ASU had a winning record (3-2) against UA through Koetter's first five seasons in Tempe, but his team's overall records were not as impressive, and that had speculation about his job security swirling toward the end of another mediocre 6-5 season in 2006.

In Tucson, Stoops' program was looking as though it was ready to turn a corner toward the end of his third season. After a 3-5 start in '06, UA rattled off three wins in a row to become bowl-eligible. But the Cats needed a fourth straight victory – this one at home against the Sun Devils – to assure that they would advance to a bowl game for the first time since their 12-1 season in 1998.

Steptoe said the emotional buildup to that year's Duel was enormous. "We won four of our last six games that year. We blew out Oregon at Oregon (37-10 the week before the ASU game)," he said. "And going from that game to play A-State when we were told that (a win) would solidify going to a bowl, we had to win that game. I felt like there was added pressure, and it was pressure that we weren't used to.

"We were always used to playing that game at the end of the year, but it not leading to anything. Now that it meant something, things changed."

Pregame pandemonium

One memory that has stuck with ASU wide receiver Chris McGaha (2005-09) from his first game against UA is that of a brutal pregame Sun Devil injury.

Only the injury wasn't suffered by a player but by the team chiropractor.

"He got blasted in the face with a glass bottle, and he had to get stitches," McGaha said. "He was just walking, and (UA fans) saw he had on an ASU shirt, and out of the stands, a bottle comes flying and hits him in the side of the face."

Catanese said emotions were running extremely high among the Wildcat crowd before the '06 Duel in Tucson. "I remember walking into that stadium, the adrenaline rush, and obviously there's a little bit of fear there," he said. "I've got to hand it to UA: They do put up a pretty good home-field fan base.

"In Tempe, obviously you have a lot of ASU fans, but you have fans from the other schools, and against UA, there was a lot of red and blue there. But (in Tucson), UA only gives ASU fans that little sliver in the corner of the end zone. So it was definitely an imposing feeling from the UA fans."

But any intimidation that the Devils might have been feeling didn't show up on the Arizona Stadium scoreboard.

Carpenter carves up Cats

There were probably plenty of UA fans who were in the mood to throw things after the '06 Duel's first 15 minutes.

Carpenter threw three first-quarter touchdown passes – a 26-yarder to McGaha, a 38-yarder to Lewis and a 7-yarder to Miller, a future NFL standout – to put ASU on top, 21-0.

"Rudy's probably one of the slowest people on our team, but he'd still be elusive in the pocket. He'd make something out of nothing," McGaha said. "And he's probably one of the smartest quarterbacks that I've ever played with, because he probably knows the offense better than the guys who invented the offense. If you could learn Koetter's offense, you can pretty much learn anybody's offense."

Stoops still isn't sure why the Wildcats came out flat in such an important game. "With so much on the line, I don't know if it was just too much," he said. "We hadn't been in many big, meaningful games before, and maybe we just didn't handle it very well."

The Cats' defense eventually settled in, and their offense finally found some rhythm. On UA's first possession of the second quarter, Tuitama, who had been hampered by injuries throughout his sophomore season, threw a 6-yard touchdown pass to Steptoe to cut the ASU lead to 21-7.

"My sophomore year, I was troubled a lot by concussions," Tuitama said. "That was just the most frustrating year that I've ever been a part of, especially when it's concussions and it just has to do with your head."

Tuitama's frustration was compounded halfway through the third quarter when a hit knocked him out of the Duel for the second straight year. "I got kind of sandwiched, I thought. I got hit from both sides," he said. "At first, I was just rattled and on the sidelines, and I was just trying to go back in. But the training staff took away my helmet because they knew what happened."

Diagnosis: another concussion. Tuitama wouldn't return to the field. "For me, yeah, I wanted to go back in. But that's just the nature (of concussions)," he said.

Senior QB Adam Austin took Tuitama's place and threw a touchdown pass to wide receiver Mike Thomas in the final minute of the third quarter to get UA back within seven points. But once again, Steptoe said, there just wasn't an adequate replacement for Tuitama.

"I thought Adam Austin came in and played pretty well, but I felt like if we would've had Willie, it would've been a lot different outcome in that game," Steptoe said. "The whole season, he was battling concussions, and that was the main thing that kept him out of that game, and they wouldn't let him go back in."

Arizona didn't score a point in the fourth quarter, and the Devils eliminated any possibility of a Wildcat comeback when running back Dimitri Nance scored from 1 yard out with less than eight minutes to play, completing a 28-14 ASU victory. The Devils enjoyed a balanced offensive attack from Carpenter and future Washington Redskins running back Ryan Torain, who rushed for well over 100 yards.

Catanese was surprised at the game's lopsided nature, especially in the first quarter, given the talent UA had on offense. "They had Willie, (running back) Chris Henry, Steptoe and Mike Thomas. They had a good squad," he said. "So you're kind of wondering what team is going to show up. Luckily, we got on them fast, and it's hard to come back from 21 points down."

Palmer said a bit of complacency may have set in among the Wildcats following their three-game winning streak. "I think we were a little ahead of ourselves, thought too much of what we had already accomplished," he said.

To make matters worse, the Cats were not invited to a bowl game, leaving them without a postseason appearance for the eighth straight year. "That one hurt. It stung," Stoops said. "We were 6-5 and could've been 7-5, but we ended up 6-6 and didn't go to a bowl. They must have had too many bowl-eligible teams that year."

Koetter leaves to mixed reviews

During the '06 Duel's postgame handshakes, Stoops recalled, Koetter told him something that he certainly didn't expect to hear.

"I don't know how he knew or why, and whether he said, 'I'm fired,' or 'I got fired,' I can't remember. But I remember him saying something to that effect after the game," he said. "And I was just like, 'Wow.' I was shocked."

Whether it was just a feeling he had or was based on information that only he was privy to, Koetter was correct: After four wins in six Duels, his time in Tempe was over. The ASU athletic department did allow Koetter to coach the Devils in the Hawaii Bowl, where they lost to Hawaii in Honolulu, 41-24, before he was dismissed and replaced.

Player reactions to the firing were mixed. "I don't think he was necessarily given a fair shake, but I think what it really came down to was Coach Koetter was still winning, but nobody wanted to play for him," McGaha said. "It was kind of like, even though we had the talent and he could do the recruiting and run the offense, he couldn't make his players rally around him and play good football, and I think the administrative staff called him for that. I think he struggled with the criticism from fans, as well."

On the other hand, Catanese said he enjoyed Koetter's no-nonsense approach. "I liked playing for Dirk. I felt like he was kind of all business, all the time," he said. "He didn't just recruit football players; he recruited men. He wanted guys who were going to be successful on and off the field. I think he was also concerned about making sure his guys were going to be successful when football was over.

"I've always liked and respected Dirk Koetter. I just think the cookie didn't crumble in his favor all the time."

Stoops said he came to respect Koetter as a formidable opponent. "I really liked Dirk. I thought he was an excellent football coach, did a great job and was a great offensive mind," he said. "I always thought the matchups were tough with them. We played them well, but I thought he did a great job."

ASU turns to former national champ

In its pursuit to once again become a national championship contender, ASU decided to hire a two-time national champion.

The Devils' choice to replace Koetter, Dennis Erickson, won national titles at the University of Miami in 1989 and 1991, spent time in the Pac-10 as the head coach at Oregon State and also spent several years in the NFL as head coach of the San Francisco 49ers and Seattle Seahawks.

ASU wide receiver Kyle Williams (2006-09) said Erickson brought a more casual atmosphere to the program. "Coach Koetter was more of a hard-nosed, in-your-face guy. If you messed up, he was going to let you know in a serious way," he said. "Coach Erickson would get on you, but you could tell he was more laid back about the players and winning in general.

"The No. 1 difference, I think, was a lot more guys felt more comfortable (under Erickson). Don't get me wrong: Both were great coaches, and I was happy to play for both of them. But I think it was a little change in the coaching style that may have better suited our team at the time."

Stoops said Erickson was more of a pass-oriented coach than Koetter was. "Dennis was a little more free-wheeling with the ball. He liked to spread it and throw it," he said. "Dirk was a little more controlled in that element of the passing game."

One thing that both Koetter and Erickson did well, according to McGaha, was get their players ready and excited to beat the Wildcats. "When I came here, (Koetter) said, 'All you have to do is beat UA.' Erickson came in with the same motive," he said. "He knows that it's a heavy rivalry we have, and it's bragging rights for the whole year, whoever has the cup."

Dan Cozzetto, who returned to ASU as Erickson's tight ends coach in '07, was able to fill Erickson in on the rivalry. "I said, 'You've got to understand something: We've got to win this game,'" he said. "I said, 'It's kind of like Miami-Florida State, and it's intense as anything you've ever seen.'"

And UA fans living in the Phoenix area were more than happy to confirm for Erickson the serious nature of the Duel in the Desert.

"I live on a golf course, and I've seen some UA golf balls thrown in my yard," he said. "And then you walk around, and if there's a UA fan, I've had them make remarks during the year or the spring. There's no question about it: You hear it all the time."

A second chance to go bowling

Arizona's 2007 season leading up to the Duel was almost a carbon copy of the '06 campaign – a slow start followed by three straight wins, including a victory over Oregon before the ASU game.

The only difference was that this time, the five-win Wildcats were 100 percent certain that they had to beat the Sun Devils in order to advance to a bowl game. And it wouldn't be easy going on the road against an ASU squad that Erickson had humming along with a 9-2 record in his first season – though the Devils had lost 2 of 3 going into the game.

But UA began the '07 game in much more promising fashion than it had the '06 Duel, scoring the game's first touchdown off a pass from a healthy Tuitama to future NFL Pro Bowl tight end Rob Gronkowski to take a 7-0 first-quarter lead in front of a packed, gold-clad Sun Devil Stadium crowd.

"He's a great blocker, but at the same time, he's fast, he has great hands and knows how to use his body to keep guys off him, and he just has a knack for the ball," said Tuitama of Gronkowski, who only played one full season as a Wildcat before going to the NFL. "It's just one of those things where he had a lot of God-given talent and he knew what to do with it."

Carpenter led ASU back by completing a 14-play drive with a 3-yard TD pass to wide receiver Tyrice Thompson to tie the score at 7-all five minutes into the second quarter.

Later in the quarter, McGaha caught a pass that was reminiscent of the extraordinary grab by John Jefferson 32 years earlier. On first-and-10 from the UA 32-yard line, Carpenter threw deep to McGaha, who made a leaping catch over his head while defended by UA cornerback and eventual San Diego Chargers first-round draft pick Antoine Cason. McGaha came down in bounds near the Wildcat sideline and just short of the goal line.

"That was probably one of the top three catches that I've ever seen in my life," Williams said. "He caught the back of the ball like that. I thought it was a touchdown just because he rolled in (to the end zone)."

McGaha said it was the most meaningful catch of his collegiate career - especially coming against Cason, a 2007 All-American. "I get past him, I look up, and (Carpenter) throws to the outside shoulder near the sideline. When I went around Antoine, I kind of went up towards the sidelines, so I knew I didn't have much room. So when I went to go get it, I just stretched as hard as possible.

"It hit my hands and spun out, and I ended up catching the tip of it. And I remember falling back and just tucking it, and I landed on my head for the most part. I got up and saw stars."

After an instant-replay review that wasn't available after Jefferson's catch, officials confirmed the play as a completed pass. "I had no doubt it was a catch and I had landed in bounds, because I had rolled over the (goal-line) pylon," McGaha said.

Remarkably, UA was able to keep ASU from scoring a touchdown on that drive, although a field goal by kicker Thomas Weber gave the Devils their first lead, 10-7, with three minutes to play in the first half. But the catch played a bigger role in terms of momentum than it did on the scoreboard. "That was really the big play (of that game)," Erickson said.

Rudy being Rudy

UA linebacker Xavier Kelley (2005-09) said Carpenter, who threw for almost 250 yards without an interception in the '07 Territorial Cup game, had a reputation for running his mouth before and during games, to the point that it might have thrown the Wildcat defense off at times.

"We all had our personal opinions about Rudy. Everyone wanted to pretty much get their share of the guy," he said. "He was really passionate about what he did. For some reason, he really hated us, and we really hated him. That might have been some of our issues on defense – we focused so much on one guy that we lost focus on our job responsibility."

That loss of focus, according to Kelley, was at least partially a result of a pregame quote from Carpenter. "(He was quoted in) all those newspaper articles before the game about how we don't stand a chance and he's going to do this, he's going to do that," he said. "I'll give him credit: He's a ballsy guy. Especially in a rivalry game, to go out and openly mock the competition, it's pretty ballsy."

McGaha acknowledged that Carpenter had a reputation for talking a lot. "Rudy's going to basically talk (expletive), just because that's Rudy. That's what he likes to do," he said. "His perception as far as being a jerk, being a person that's rude – that might be him on the field, and if you talk to him, he's going to tell you like it is, but he's a really nice guy. His perception on the field is skewed for who is really is. When you get off the field, he's just a cool dude."

Tuitama said his respect for Carpenter was established before they joined the collegiate ranks. "Myself and Rudy, we were at a camp together, so I actually got to really meet him and really talk to him," he said. "A lot of people don't like him, but to me, he was a great quarterback. He went there and did great for his teams.

"I have no problems with Rudy at all. To me, he was a great competitor, and that's what you want from a quarterback."

Devils "hold on to (their) rear ends"

It was two fourth-quarter possessions that ultimately tilted the '07 Duel in ASU's favor.

Carpenter's 20-yard TD pass to wide receiver Michael Jones put ASU ahead, 20-10, with less than five minutes left. On UA's next possession, Tuitama moved the Cats down to the 2-yard line before throwing an incomplete pass on fourth-and-goal, giving the ball back to ASU.

The Wildcats scored a touchdown with less than a minute to play on a 4-yard Tuitama pass to running back Nic Grigsby, but the Devils recovered the ensuing onside kick and ran out the clock.

For the second year in a row, ASU dashed Arizona's hopes of ending its lengthy bowl drought, and the win was enough to send the 11th-ranked Devils to the last bowl game the Wildcats had been to - the Holiday Bowl – though they came up short against Texas, 52-34.

Erickson survived his first Duel, but it wasn't a cakewalk. "Obviously, going into that game we were the favorites and had a good season going, but we had to fight for our lives to get out of it. That's how all those games are. It's unbelievable," he said. "That particular day, we were the better football team, I believe, talent-wise, but we had to hold on to our rear ends to win it."

Williams still has a large memento from his first Territorial Cup victory in Tempe. "I actually have the big panoramic picture of that stadium from that game, and it was packed," he said. "We were a good team that year, we had a good record, and we were hot. And we won, of course, so that's all good."

In his third attempt, Tuitama was finally able to complete a game against ASU, but he still wasn't able to get a victory under his belt. "Sometimes you just do as much as you can, and it's still not enough," he said. "I thought we did a good job of just fighting and battling, but we just couldn't come away with a win."

UA defensive back Corey Hall (2006-09) said the loss in '07 was more difficult to swallow than the '06 defeat because the Wildcats had a better chance to win. But he said he and his teammates went back to the locker room with their heads held high, sensing that the rivalry's tide was about to turn.

"Going into the locker room, we definitely felt like, 'OK, we've got another year, get at them next year,'" he said. "We made a promise to one another to have a great season and a great offseason and get to the Rose Bowl. I think that game set momentum for the offseason and the next year."

UA wouldn't make it to the Rose Bowl in 2008. But much like the Devils' 1996 Rose Bowl team, the Cats decided that, after losing three straight to their rivals, enough was enough.

"The big thing was just getting yourself in position, and eventually you'll knock the door down and get through," Stoops said. "And that's what happened the next year."

Vegas on line for winner of December Duel

The 2008 Territorial Cup contest was set for Tucson on a later-than-usual date of Dec. 6, and UA was favored to defeat ASU for the first time in the Mike Stoops era.

That's not to say the Wildcats were having a phenomenal year, but it was their best since their 12-1 season a decade earlier. They opened the season 6-3, then suffered tough back-to-back losses, including a last-second home defeat to Pac-10 leader Oregon State.

But for the third straight season, a win over ASU would assure UA of that elusive bowl appearance.

"That game was very personal for me, being a senior captain and never reaching a bowl game in my career," Kelley said. "Me, Tuitama, Mike Thomas – we had a talk, and it was just one of those, 'We are not going to lose to these (expletives) again,' because for one, we knew we were so much better than we were in the past. And they had kicked us out of a bowl (the previous two seasons), and we had the opportunity to do it to them."

ASU's '08 season shared quite a likeness to Arizona's '06 and '07 campaigns – a slow start (2-6) followed by three straight wins, putting the Devils in a situation that was quite familiar to the Wildcats: win the Duel, earn a bowl berth.

Ryan Finley, UA football's beat writer for the *Arizona Daily Star* from 2006-12, said the Las Vegas Bowl selection committee announced its intentions to invite the winner of the UA-ASU game before it began.

"That was a huge motivator for the (Wildcats) heading in," he said. "The thing I remember was the (UA) marching band learned 'Viva Las Vegas' for that game.'"

UA's D sends a message

In the first quarter of the '08 Duel, Williams got hit so hard that it ended his collegiate career in a completely different sport.

"The No. 1 thing I remember probably from the whole rivalry was in this game when I got absolutely crushed running a little bubble screen," he said. "I think it was No. 21 (Corey Hall). He came up and hit me as hard as I've ever been hit my entire life.

"There's no way to explain it. I think I had a bruised sternum for two and a half months after that."

That was especially bad news for Williams who, like his brother at UA, was also a member of his school's baseball team. In fact, baseball runs through the blood of the Williams family, as their father Ken is the executive vice president for the Chicago White Sox.

"When I was trying to get ready for baseball, I would swing the bat and my rib heads would pop out," he said. "They had to sit me down for baseball, which ultimately just ended (my baseball career) altogether. I couldn't get healthy enough because I got hit so hard."

Hall said he was out to send a message to the Devils in his junior year. "Rudy Carpenter threw a pass on the flat, and I made a big hit on Kyle Williams," he said. "I got super excited, and I guess too excited, because I got a (penalty) flag thrown at me."

Like many athletes in previous Duels, Williams remained in the game only because it was against his team's most hated rival. "I want to say that, maybe if it was SC or Oregon, I'm staying in, but if that was against a lot of teams where it's not a rivalry or the biggest game, I might have to sit down because of truly not being able to breathe," he said.

"I was pretty messed up on that one. He got me good. He knows he got me good. I think I'm going to be on UA's highlight film for a number of years because of that hit."

Wildcats' "horrible" first half puts Devils ahead

Arizona opened the scoring in '08 the same way it did the previous year: with a touchdown pass from Tuitama to Gronkowski. The 17-yard play gave UA a 7-0 lead with less than a minute remaining in the first quarter.

But the Wildcats were a frustrated bunch the rest of the half. Weber's 40-yard field goal put ASU on the board four minutes into the second quarter, and Carpenter's 2-yard TD toss to tight end Andrew Pettes gave the Devils a 10-7 lead with six minutes left in the first half.

Neither team mounted a serious offensive threat the rest of the half, and the Cats went into the locker room at halftime wondering what the heck had gone wrong.

"We played horrible in the first half. I mean, we stunk up the joint," Stoops said. "I think it's just the pressure and the nerves and understanding the importance of the game, and we just didn't have a lot of experience in meaningful games to some extent.

"I thought we had the better team. That's what I told them at halftime: 'We can't play any worse than that, and we're still only down 10-7. Just relax and do what you guys do.'"

Tuitama also knew his offense was capable of playing much better. "We were confident, but at the same time, we were just kind of mad at ourselves because we just felt like we had a whole bunch of opportunities there in the first half that we just didn't capitalize on," he said.

Carpenter under assault

Arizona got its offense going at the beginning of the second half with a 6-minute drive that ended with a 10-yard TD pass from Tuitama to wide receiver Delashaun Dean, giving the Cats a 14-10 advantage.

Led by cornerback Omar Bolden and defensive lineman Lawrence Guy, both future NFL draft picks, Arizona State had an outstanding defense in 2008. But its offense struggled, primarily due to a lack of protection for Carpenter.

"It was ridiculous. He'd drop back and just let go of the ball and get hit every single time," McGaha said. "We had a young offensive line and guys that didn't really know what they were doing, and it didn't help our offensive chemistry. It was bad."

After the Wildcats took the lead, Carpenter connected with Williams on a 31-yard pass play. But two plays later, Carpenter, who had plenty of time to throw, acted as though he was expecting to be hit at any moment, which resulted in a hasty pass that landed right in the hands of UA defensive back Marquis Hundley, who returned the interception 42 yards to the ASU 34-yard line.

Palmer said the UA defense could sense that Carpenter was wary of being hit. "I think that he was definitely rattled," he said. "He was banged up a lot that whole year, and we had a great young defense, so we really got after him. We showed up on defense throughout that game."

In addition to the interception, Carpenter was sacked three times in the '08 Duel. "It's going to mess with you mentally if they're just blasting you every play, because you know your offensive line isn't going to pick them up," McGaha said of his senior quarterback.

Four plays later, UA scored again on an 11-yard run by Grigsby to go ahead 21-10.

Money Mike takes it to the house

ASU couldn't escape from the shadow of its own end zone on its next possession and was forced to punt from deep in its own territory.

A low punt by Weber was scooped up at the UA 48-yard line by Thomas, who ran backwards for several yards to escape pressure, then darted down the Sun Devil sideline. He received two devastating blocks from his teammates that knocked ASU would-be tacklers to the turf, one from defensive back Orlando Vargas and another from freshman wide receiver Juron Criner.

The floodgates had opened. Thomas' 52-yard return put the Wildcats ahead 28-10, and they never looked back.

Williams remembers the Thomas punt return for its impact on a team and an individual level. "We were actually going head to head for the (title of) lead punt returner in the conference. I think we were tied or a decimal away from each other as far as punt-return average," he said. "So it was a huge deal for us because we wanted to win this battle. And he took it away with that punt return.

"He caught it, went down the left sideline and took off. And that kind of was the momentum shift in the game that got them going and kind of threw us under."

UA added a 49-yard field goal by kicker Jason Bondzio early in the fourth quarter to cap its 31-10 victory, cueing the UA band to play that old Elvis Presley hit, "Viva Las Vegas," on a continuous loop in the game's final minutes.

Tuitama said the win, which featured the Wildcats' biggest margin of victory over the Devils since 1964, played out the same way that many games did for UA that season. "My whole senior season, we were a second-half team for some reason," he said. "There were games where we were down, and in the third quarter, we'd just explode. That's pretty much what happened in that game. It was just one of those games where everything kind of came together."

Arizona defensive lineman Ricky Elmore (2007-10) said the win was a validation of everything his teammates had worked for. "All I really remember is we hadn't been to a bowl ever, and it was a perfect opportunity to beat a rival to get to a bowl, so it was like a win-win for us," he said. "It was a good feeling. I just remember after the game celebrating with my teammates, and the Las Vegas Bowl (representative) came into the locker room to invite us to our first bowl game in 10 years."

Also presented in the UA locker room for the first time since 2004: the Territorial Cup.

Stoops still finds it difficult to decide which was more significant: the blowout win over ASU or the 31-21 Las Vegas Bowl victory over BYU several weeks later. "I think they were equal," he said. "They were both significant in a lot of ways. Just being able to finish the season like that and go into a bowl game – we reversed the fortune on them and knocked them out of a bowl game that year.

"To end it that way and to do what they did to us, to do that to them for the first time – I thought that was significant for our players."

Tuitama said he would've considered his time in Tucson incomplete if he had gone 0-4 against the Sun Devils. "I would've definitely thought that, yeah, without a doubt – not just for myself, but all the rest of the seniors and even some of the juniors that had been there," he said. "It's not like we ever really got blown out (by ASU); it's just that we couldn't make enough plays to win.

"Especially for us, our senior year, being able to get that win and go to a bowl game for the first time in 10 years - that was huge, especially for all the seniors and guys who had been there and who worked hard and had been so close. To finally get to that point and beat those guys and keep them home – that whole part of it was huge."

The Wildcats dealt one final blow to the Sun Devils that season: On the Las Vegas Bowl's final play, Thomas broke Hagan's all-time Pac-10 receptions record.

QB carousel

With Carpenter gone in 2009, ASU dealt with a lack of stability at the quarterback position – and with a 4-7 record and a five-game losing streak, Erickson decided to start freshman QB Samson Szakacsy instead of senior Danny Sullivan in the Duel.

The Wildcats didn't share the Devils' QB issues following Tuitama's departure, as sophomore Michigan State transfer Nick Foles won the starting job in UA's third game of the season and posted outstanding numbers in the Cats' new spread offense. Though UA was coming off a double-overtime loss to top-10-ranked Oregon the week before, Foles had the Wildcats in position to finish second in the Pac-10 and earn a trip to the Holiday Bowl with wins at ASU and the following week at USC.

"They're both great throwers of the football. That's what I remember about them," said Stoops of Tuitama and Foles. "They're both great competitors. Both would stand in the pocket and deliver the ball, so they're both very courageous players, which is what I liked."

Foles, however, was nursing a broken bone in his non-throwing hand going into his first Duel, which - combined with the Devils' ongoing woes on offense - made for a sloppy affair that Saturday afternoon in Tempe.

ASU and UA combined for less than 600 total yards, 13 penalties (10 by ASU) and two missed first-half field goals in the '09 Duel. But two plays allowed the Cats to separate from the Devils in the first half: a 67-yard run by running back Keola Antolin in the first quarter and a blocked punt returned for a touchdown by Vargas in the second.

With ASU trailing 14-0, Erickson decided to hand the reins over to his senior QB, Sullivan, midway through the second quarter. "We weren't producing offensively," he said, "and Szakacsy came in and started the game and did some good things, but he made a lot of mistakes.

"Danny was a senior, he'd been around, and he played a lot that season. I just made the decision that we were going to go with him because he's a guy that can make some plays."

It took a while, but Sullivan brought the Devils back to life. Trailing 14-3 in the fourth quarter, he led a 96-yard drive that ended with a 44-yard touchdown pass to Williams.

"We didn't play very well offensively, and neither did they for the first three quarters," Stoops said. "I think their quarterback came in and did some unbelievable things in the second half, particularly in the fourth quarter. He threw some balls that were pretty special plays to get back in the game."

After a 30-yard field goal by UA kicker Alex Zendejas, the nephew of Max and Luis who made his Duel debut in '09, Sullivan moved ASU down the field again. And on a pass that was originally intended for McGaha, Sullivan found Williams sprinting from left to right in the back of the end zone on fourth down.

Williams' diving catch was comparable to Jefferson's in '75 and McGaha's in '07, and it tied the game with just over two minutes left in the fourth quarter.

The play was Williams' idea. "If you can believe it, it was the same play that I scored my first touchdown on in Colorado, but I was going the opposite way, right to left instead of left to right," he said.

"I went to Danny first and I said, 'We need to run this.' And he was like, 'I like it,' so we went to Coach E. and said, 'This is what we need to run.'

"I just tried to get over there as fast as I can, and Danny rolled out to the right, and I think he made the best throw of his college career, because he put that thing right on the money. It was perfect. He couldn't have thrown a better ball."

For that moment, Williams could not have scripted his final game in an ASU uniform more perfectly. "For about two minutes, it was an ideal situation. It was the perfect ending to a career, in a sense," he said. "For about 2-3 minutes, it was one of the best moments of my life.

"And then it was immediately followed by one of the worst, just like that."

Hero to heartbreak

Williams was still the team's punt returner in '09, and after his game-tying TD, the senior was eager to make one more play to cement his Sun Devil legacy. That chance came when ASU forced UA to punt with just over a minute left in the fourth quarter.

Hall, who leveled that devastating hit on Williams a year earlier, couldn't believe what he was seeing.

"I remember going through my head, 'We can't let this happen,' me being a senior and losing to them my first two years," he said. "We had pretty much a legit, great season, and to give ASU that game when we felt like we were clearly the better team that year – it'd be unfortunate for them to take that cup home when we were on their field and could take it from them."

Stoops said he feared the worst for the Wildcats as they were lining up for the punt. "Kyle Williams made a great catch in the back of the end zone," he said, "and then we got the ball back with maybe two minutes to go and we went three-and-out, and I said, 'Oh, geez,' he said. "They had hurt us on punt returns in other games we played with them."

Williams was ready to hurt the Cats again. "I was already in coach's ear: 'I'm ready to make another play. I want this game. This is it. This is my career,'" he said.

Erickson remembers storm clouds moving over Sun Devil Stadium right before the punt. "I remember the wind was really weird that day, and it started raining," he said.

Maybe the weather had an impact on what happened next. Or maybe it was simply a case of foreshadowing. On fourth down, Williams lined up to field UA punter Keenyn Crier's kick at the ASU 22-yard line.

Williams remembers the play just as well as his touchdown a minute earlier:

"I wanted to save field position because it was a tie game, and all we needed was a field goal, so if I was able to fair-catch it where I was, we would've been in some pretty good field position, and we had a good kicker," he said. "So I'm back there, and it started off like it was going to be a deeper punt, and due to the (weather) conditions, that kind of knocked it down a little bit, so I had to start coming up on it.

"I called for the fair-catch signal, and as I was running up, (UA cornerback Mike Turner) was running down, and our corner who was blocking him was also running down, so we're kind of on a collision course toward each other.

"So, as we're getting closer to each other, I'm under it and I've got a beat on it, and I'm going to fair-catch it. It got to right when the ball was there – I was almost certain that we were going run into each other or it was going to hit him, and it was going to be a bang-bang play that was going to happen.

"At the very last second, when it started to get hot, all three of us were within a 3-4-yard radius to each other. I kind of backed off it a little bit because I was camped under it ready to catch it, so I kind of pulled my hands back a little bit and I started to jump back."

The ball hit Williams' fingertips and then took a very unlucky bounce off his foot. "When it hit my foot, it literally bounced right into (Turner's) breadbasket, almost like I kicked it right to him," he said.

Turner's recovery of the muffed punt not only gave the Wildcats the ball but put them in field-goal range. All they had to do was run down the clock to give another Zendejas the chance to rip out the hearts of Sun Devil fans on a last-second kick.

Alex makes his mark

Following its stroke of good fortune, UA was able to move the ball a few yards closer for Alex Zendejas, who came on for a game-winning 32-yard attempt on the same field that his uncle, Max, had dashed ASU's Rose Bowl hopes 24 years earlier.

Alex, who went to high school in Glendale, said he was excited for his moment as soon as the Cats recovered the muffed punt. "I was in shock at first that it actually happened, but once it did, I got my snapper and my holder ready, and I took a couple practice (kicks)," he said. "I was actually really excited because I had a lot of family there and a lot of people watching."

Zendejas said his mind went blank before he took the field on that rainy afternoon. "You don't put as much thought into it as people would think, I guess," he said. "From there, it was all just in my head: 'I'm going to make it.' I had the confidence."

When the moment came, the snap was good, the hold was good and so was the kick. UA escaped with a 20-17 win, Zendejas ran around the field with his arms raised in triumph, and Stoops looked for someone to hug on the sideline to celebrate his first rivalry win in Tempe.

"Just seeing it going through was a really good feeling," Zendejas said. "I was just happy to be on that field and be out there with my teammates."

UA went on to beat USC in Los Angeles to earn that second-place conference finish, although the Wildcats were blown out by Nebraska, 33-0, in the Holiday Bowl.

Nonetheless, the eight-win season was Arizona's best since the Dick Tomey era. "The way we ended that year was pretty special. To go on the road and win two games like that, we started to feel better about ourselves going on the road and winning big games and rival games," Stoops said. "Those are important factors in continually building your program."

With his second straight win over ASU in tow, Stoops triumphantly put his index finger in the air as he trotted off Sun Devil Stadium as UA head coach for the last time.

The legacy of Kyle Williams

Williams could only watch from the sidelines as Zendejas' kick sailed through the uprights to end his Sun Devil career.

"To be totally honest with you, there's still not a word that I can find that can describe the feeling at that moment (after the muffed punt)," he said. "It was like, 'That didn't just happen. There's no way.' And I always go back to it, and I think, 'What if I'd made a different decision?'"

Erickson, who said the '09 loss to UA was one of his toughest as a head coach, said he felt terrible for the outgoing senior. "I hugged him and told him I love him," he said. "He didn't try to muff it; he was trying to make a play, and that happens. He had a lot of support, and I felt very bad for him."

Healey said he got to know Williams well during his four years in Tempe. "He's a great kid, a great interview, always well-spoken, and made so many big plays for the Sun Devils in his career. And he made big plays in that game," he said. "That touchdown catch to tie the game was a remarkable catch.

"But fate can be cruel sometimes. It's funny: Over the years broadcasting sports for Arizona State, I've seen some great student-athletes at ASU who had great careers end their careers on plays or games that went the other way. It almost seems like a cruel twist of fate, if you will, in that way."

McGaha said he and Williams are still good friends – "we're on a family plan on our cell phones," he said – and remembers telling Williams that the muffed punt wouldn't have meant anything if not for his heroics earlier in the fourth quarter.

"I told him, 'You had a great game. We didn't lose the game because you made one mistake,'" he said. "When you lose a football game, there are a lot of factors, and it doesn't come down to just one dropped punt. Yeah, that's part of it, the mistakes, but it's not just one single mistake that wins or loses the game."

Even worse for Williams was the treatment he received from some ASU and UA fans after the game. "When I got to my house, I had stuff on my doorstep (from ASU fans) telling me about how it was on and they were going to fight me and jump me," he said. "I had UA fans blowing up my Facebook and my phone

– somehow my number got out – and I had 140 text messages from UA and ASU fans getting into me.

"It was a pretty big deal and a pretty tough time at first. It's bad enough already for that to happen, and the backlash from everyone was just icing on the cake."

To Williams' surprise, the majority of the support and encouragement he received after the game came from Tucson. "It wasn't all negative. I actually had a lot of UA people who contacted me just like the people who were trying to tear me down and say, 'You know what? I'm a Wildcat and I'm happy my team won, but the way you played against us for four years, you shouldn't be remembered like that, and you shouldn't remember your career like that,'" he said. "I didn't want to hear it at the time, but looking back on it, for all the bad stuff that I got, I did get some good stuff back."

Two years later, Williams, who was selected in the sixth round of the 2010 NFL draft by the San Francisco 49ers, experienced similar agony on a bigger stage. He fumbled a punt for the 49ers in overtime of the 2011 NFC Championship Game, leading to a game-winning New York Giants field goal that ended San Francisco's chances of advancing to the Super Bowl.

Williams didn't hide from the cameras after that game; he handled the situation with as much maturity and responsibility as he showed in the aftermath of the '09 Duel.

"When it's all said and done, in the situation we were in, you've got to take care of the football," he said about the ASU loss. "I tell people I'm not afraid to talk about it, because it's something that happens and something that I'll live with forever. It was just such a big moment, it could've gone one way or another, and it turned for the worse.

"When I go back to it, I'm forced to kind of chalk it up as, you know, that's football – but at the end of the day, you've got to catch that ball. You're back there because you've shown consistent hands and you've got the trust not only of your team but your community. It was my fault. It was a decision I made, and it cost me."

After Williams' fumble in the NFC Championship Game, Alex Zendejas posted the following message on his Facebook page:

"No one should be judged on their worst day."

Zendejas' sympathy was understandable: By the end of the 2010 Duel in the Desert, he had felt Williams' pain.

Reversal of fortune

ASU's bad luck on special teams carried over from the '09 Duel to its 2010 season, as the Devils lost two games due to missed extra points. In their third game of the year, a blocked Weber PAT in the fourth quarter resulted in a one-point loss at highly-ranked Wisconsin. Several weeks later, at USC, another blocked extra point was returned by the Trojans for a two-point conversion, which proved to be difference in another one-point defeat.

The Sun Devils were just 5-6 when they headed to Tucson that season, but four of their losses were by four points or fewer. And they had gained some steam the previous week, putting up 55 points in a 21-point home win over UCLA.

Sophomore quarterback Brock Osweiler was called upon to lead the ASU offense late in the season after starting QB Steven Threet was sidelined with an injury that would end his career. Osweiler made an immediate impact, throwing for nearly 400 yards and four touchdowns after coming on in relief in the win over the Bruins.

ASU wide receiver Aaron Pflugrad (2009-11) said the Devils were focused heading down to Tucson. "We had come off a victory against UCLA, Brock had played really well, and we were all really excited to get out there," he said. "We thought if we won, we were going to get a bowl game – and it was (against) UA, also."

The Wildcats opened 2010 with a 7-1 record and were ranked as high as No. 9 in the AP poll before struggling late in the season, losing three straight games – and surrendering over 100 combined points in those games – before hosting the Duel.

Foles vs. Osweiler

The first half of the 2010 Duel was forgettable. Weber's two field goals – including one from 52 yards in the first quarter – accounted for the only scoring, and ASU went into the locker room with a 6-0 advantage.

Foles got the Cats going in the third quarter, connecting with Criner, a 2010 All-Pac-10 selection, twice on touchdown throws of 28 and 52 yards to put Arizona in control, 14-6.

"(Foles) rose up after halftime. He took the team on his shoulders and said, 'We're going to go out there and score points, and we're going to win this game,'" said UA center Kyle Quinn (2008-12). "He definitely did everything he could to make sure we had the best chance to win the game. That really was one of the best performances for one half of football by a quarterback."

But the 6-foot-8 Osweiler put on a worthy performance of his own by keeping plays alive with his feet, repeatedly avoiding what looked like sure sacks. "We'd get after him a few times and he'd be scrambling and dodging tackles, and for a guy his size, we didn't think he could do that," Elmore said.

Osweiler did make some mistakes, though, and many Wildcats still regret the number of potential interceptions that their defense dropped in the 2010 Duel. "I think we should've won the game with all the turnovers we should've had," Elmore said. "But then again, (Osweiler) did a good job keeping the ball alive with all the opportunities he had."

Instead, it was the Sun Devils who took advantage of turnovers. With the Wildcats leading 14-9 early in the fourth quarter, UA running back Greg Nwoko fumbled at midfield, and ASU linebacker Oliver Aaron scooped it up. On the Devils' ensuing possession, Osweiler connected with wide receiver Mike Willie in the back of the end zone for a touchdown, then threw for a two-point conversion to wide receiver Kerry Taylor to give Arizona State a 17-14 lead.

"I don't think it was (Osweiler's) best game throwing it, but he made some big throws. He just kind of willed us to win that game," Erickson said.

A fourth Weber field goal made the score 20-14 ASU with 2:59 remaining in the fourth quarter. But Foles, who had led Arizona to a pair of late-game comebacks earlier in the season and battled back from a dislocated kneecap that kept him out of three games in the middle of the year, completed seven passes, including four to wide receiver David Douglas, on UA's final possession of the fourth quarter. His 5-yard throw to Douglas in the end zone tied the game at 20 with just 27 seconds to play and the extra point pending.

"That would've been Nick Foles' crowning moment as the Arizona quarterback," Finley said. "He had played so poorly in the Holiday Bowl the previous year, and he obviously had that knee injury and had not played much. That rally would've been one of those things that he would've been known for, I think."

But as fate would have it, Foles' last-minute heroics would become a footnote to one of the rivalry's most bizarre endings.

What goes around comes around

After a pair of deflating one-point losses earlier in the season, two words were going through Erickson's mind when 23rd-ranked Arizona scored what appeared to be the game-winning touchdown.

"Déjà vu," he said. "All of a sudden you're thinking about, with 30 seconds, how we're going to get back."

Healey, who had called his share of gut-wrenching Sun Devil losses to the Cats, was thinking the same thing. "I think my thought process was along the lines of, 'Here we go again. Another disheartening loss,'" He said. "This was going to be the cruel way to cap a frustrating season – another close-but-no-cigar game for the Sun Devils, who made a living out of losing those heartbreakers in 2010."

On the other side of the media aisle, Finley sat in the press box and remembered several extra points that Zendejas had missed throughout the season. "We had watched him kick all year," he said, "and I hate to sound like generic media cliché guy here, but in this game, so many funny things happen. Anything in this game can happen, to the point that when they do connect on routine things like a short pass or making an easy tackle or a chip-shot field goal, you're almost surprised. And the way I felt with Zendejas was, 'Let's see if he can get this thing through the uprights.'

"As a guy on deadline, I was pretty smart to where I didn't start writing the 'Arizona wins' story just yet. I think it was 9 at night and I had about 20 minutes to file it, but I wanted to sit there and watch. And I think it was one of those moments in the press box when everybody kind of stops. I think I closed the lid to my laptop and was thinking, 'I want to watch this and see what happens.'

"And sure enough, he misses."

Defensive end James Brooks singlehandedly redeemed the Sun Devils' season by getting his hand up and blocking Zendejas' PAT.

"At that point, obviously it was thrilling to see from a Sun Devil perspective because it was such a huge play, and you realize the irony that a team that had lost two games by a margin of blocked extra points this year had just kept its hopes alive by blocking one," Healey said.

"At that point, you figure the extra point's automatic. And then, all of a sudden, James Brooks steps into the spotlight, and that's a great moment."

Zendejas has replayed the kick in his head many times. "I kicked it, he blocked it. I watched it plenty times running through my mind. It happened, and there's nothing you can do about it," he said. "I give him credit. He got up there, and it probably wasn't the best kick on my part, but it happened."

Erickson said Lady Luck was finally smiling on his team. "All of a sudden, the football gods were on our side in that particular game," he said. "We get one blocked against SC and one blocked against Wisconsin. It could've been a different season.

"But I think God looked down and thought we suffered enough. I know he looked down at me and said, 'That gray-haired dude's really suffered.'"

The block sent the game to overtime – a first in Duel history - and Stoops and his team had no choice but to try to refocus.

"Missing the extra point, it really hurt us," he said, "but we kind of regrouped and finished the game, and I thought we'd win in overtime. We were moving the ball. Nick got hot in the fourth quarter, and everything he threw was right. So I felt good going into the overtime."

The two teams traded field goals in the first OT – Zendejas shook off the block to connect on a 19-yard try, and Weber, on what would have been the final play of his collegiate career if he'd have missed, sent a 40-yard attempt straight through the uprights for his fifth and final make of the game.

Weber (2007-10), a 2007 All-American, had struggled throughout his senior year but made up for it - and then some - with his 5-for-5 performance that night in Tucson. "I started to struggle because you start thinking too much," he said. "I think it was just the support of my coaches and teammates, the entire coaching staff – they picked me up, and (I got) the opportunity to repay them and uphold my end of the bargain."

ASU got the ball first to start the second overtime, and Osweiler's 19-yard pass to Taylor set up a 2-yard rushing touchdown by running back Cameron Marshall, with Weber's PAT giving the Devils a 30-23 advantage.

Foles once again had an answer. A lateral that Douglas took in for a touchdown from 9 yards out pulled the Wildcats to within one point, meaning they were an extra point away from sending the game to a third overtime.

But before the attempt, Zendejas said, he committed what kickers consider a cardinal sin. "I remember going into that, I did what kickers weren't supposed to do: I thought about the last one," he said. "So instead of going through the same technique I usually do, I thought, 'I have to get this one higher,' because the last one got blocked. That's one of the big things I learned since that kick: Every kick you have to hit the same."

As a result, Zendejas' kick was low, and Brooks once again deflected the ball, sending it wide right and just short of the crossbar. The Sun Devil sideline and fan contingent at Arizona Stadium erupted, while the Wildcat fans, including the 10,000-strong "ZonaZoo" student section, stood as one in disbelief.

Final: ASU 30, UA 29 in double overtime.

Healey was happy to see a crazy Duel finish, at long last, go in Arizona State's favor.

"I guess you can sum it up by saying that's the kind of play that went Arizona's way from 1982-90," he said. "So maybe not only were the Sun Devils due to have that kind of a play because of what happened to them in the 2010 season, but for those of us who have been around long enough to remember, maybe that's the kind of play that Arizona State was due to have after seeing UA get plays like that for nine consecutive years in the '80s and early '90s."

Pflugrad said it was about time that his team got on the winning end of a one-point game for the first time that season. "I remember Coach Erickson saying something after the game about karma and everything because we had lost two (games) on extra points," he said. "For us to get the block, that was awesome."

ASU linebacker Colin Parker (2007-11), son of former Sun Devil standout Anthony Parker, had the same thought cross his mind. "The first thing I thought about when we blocked the first one was something finally went *our* way," he said. "And having it go the other way just made it 100 times better."

The ASU players took their celebration to the corner of the field where their fans were located. Weber took Sparky's pitchfork and thrust it into the turf in the south end zone – a longtime Sun Devil custom following a road win.

"It was just that feeling that we'll remember forever, being our last game," Weber said. "It definitely doesn't change the fact that we could've had a much better season, but for us in our last game, it was great."

ASU finished the season 6-6, and while the Devils were not invited to a bowl game, Erickson said their postgame celebration in a cramped Arizona Stadium locker room was like few others he had witnessed in his coaching career. "It was unbelievable," he said. "The season had been a tough season, but we'd won a couple in a row and we had some momentum going. It was fun is what I guess I could say."

On the UA side, Stoops pointed to missed opportunities throughout the game on which the Wildcats failed to capitalize. "I think we didn't help ourselves. We dropped three interceptions in the first half right in our hands, and that hurt us," he said. "We seemed depressed a lot in that game. It was a weird, freaky game.

"We scored with, what, 29 seconds to go? And I thought, 'Wow, what a great way to end the season.' And it was really disheartening. That will probably go down as one of my hardest losses ever. That one hurt in a lot of ways. We were kind of struggling through the end of the year. It just hurt our momentum, and that's been the hard thing at Arizona, to sustain momentum. That really hurt our momentum as a program."

The Cats' hangover from the loss persisted through their appearance in their first Alamo Bowl, where they were soundly defeated for the second straight time in a postseason game, this time 36-10 by Oklahoma State.

Zendejas looks back, forward

Like Kyle Williams a year earlier, Alex Zendejas placed the blame for what transpired at the end of his team's heartbreaking Duel defeat on his own shoulders.

"The second kick, I threw my technique off by trying to get it higher than the first one, so that was my fault," he said. "I take full responsibility for that kick."

And like Williams, Zendejas said he received his share of nasty comments from fans but also got a great deal of support. "I had a lot of people come to my side and encourage me," he said. "My family was the biggest part. My dad, my mom, my brother, my uncles – they all came to my side and told me that that's the life of a kicker sometimes. They've all had their ups and downs, they've all had game-winners, and they've all missed plenty of times. So they were just, 'Let it make you stronger. Let it be the fuel behind everything to keep going.'"

But Alex said the 2010 Duel continued to play with his head in his senior season in 2011, and that contributed to him losing his starting job.

"As much as I didn't want it to, in the offseason I heard a lot of stuff, and I wasn't as prepared for what I was going to be going through," he said.

"It's still something I think about. I can't take it back. I wish I would've bounced back better than I did."

If there's one athlete who's experienced the highest of highs and the lowest of lows in the Duel in the Desert, it's Alex Zendejas. "For me, you've got to take the bad with the good," he said. "2009 was a great feeling, especially to (kick the game-winner) there in their stadium. For all the reasons that was so great, those were the same reasons that the 2010 game wasn't as great. I had a lot of people that I knew at Arizona Stadium, and having to go to class the next day, it was rough.

"But at the same time, I'm still trying to learn from it, still trying to go forward. I'm not going to let what people have to say bring me down or discourage me, and I know what I'm capable of doing. I have the uncles, the dad, the people to be supportive, help me out and keep pushing forward."

Stoops dismissed in midseason

The hangover the Wildcats experienced following their 2010 Duel loss lasted well beyond their bowl game; it festered into the 2011 season in the new Pac-12 - and it cost Mike Stoops his job.

The Cats opened 2011 with a 1-5 record and had lost 10 of their last 11 games dating back to the previous year. And just like Mackovic eight years earlier, Stoops was let go halfway through a disappointing season.

Byrne said his decision to make the midseason change was the right one. "I think it's really important that you're upfront and you're honest with your coaches, and we had made a decision to change the leadership there, and I wasn't going to be dishonest with Coach Stoops," he said. "And then I also felt (we had) the ability, like we talked about publicly, to calm our program down a bit and maybe put our seniors in the best possible position to go to a bowl game – which didn't happen, unfortunately. And it allowed us to get in front of the (head coaching) market and get ahead of what's often a busy offseason."

Heavner, whom Stoops brought back as a graduate assistant for the 2011 season, had seen this movie before – only this time the scene wasn't as bleak as it was after Mackovic was replaced in the middle of the '03 season.

"With Coach Mackovic, the program was kind of going downhill, so at workouts, it wasn't that intense. Some guys didn't really care, and I didn't really understand that as a freshman," he said. "With Coach Stoops, he had a mentality that every day was a work day and everything we did was geared toward preparing us for the game. And that's what was established in day one with him.

"Everybody respected the heck out of that guy because of his résumé, what he'd done before. Obviously, winning a national championship (at Oklahoma), he knew how to do stuff. And his knowledge and passion for the game, you could feel it every day."

Tuitama recognized that many Wildcat fans were put off by Stoops' displays of emotion and intensity on the sidelines. But it was that passion for the game that many of his players enjoyed.

"I loved playing for Coach Stoops," Tuitama said. "A lot of people look at him when he's on the sideline and things like that, but that's who he is. He's a good coach, and I'd rather have a coach that's passionate and not afraid to show it. He doesn't care what other people think of him; he just wants to go out there and get wins. I think Coach Stoops is a great coach and he's going to have a great career."

Finley got to know Stoops for five years through his coverage for the *Star*. "Mike Stoops is just a different dude," he said. "The players loved him, and he bonded well with guys that came from horrible situations because he came from a horrible situation. He was a big fan of the underdog, and certainly that does not get reported or talked about enough.

"It was the people in his own building that I think he had a hard time connecting with and establishing any kind of a rapport with, and I think that's what ultimately got him fired."

After having several months to reflect upon his time in Tucson – and just hours before he publicly accepted an offer to rejoin his brother, Bob, at Oklahoma as defensive coordinator – Stoops was asked whether he left the UA football program in better shape than it was in when he arrived.

"Oh, without question," he said. "We took over a very dismal place and did it with very few means – no football facility, money was always an issue. But you know what? Our coaches and players never wavered in their goals to rebuild this thing through hard work and toughness, and I think that's what our program was built on, and we certainly tried to instill that in our players every day.

"I feel very good about what we were able to accomplish. Going to the next level is a very difficult step, and that's one that I hope Arizona is able to take over the next several years."

Kish picks up the pieces

The decision to let Stoops go left many UA players stunned. "It was shock. Nobody expected that to happen the middle of the year," Quinn said. "A situation like that just doesn't happen every day in college sports, and to have your coach get fired in the middle of the season, it definitely took us some time to digest what happened. But you can't live in the past. You have to move forward, especially in the middle of the season like we did."

As in 2003, Arizona selected its defensive coordinator – or in this case, its co-defensive coordinator – to lead the team for the rest of the season. And just like Mike Hankwitz, Tim Kish had never been a head coach.

"I have great respect for him. He was with me for 10 years, and his dad was my high school basketball coach, so I've known him for a long time," said Jim Young, who coached with Kish at Army. "I think he's a very personable individual and an excellent recruiter, and he emphasized (to the UA players) enjoying themselves and having fun, which I think took some of the pressure off of them."

Quinn agreed that everyone was wound up a little too tight earlier in the season. "Coach Kish really just brought us back down to the basics. We had a lot of fun at practice and just got back to having fun," he said. "Practices were much looser. We still worked hard – our work ethic never changed – but the way we approached practice changed and how everybody just went out there and had fun."

The Wildcats responded with a 48-12 pounding of UCLA at Arizona Stadium in their first game without Stoops, but their struggles soon returned, as they dropped their next three games, including back-to-back double-digit losses to the two newest members of the conference, Utah and Pac-12 basement-dweller Colorado.

But a Territorial Cup victory is always the perfect antidote for a disappointing season – and UA's interim coach understood that.

In fact, Kish duplicated a Jim Young tactic just days before the game. "He showed us videos of ASU – just old clips of how they really hate us, just (to show) how the rivalry is and get the young guys caught up a little bit," said Antolin (2008-11).

UA linebacker Derek Earls (2010-11) specifically remembers the video showing Weber thrusting the ASU pitchfork into the UA end zone following the Devils' double-overtime win. "That got people going," he said. "That got us motivated when we played them, just knowing how they disrespected us."

Kish also utilized the two members of his coaching staff who had played in the rivalry – Joe Salave'a, UA's defensive line coach, and former defensive back Jeff Hammerschmidt, Arizona's special-teams coordinator and defensive line coach.

"Coach Joe came up and talked to us. He had a great play (against ASU) back in the '80s," Quinn said. "Then Coach Hammerschmidt came up and talked, and Coach Hammerschmidt's an amazing motivator. He got up there yelling and screaming and getting us fired up for practices."

Earls said the coaches also inserted some brand-new defensive schemes that week. "When we played ASU, we played out with stuff that we never showed before at all," he said.

With all the motivation and game-plan retooling that his coaching staff could muster, Kish took his 2-8 squad to Tempe to try to end a turmoil-filled season in triumph.

Devils look to "Black Out" Cats

With a new pitchfork logo and revamped uniforms, the Sun Devils opened the 2011 season with a 6-2 record, including a 21-point win over USC and an overtime victory against Missouri on national TV at Sun Devil Stadium, a game in which ASU debuted its all-black uniforms and encouraged its fans to wear black, as well.

But like Arizona a year earlier, ASU faltered down the stretch, losing two straight games to unranked teams before hosting the Wildcats in front of another "Black Out" crowd.

And the Devils had plenty to play for – namely, a chance to win the first-ever Pac-12 South Division title, which would earn them a spot in the inaugural Pac-12 championship game, with the winner of that game guaranteed a spot in the Rose Bowl.

But in the 2011 Duel, the motivated Wildcats struck first. A 48-yard pass from Foles to Criner – who had surpassed "T" Bell as Arizona's all-time receiving touchdowns leader – set up a 1-yard TD rush by Antolin on their first possession. After UA cornerback Shaquille Richardson intercepted an Osweiler pass, Foles threw an 11-yard touchdown pass to freshman running back and Tucson native Ka'Deem Carey to extend the lead to 14-0.

ASU responded by finding the end zone on its next three possessions. Marshall's 2-yard touchdown run and an 11-yard TD pass from Osweiler to wide receiver Gerell Robinson tied the game at 14-14 in the second quarter.

And after Osweiler's 58-yard pass to Pflugrad set up a 22-yard Marshall TD run, giving ASU a 21-14 advantage, the black-clad fans were riled up.

"It's always fun to make a good play in the rivalry game, but once again, just the intensity of the game and how the whole state of Arizona was up for it (was memorable)," Pflugrad said.

UA kicker John Bonano's 43-yard field goal in the half's final seconds trimmed the ASU lead to 21-17. The Devils came out moving the ball again in the second half, but the Wildcat defense kept them out of the end zone and forced them to settle for field goals. A 22-yard yarder in the third quarter and a 27-yarder early in the fourth by Alex Garoutte pushed the ASU lead to 27-17 but allowed UA to stay within striking distance.

Weekend at Beirne's

With the Wildcats trailing by 10 points in the fourth quarter, Foles found senior wide receiver Gino Crump, who dodged several Devils on his way to a 33-yard score that cut the UA deficit to 27-24.

"The thing that disappointed us the most is we gave away stuff – missed tackles and blown assignments, stuff that we didn't have to give them," Parker said. "We felt that, had we played a more disciplined game, a better ballgame, that the game was ours."

The Wildcats got the ball back a few plays later and were inching closer to taking the lead. But on a first-down play from the ASU 30-yard line, Foles collapsed to the ground in pain, injuring his lower back as he turned to hand the ball to Antolin. He was forced to leave the game and wouldn't return – which gave senior and seldom-used fifth-year quarterback Bryson Beirne a crack at the Sun Devils in his final Territorial Cup contest.

On just his second play, Beirne threw a screen pass to Criner, who, like Crump earlier in the fourth quarter, eluded several ASU defenders as he broke free for a 23-yard touchdown, giving Arizona a 31-27 lead with just over five minutes to play.

Foles (2009-11), who was selected by the Philadelphia Eagles in the third round of the 2012 NFL draft, was thrilled to see Beirne get his moment in the spotlight.

"It was amazing. If there's anybody who deserves it, it's him, just for what he's fought through throughout his career and this season," he said. "He's my brother, and just to see him going in there – I looked at him and he looked at me, and he said, 'I'm going to go in there and win this thing.'"

Beirne said he didn't need to play in that game in order to consider his collegiate career complete - but he also said he's a believer in destiny. "I'm a firm believer that my Heavenly Father – whatever he wants, it's going to happen," he said. "I don't really look for any validation. I'm going to work hard no matter whether I do play or don't play.

"I just got the ball and threw it to Juron. He had to make that first guy miss, and the made the second guy miss, and it was probably three, four, five more guys (he avoided), and he just sprinted to the goal line.

"I almost tackled him. I was just so stoked that he did that."

Criner (2008-11) was grateful to be on the receiving end of Beirne's career highlight. "That meant a lot to him, and for me to be able to finish it for him, it meant a lot," he said. "He's always been able to make plays in practice, and he knows he doesn't play much, but you see him going in practice like it's a game, and I knew he was ready for it."

Stoops watched the 2011 Duel on television and was elated to see Beirne get his due.

"I mean, the kid, he'd been a great team guy," he said. "He's been like a coach to these guys, to Willie, to Nick. He was kind of the glue that held everything together with those guys. So it was very fitting that he threw the winning touchdown. I was so happy for him. He deserved it, and it's a great lesson of perseverance.

"Good things happen to good people – that's what I always believe – and certainly it did in that instance. That's a memory he'll always have, and I think it's pretty special."

Last-minute mayhem

UA defensive back Jourdon Grandon intercepted an Osweiler pass on the next series and returned it into ASU territory, but the Wildcats were forced to punt the ball back to the Devils, who then had 79 seconds to go 80 yards to avoid the upset on their home field.

Osweiler was ready to break the Cats' hearts again, completing five passes for 65 yards in just over a minute. His 20-yard completion to Marshall moved the Devils to within 15 yards of a victory with less than 15 seconds left in front of 70,000-plus ASU fans and a smattering of Wildcat fans who were all standing during the game's final moments.

On first down, Osweiler's pass was knocked away by Grandon, giving the Devils one last opportunity with just four seconds left. As broadcaster Tom Leander noted on the Fox Sports Arizona telecast of the game, the recipient of the Territorial Cup would be decided on the game's final play for the third consecutive season.

And for the third consecutive season, the visitors left the home fans dejected. Richardson knocked away an Osweiler pass intended for Willie at the goal line as time expired, allowing the Wildcats to hold on and do what the Devils had done to them the previous season – go into hostile territory with a losing record and come out on top in the Duel against a team with a winning record.

After the game, UA attempted to exact revenge for the 2010 pitchfork incident by sticking its flag on the new ASU pitchfork logo in the middle of the field. A few Devil players prevented the Wildcats from doing so, and the flag ultimately made its way into the Sun Devil student section, where it was promptly torn apart – but that didn't put a stop to the celebration that ensued.

Bearing down

For UA, months of futility and frustration were immediately forgotten.

"That game was really – I still can't put a word on it," Quinn said. "The feeling of winning that game on their field was just amazing. With the season that we had, everything that went on with the coaching staff, it just wasn't a good year for us. We didn't perform like we wanted to. But to be able to go up there and beat a team that was favored to do all these great things and to beat them on their field in front of a sold-out crowd like that, that was really special."

The Wildcats went back to the visiting locker room and twice sang "Bear Down, Arizona" loud enough to be heard in the adjoining press room.

After the game, Kish said the Cats "did everything we asked of them" that night. "They prepared themselves as well as they did all year – and they should. It's a rivalry game. It means a lot," he said. "And I just couldn't be happier for the seniors and the university and the City of Tucson."

Quinn momentarily left the locker-room celebration to show off the Territorial Cup – the replica, of course – to Kish in the press room.

And it was a special night for UA's backup quarterback. "(Waiting) five years, and to get a chance to beat ASU, senior year, up in Phoenix on their field – you can't ask for something like that," said Beirne, who started the Cats' final game of the season the following week, a 45-37 home win over Louisiana-Lafayette. "It was placed upon me, and I'm grateful it was."

One of UA's biggest cheerleaders that night was its former head coach. "I was certainly cheering and got excited in the fourth quarter," Stoops said. "At the beginning of the year, Arizona State was playing so well, and they deteriorated as the year went on for whatever reason. We knew it was going to be a tough game, but I was glad to see them go out and compete. They played hard, and that was good to see."

And while Alex Zendejas didn't play in his final game against ASU, he said it was gratifying to be able to celebrate with the team as a senior.

"That was a great game, just being a part of it, being on the field with my team, and just getting the win," he said. "I'd have to say that two of my best college memories were in ASU's stadium – the 2009 kick, obviously, and then (the 2011 game). It was a fun game to be a part of. My teammates went out there and took care of business."

The end for Coach E.

Osweiler (2009-11) decided to forgo his senior season and declare for the 2012 draft, where he was picked by the Denver Broncos in the second round. Like Quinn, he struggled to articulate his thoughts on the game, albeit from a much different perspective.

"No words can explain it," he said. "We had plenty of opportunities. I feel like we didn't capitalize on them. We worked extremely hard to find the team that had so much confidence during summer workouts, and just for whatever reason, we can't grab on to that."

Erickson said the list of things that went wrong for ASU that night was almost too long to recount. "Golly, there are just so many things that happened in that game," he said. "We turned it over way too many times, and I think that was the biggest difference in that game. But we still had an opportunity to win.

"That was probably one of the most devastating losses I've been involved in. Losing a rivalry game like that was really tough. Where we were at in our season made it even tougher."

With ASU's late-season struggles came speculation that Erickson would be asked to leave at the end of the season. The UA loss, combined with a home loss to Cal the following week, kept the Devils out of the Pac-12 championship game and convinced ASU's leadership to go another direction.

"Dennis was coaching his fifth season at Arizona State, and there was a progressive plan all along that, by the time we reached the 2011 season, we'd be an equipped football program and, in this case, compete for the (South) Division title and potentially a spot in the Rose Bowl game," said former ASU athletic director Lisa Love. "We were pointed in a particular direction, and all arrows looked like we were (getting there) until the month of November, and then it appeared that we were more competitively fragile than we should have been. And so, that raised doubts about where we would be going beyond those years, so that's when I decided it was time to make a change."

Love was also replaced shortly after Erickson's firing.

Months after his dismissal, Erickson was asked the same question that Stoops had been asked: Did he leave the Arizona State football program in better shape than it was when he arrived?

"Without a question," he said. "Unfortunately, we didn't win enough football games, so that's the bottom line. I've been in the business a long time, and I understand that. But I'm proud of what we did there, and the new coach – he's got some things to work with."

Starting over again

Just as they did after the 2000 season, both schools hired new coaches following their respective 2011 campaigns, as former Rice, Tulsa and Pittsburgh head coach Todd Graham was selected to take over the Sun Devils, while former West Virginia and Michigan coach Rich Rodriguez was picked to navigate the Wildcats through their next chapter. Graham and Rodriguez coached together for two seasons at West Virginia.

Erickson's rivalry counterpart from 2007-11 knows both men, and he believes they'll both inject plenty of their own flavor into the Duel.

"I think this rivalry will take on new meaning with Rich and Todd," Stoops said. "I don't think there's any love lost there, and they're pretty similar people. They're both very stubborn. So this is going to be an interesting new series of games."

CONCLUSION

An unusual thing happened at Arizona Stadium at the end of the first Duel in the Desert for both Todd Graham and Rich Rodriguez.

Sure, there were plenty of familiar aspects to the 2012 game. For one, the Duel returned to what many believe is its proper date: the day after Thanksgiving.

There were also the usual pregame taunts from fans inside and outside of Arizona Stadium.

There were plenty of unlikely special-teams plays, such as a two-point conversion by a UA kicker and a late blocked punt to set up an ASU touchdown.

There was a visiting team winning for the fourth straight season – this time it was the Sun Devils overcoming a 10-point fourth-quarter deficit to pull out a road victory.

There were new heroes created. Sophomore Taylor Kelly, who exchanged text messages with fellow Idaho native Jake Plummer throughout the season, made some big plays down the stretch and didn't have a single turnover in his Territorial Cup debut. "I like it when he gets out of the pocket – he reminds me a little of myself when he runs around out there," Plummer said. "I thought he played really well, had a great year, and definitely did a good job (against UA)."

Kelly outdueled Wildcat senior Matt Scott, who threw for three touchdowns but also committed four turnovers and experienced the heartbreak of so many athletes before him in losing in his final appearance in the Duel.

There was a celebration with the Territorial Cup, as Graham high-fived ASU fans with one hand while holding the cup in the other after the game.

And there was even another color controversy, as ASU wanted to wear a certain uniform combination for the UA game but had to ask the host team permission to do so. "When we saw that (the Wildcats) were doing all-red uniforms, we thought it'd be neat if we wore our all-black," said ASU associate athletic director of media relations Mark Brand. "So when we called and asked them, they said no. So we called the (Pac-12), and they said that was the first time anybody's ever denied anybody."

But as the clock ticked down to zero in ASU's 41-34 win, which gave both first-year head coaches a final regular-season record of 7-5, 50,000-plus fans witnessed something unusual on the field.

No pushing. No shoving. No jawing. No flag-planting at midfield.

None of that stuff - just handshakes and congratulations all the way around.

In fact, one might say that the 2012 Territorial Cup postgame scene was pretty darn cordial.

The Devils did continue their tradition of stabbing Sparky's pitchfork into the other team's end zone – this time, outgoing senior Cameron Marshall, who scored on an 8-yard run following a blocked punt by safety Kevin Ayers to give ASU a late lead, got the honors.

"We definitely talked about (getting payback) after losing a close game we should've won (in 2011), and we talked about how disrespectful they were to us at the end of the game – the feeling of them wanting to jump on our logo – and how we weren't going to experience that anymore," Marshall (2009-12) said. "I said to myself after that game when I was a junior that I'd never experience that feeling again as a Sun Devil, to have a UA Wildcat stomping on my logo and have the opportunity to say they beat me."

That postgame disrespect played a role in the Devils' desire to end the 2012 Duel on a classier note. ASU linebacker Brandon Magee (2008-12), who was named Pac-12 Defensive Player of the Week for his performance against UA, said Graham and the veteran Sun Devil players talked about it earlier that week.

"To see them put the flag in the middle of our 'A' (in 2011), dance in the middle of our field, and being so disrespectful and all that, that really got us fired up. And we decided that when we won, we weren't going to do all that," he said. "We were just going to walk off the field and celebrate with our fans.

"We walked in there as a winning team with character. Todd Graham really pushed the guys to play like that. And if we would've danced on that field – I guarantee you, anybody who would've done that would not be playing in the bowl game."

But the display of respect didn't just come from ASU's side. Kyle Quinn said he was happy to see his teammates on the UA side reciprocate – not just after the game but during the on-field battle.

"There wasn't much trash talk during the game, either. There was the usual smack talk – a guy makes a play and gets into your face – but that's normal football. But the extracurricular stuff – the extra shove, the extra push, the taunting penalties – those didn't happen," he said. "That's really a credit to Coach Graham and Coach Rodriguez for keeping both teams' attention on the game and not the side conversations and side acts that go on in a rivalry game.

"Some people get caught in the moment because it's a rivalry game and there's so much emotion, so much passion for the game on the field, but the purpose of every college athlete is you have to represent your university and your conference with class. Getting into a rivalry game where it's blood, sweat and tears, and you're fighting for your state, you have to remember you represent more than just yourself; you represent your university, your coaching staff, your administration and everybody when you put on your jersey and represent your (team) logo, whether it's ASU or UA.

"(It's important to) keep it classy and make sure we're out there shaking hands with each other and telling each other, 'Good game,' and not having a shoving or shouting match. That's just not part of football."

Rodriguez said the 2012 post-Duel scene was representative of what he expects to be the norm as long as he and Graham are in charge.

"It's an extremely emotional game, and for your players, if they're not upset after the game when they lose and really happy when they win, there's something wrong," he said. "But at the same time, once that final whistle blows, you've got to show respect to your opponent no matter who it is and do things the right way, and our guys will do that.

"Certainly sometimes, there are some emotions that carry over, and they probably have in the past. But it's still a game, the guys have battled hard, and they should show respect for each other."

∞

In a hyped, emotion-fueled and often nasty game such as the annual Duel in the Desert, respect doesn't always come naturally. And despite the display of respect in the aftermath of the 2012 Duel in Tucson, the fact is that, for many former UA and ASU athletes, that attitude has never come.

But there is a contingent of former ASU and UA players who, in the appreciation of their opponents' efforts and the spirit of sportsmanship, managed to become friends after their collegiate careers.

"Here's the funny thing: You really don't like these people down in Tucson. You grow to despise them. It's amazing to have so much animosity toward someone you don't know personally," Ron Pritchard said. "And when you're out of school, a lot of these guys become your friends."

On the first Monday of every month, dozens of former athletes from the Grand Canyon State, including ASU and UA football players and coaches from the 1950s and '60s, meet in downtown Phoenix. They share memories of their careers – many played other sports in addition to football – and for a fee of $7.50 to cover lunch, they reminisce about some of the battles they had with each other along with a number of other topics.

UA and ASU greats such as Eddie Wilson, Ralph Hunsaker, Fred Rhoades and Ron Cosner often show up. Even Frank Kush is known to stop by once in a while.

The tradition was started over a decade ago by longtime Kush assistant Larry Kentera and former Phoenix Union basketball coach Ed Long. "We all talk about what's going on presently in the world of sports, and sometimes that involves ASU and UA," Wilson said. "They visit about old times and say, 'Do you remember so-and-so from ASU?' It's a great range of diversity."

Oddly enough, Rhoades said, the Duel in the Desert is typically not a topic of conversation, as those who competed in it seem to be content to let the past remain the past. "We never talk about the rivalry. We just know that we played each other and we think that each other did a good job," he said.

Wilson said the mutual respect that allows players who wore different collegiate colors to come together and break bread should be shared among all former UA and ASU athletes, regardless of whether they bleed red and blue or maroon and gold.

"I think they all should respect one another because they're all part of the same brotherhood," he said. "They all had pain. They all had excitement and thrills. They all had good moments and they all had bad moments."

Wilson hopes that the younger players who have yet to adopt that mindset will do so later in life. "I think when you age, you become more mellow in that respect," he said. "It disturbs me that, after their playing days are over, they can't meet somebody and have respect for that person for what they've done."

The Crum family is among the most fervently pro-Wildcat clans you'll ever meet. Moose Crum and his son, Bob, played on the UA football team, and Bob's son, Cassidy, was a member of the Wildcat volleyball squad.

And while he's maintained his rooting interests since his playing days, Bob said he's developed some lifelong friendships with former Sun Devils. "I have some very good friends who are ex-Arizona State players," he said. "I'm always glad to beat 'em, but I have a ton of respect for the great athletes and great teams that they've had."

Case in point: One of Crum's good friends is Steve Matlock, whom he competed against in the Duel and even before then during their high school days in Phoenix, as Bob went to Sunnyslope and Steve attended Alhambra.

The year after Matlock's final season at ASU, he and his family went down to Tucson to attend the '74 Duel. "It was the first time I had been in the stands at UA since I was recruited down there," he said, "and sure enough, we were gathered in the middle of the UA section in the south end zone."

Matlock and his family were decked out in Sun Devil gear, which didn't go over well with some of the more rabid Wildcat supporters. "There were comments going back and forth, but I had my folks there, and I wasn't going to say anything," he said. "And finally, it got a little heated, and one of the guys in the row behind us popped off about me because I had my letterman jacket on."

Long story short, the fan proceeded to question Matlock's manhood. "And my dad, who was a big guy, jumped up, spun around and hit this kid," he said. "He was probably 20-21 years old, a college kid, and he just ripped this guy – KO'd him on the spot.

"Well, needless to say, all hell broke loose at that point. I moved my mom and my future wife, got them all out of the way, and my dad, my brother, my brother-in-law and I just kicked the (expletive) out of about six guys in the UA south end zone. Fortunately, because it was a total upheaval, security came over and busted it all up."

Understandably, Matlock and his family reconsidered the wisdom of attending future Duels in Tucson. "At that point, I said, 'Gosh, I don't think I'll ever come to another game down here. That's ridiculous,'" he said.

But Matlock relayed the tale to his friend, Crum, who vowed that Matlock would never again receive that kind of treatment in his alma mater's stadium. "We both had gotten married and started having kids, and when that happened, he said, 'You come on down and I'll treat you and your whole family,'" Matlock said.

"And as the families expanded – he has five kids, I have three – I started bringing him up (to games in Tempe), and it was just a great time."

For 25 years, Matlock and Crum's pregame tailgates were an annual event. In fact, when Matlock was the president of ASU's Varsity 'A' Association, he spearheaded a joint ASU-UA tailgate party for the Duels at Sun Devil Stadium.

During the tailgates outside the stadium and during the games in the stands, Matlock and Crum – whom Matlock affectionately calls "Crum Bum" – had each other's back. "I would be responsible to tell Sun Devil (fans), 'Back off, these are our friends,' and vice versa down there," Matlock said. "And we'd help each other out of the stands without having any problems."

Matlock has kept in touch with many friends, both Sun Devils and Wildcats, from his high school days. As he and Crum got married and had kids, their families became close, and they've even helped each other to grow in their spiritual faith.

"We ran around together and had a great time, and we still do," he said. "The rivalry, it was a great football game, but more importantly, there were some great friendships created between the UA and ASU players, even though the fans probably wouldn't accept that in most cases. But it was something I'm glad we did, because there were some good guys down there."

Many coaches, players and analysts have noted that the fans are usually the ones who take the nastiness of the rivalry to another level. But Tim Healey said that, in the grand scheme of things, the Duel has been surprisingly civil on the field.

"It has always been super intense, as intense as any college football rivalry in the country, and I hate to say it, but at times I think it's as hate-filled among the fans as any rivalry I've ever seen. I got that sense when I moved here in 1983, and I think it's about the same today," he said. "It changes and goes thru ebbs and flows in terms of which team is better, but in terms of the feelings that exist between the two schools, the two programs and, heck, the two towns of Tucson and Tempe, I don't really know that a whole lot has changed since I've been here.

"But I would add a footnote that, as nasty and hate-filled as it is, for the most part, I'd say most of the games they've played in have been cleanly contested. Certainly (it wasn't) in the game in 1996 when ASU's Rose Bowl team clobbered the Wildcats in Tucson, and there was an incident when some of the players danced on Sparky (in 2001). But I think it's kind of interesting for a rivalry that's as passionate as this one that, for the most part, most of the games have been cleanly contested."

So maybe – just maybe – the camaraderie that the coaches and some of the former players from the state's two largest learning institutions enjoy will eventually trickle down to the fans and reflect the spirit of those first two teams that met on Thanksgiving Day 1899 and played a hard-fought game on a dusty field yet openly respected and appreciated each other before and after the battle.

"It's a great sports tradition, and I think it's a shame that it's gotten as nasty as it has," Rob Spindler said. "Frankly, we have much more in common as the two great institutions of higher education in Arizona than we have to be mad at each other over. There's no reason we can't fight hard on the football field and work together as institutions of higher education."

Jay Dobyns and John Mistler both went to Sahuaro High School in Tucson, but Mistler decided to go to ASU while Dobyns stayed in town to play for UA. Dobyns said that while in high school, he idolized Mistler, who was a senior when he was a freshman, and the two men remain very good friends.

Mistler said he's among those pleased to see the mutual display of respect facilitated by coaches Graham and Rodriguez. "It's not driven by, 'Look at those guys, we hate them. Those are just a bunch of thugs on the other side,'" he said. "Both coaches respect the other teams, and they respect the rivalry."

Dobyns is as loyal to the red and blue as anyone, but he said a great rivalry can't come without respect, not only for the opposing school but for the great athletes and coaches who came from there.

"If there's no respect, what kind of rivalry is it?" he said. "I don't care what school you like – if you can't admit Coach

Kush is a legend in college football, let alone in the state, you're delusional."

And if the legendary ASU coach who'd rather walk home from Tucson than lose to UA can adopt that same kind of attitude toward his archrival, anyone can.

"I think it'll always be a great rivalry game," said Kush. "I really kind of enjoyed it, and it got to the point where I got to know a lot of the guys down there, and I had a good relationship with those people. I have a great deal of admiration for both institutions."

ACKNOWLEDGEMENTS

The first thing this Wildcat has to do is send out a big thanks to the athletic department of Arizona State University.

Mark Brand, Doug Tammaro and Kevin Miniefield were instrumental in helping me get in contact with so many of the great Sun Devil players and coaches I was privileged to interview for this book, and they were kind enough to give me a press pass to the 2011 Duel in the Desert. They all saw the value in promoting the rivalry and the university through this book, and I'm truly thankful for that.

Down south, Frankie Acosta and Molly O'Mara at UA's athletic department assisted me in setting up conversations with former and current Wildcat greats, and Greg Byrne's assistant, Brenda Filippelli, provided me with valuable information.

I also need to thank two of my old bosses at the *Arizona Daily Wildcat*. Ryan Finley connected me to several players and coaches who I was lucky enough to speak with, and Brett Fera helped me cover the 2011 Duel in the Desert.

This book wouldn't have looked nearly as tidy without the copy editing work of Matt Swartz at Fox Sports Arizona. Matt went above and beyond in his edits and caught some bonehead mistakes.

Thanks to Jason Wise, ASU's photographer, for all of his hard work in digging up some great rivalry pictures from the dusty ASU archives, and thanks to Rick Wiley at the *Arizona Daily Star* for doing the same.

Thanks to Jim Johnson, my fellow author and one of my favorite journalism professors during my time at UA. I appreciate all of his advice and guidance throughout this lengthy process.

I can't thank my good friends Travis and Jena Clark enough for all their help in promoting the book. Travis designed the Web site I used to promote the book, while Jena created the amazing Old West-style book cover. It's so good to have talented friends.

Thank you to the 150-plus former and current players, coaches, and Duel in the Desert experts who took the time to chat with me – especially Juan Roque and LaMonte Hunley for their Forewords. The completion of this book has been a two-year process, but because of all the talented athletes I had the honor to speak with – many of whom I've seen play in person at the collegiate and/or professional level – it was a joy and well worth the time.

Thanks to my cairn terrier, Zeek, for keeping me company during all those long work-from-home days. I can't imagine how boring the house was before he came along. Adopting him was one of the best decisions Jennie and I ever made.

And speaking of my wonderful wife: Jennie could not have been more encouraging throughout this entire process. She believed in me from start to finish, and I don't know that I would have ever gotten this project off the ground without her support. I love you and I'm excited to see where we go from here.

Finally, I have to pull a Kurt Warner (or Tim Tebow, if you prefer) and thank The Lord for helping me to see this project all the way through. He has answered so many prayers from the beginning to the end of this process, and I would be nowhere without His provision.

Made in the USA
Las Vegas, NV
01 December 2023